焦红波 主编

嵩山少林寺武术馆武术教材

第三册

西北工业大学出版社

【内容简介】 本书主要包括少林六合拳、少林炮拳、少林长护心意门拳、少林达摩剑、少林春秋大刀、少林养生功(八段锦、易筋经)等内容,对少林武术的传播发展,起到很大的促进作用。

适用于业界人士和少林武术研修者,可成为广大少林武术爱好者的良师善友、得力助手。

图书在版编目(CIP)数据

嵩山少林寺武术馆武术教材. 第三册 / 焦红波主编. -- 西安:西北工业大学出版社,2016.12
ISBN 978-7-5612-5175-1

Ⅰ.①嵩… Ⅱ.①焦… Ⅲ.①少林武术-教材 Ⅳ.①G852

中国版本图书馆 CIP 数据核字(2016)第 301526 号

出版发行:西北工业大学出版社
通信地址:西安市友谊西路 127 号　邮编:710072
电　　话:(029)88493844　88491757
网　　址:www.nwpup.com
印 刷 者:陕西金德佳印务有限公司
开　　本:787 mm×1 092 mm　　1/16
印　　张:28
字　　数:499 千字
版　　次:2016 年 12 月第 1 版　2016 年 12 月第 1 次印刷
定　　价:68.00 元

编委会成员
Editorial Board Members

主 编：焦红波
Chief Editor：Jiao Hongbo

副主编：陈俊杰　　王松伟　　王占洋　　郑跃峰
Associate Editor：Chen Junjie　Wang Songwei
Wang Zhanyang　Zheng Yuefeng

执 笔：陈俊杰
Written by：Chen Junjie

编 委：
Editorial Board Members：
阎治军　　韩新强　　王占通　　焦晓伟
Yan Zhijun　Han Xinqiang　Wang Zhantong　Jiao Xiaowei
焦宏敏　　蒋东旭　　吕宏军　　李振亮
Jiao Hongmin　Jiang Dongxu　Lü Hongjun　Li Zhenliang
景冠飞　　刘珊珊　　吴卫永　　董 伟
Jing Guanfei　Liu Shanshan　Wu Weiyong　Dong Wei

翻 译：李广升　　陈中纪
Translator：Li Guangsheng　Chen Zhongji

發展少林武術
振興民族文化

張文廣

少林拳法
修身養性

蔡龍雲

弘揚少林武術

乙酉年八月 門惠豐

為嵩山少林寺武術館武術教材題

为少林武术馆题

弘扬传统文化
传承少林武术

乙未年夏柏华

嵩山少林寺武術館

規范教材
科學发展

康戈武
乙酉秋

序

寇武江[1]

缘于工作我与同事一起到嵩山少林寺武术馆调研，在观看队员表演练功后，红波告诉我，武术馆拟出版一本少林武术教材，并希望我能为之作序。说实话，近段时间对于武术文化与旅游的研究，我虽然下了一点功夫，但对少林武术的套路招式技法学习我可是一窍不通。然而，考虑到出版教材，传承文化，规范练习，是件功在当今、利在后人的好事，我便答应了。

少林武术在河南旅游文化品牌中极具代表性，在国内外享有盛名。自北魏以来，少林武术伴随着少林寺禅宗的发展，历经1 500多年的沧桑岁月，积淀了丰富而深厚的文化内涵。20世纪80年代，国家旅游局和河南省人民政府共同投资兴建少林寺武术馆时，就依托少林寺"拳以寺名，寺以武显"的文化内涵，将演武厅列入中原旅游区重点工程项目进行建设。其目的是宣传弘扬深厚的河南文化，满足广大武术爱好者和游客学习少林武术和观看少林武术表演的要求。武术馆自1988年开馆至今，以少林武术这一独特的旅游文化为基础，积极开展少林武术国际文化交流和武术教学研究活动，推动了少林武术专项游，吸引了国内外成千上万的武术爱好者前来参观、学习少林武术，培养出了一大批高层次的少林武术专业人才，为宣传弘扬少林武术文化，促进河南旅游业可持续发展做出了突出贡献。

少林寺在历史上屡遭兵燹，几经兴衰，少林武术也屡遭摧残，濒临失传。20世纪80年代，国家对传统武术文化给予了高度重视，对长期保存于少林高僧及民间武术名师中的珍贵少林武术资料进行了挖掘收集整理，以不同的方式予以出版发行，对少林武术的传播发展起到很大的促进作用，但以教材的形式出版的则很少。

少林寺武术馆集聚着众多少林武术名家及武坛精英，他们在工作之余

---

[1] 寇武江：河南省旅游局局长。

长期致力于少林武术文化的研究,并把研究成果在实践中加以验证,不断地修正传统套路中技法理论及技法运用。本书就是他们对少林武术文化研究的成果和近30年来长期从事表演、教学、交流工作经验的积累结晶。我相信本书出版以后,一定会给业界人士和广大少林武术研修者提供一个好的参考,成为广大少林武术爱好者的良师善友、得力助手。

是为序。

2015 年 6 月 5 日

Preface

By Kou Wujiang[1]

Due to a work visit to the Shaolin Temple Wushu Training Center with my colleagues, Hongbo asked me after I watched their kungfu performance and training to provide a preface to the textbook that they were preparing to publish about Shaolin martial arts. Frankly speaking, I know little about martial arts forms and combat techniques, although I did spend some time researching martial arts culture and tourism. However, considering that the textbook would bring significant benefits not only for Shaolin cultural heritage but also for students of martial arts, I said yes.

Shaolin Martial Arts is a recognized brand for Henan cultural tourism and it enjoys a great reputation around the world. Since the Northern Wei Dynasty, Shaolin martial arts, along with Shaolin Zen culture, has been developed for more than 1,500 years. A rich and profound cultural tradition was nurtured and cultivated during this period. During the 80's of the last century, the China National Tourism Administration and the People's Government of Henan province built the Shaolin Temple Wushu Training Center based on a cultural philosophy of the Shaolin Temple, "The martial arts are recognized by the fame of the Shaolin Temple and the Temple is recognized by martial arts." The Shaolin Wushu Training Center was envisioned to play a key role in China's central region tourism project for spreading Henan's culture and meeting the peoples' desire to practice Shaolin Kungfu and watch Kungfu performances. Since 1988, the Wushu Center has carried out international communications and undertaken teaching activities based upon martial arts. Millions of tourists have been

---

[1] Kou Wujiang: Director General of Henan Provincial Tourism Administration.

attracted to visit the center and experience martial arts through specialized Shaolin tourism. Moreover, a large number of high level martial arts masters have been trained here. The center has made great contributions to the promotion of Shaolin martial arts as well as Henan's sustainable tourism development.

The Shaolin Temple has seen destruction several times in its history and Shaolin martial arts has also encountered challenges, even to the point of almost suffering extinction. In the 80's of the last century, our nation paid great attention to traditional martial arts culture, to systematically excavate and preserve the martial arts materials derived from prominent Shaolin monks and folk Kungfu masters. The materials were published through different methods to develop and promote Shaolin martial arts more effectively. However, published textbooks with an emphasis on teaching are rarely seen.

The Shaolin Temple Wushu Training Center has gathered many Shaolin Wushu masters and professionals who have devoted themselves in the long run to Shaolin martial arts culture research as well as to ensure that the research results can be put into practice; as well as continuous efforts of revising the technical theories and applications in the traditional practice sets. This textbook is the product of the accumulation of their research results in Shaolin wushu culture and the working experience through their performance, teaching and exchange over two decades. I believe that after this texbook is published, it will serve as an excellent reference to the people in the industry and to the general public who are interested in practicing Shaolin wushu.

The above serves as a foreword.

June 05, 2015

前 言

焦红波[①]

  少林武术是中国宝贵的文化遗产,是武林中的一颗璀璨明珠。它内容广博,种类繁多,技法精湛,享誉中外。习练少林武术,不仅可以强健筋骨,防身抗暴,还可以陶冶情操,祛病延年。少林武术内静外猛、朴实无华、刚柔相济、立足实战,现已发展成为海内外广为流传的健身运动之一。

  少林武术因发源于嵩山少林寺而得名。千百年来,作为少林武术发祥地的少林寺,因闻名天下的少林功夫和禅宗祖庭而被誉为"天下第一名刹"。地处少林寺的登封,因少林武术运动开展得非常广泛,也被称为"武术之乡"。为了传承与弘扬博大精深的少林武术,使少林武术以更大的步伐走向世界,1988年,作为向海内外传授少林武术基地的嵩山少林寺武术馆在少林武术发祥地诞生了。

  河南省嵩山少林寺武术馆自创办之后,中外少林武术爱好者闻讯而至,习武练功。到目前为止,嵩山少林寺武术馆已培养了世界100多个国家和地区的武术学员2万余人。武馆自建立以来还为数以千万计的中外来宾展示精湛的少林武术。同时,嵩山少林寺武术馆还应邀到世界80多个国家和地区传授少林武术,使之在世界上生根、开花、结果。

  嵩山少林寺武术馆由于地处少林武术发祥地和武术之乡的优势,汇集了众多少林武术高手在此传武研武,可谓人才济济。自建馆起,武术馆在传授少林武术的同时,还不断对少林武术进行深入的研究、挖掘和整理,并编写了许多具有代表性的少林武术文化书籍,为少林武术的传播和光大起到了重要的作用。

  当前,在传习少林武术的过程中,系统、规范的少林武术教材的缺失致使少林武术在传播过程中出现诸多对其曲解和误解的现象。嵩山少林寺武

[①] 焦红波:河南省嵩山少林寺武术馆馆长、总教练,本书主编。

术馆作为国家建立的传播、弘扬和研究少林武术的中心,有责任、有义务编写一部权威性的介绍少林武术的书籍,以便为人们系统和完整学习少林武术提供强有力的保障。

　　本次编写的少林武术教材内容分为少林武术概论、少林武术基本动作和少林武术基本套路三部分。全书系统论述和介绍了少林武术的理论和具体习练方法,是学习和研究少林武术的必备之教材。本书按照少林武术一至九段的评位要求,分初级、中级、高级三个阶段,选取了少林十八势、少林烧火棍、少林长拳、七星拳、八段锦、易筋经等作为练习的功法,从而为求取段位者顺利通过段位的考核提供最有效的途径。特别要提出的是,本书中的部分内容,是我们与国家体委武术挖掘小组和北京体育大学门惠丰教授于20世纪80年代初共同创编的,经过多年的教学实践反映良好。

　　少林武术历史悠久,技法精湛,内容博大,需要探索和研究的还很多。因而在编写少林武术书籍之时,编写人员虽竭尽全力,但书中不当之处也再所难免,敬希各位方家及广大武术爱好者不吝赐教,以使其日臻完善。

2016年8月20日

Foreword

By Jiao Hongbo[1]

Shaolin martial arts is a bright pearl and the precious cultural heritage of China. It enjoys enormous popularity throughout the world for its broad content, variety of types and exquisite techniques. Practicing martial arts can not only strengthen the muscles and bones, but also cultivate sentiments and keep healthy. Now it has become a popular worldwide sport due to its graceful and powerful movements, internal static, external fierce and actual combat experiences.

Shaolin martial arts originated from the Shaolin Temple, hence the name. It was reputed as the "No. 1 Temple under Heaven". Dengfeng city, where the Shaolin Temple was located, was renowned as the "Hometown of Chinese Kungfu" for the popular participation. In 1988, the Shaolin Temple Wushu Training Center was founded in Shaolin Village, its purpose is to inherit and carry forward the extensive and profound Shaolin martial arts.

Numerous enthusiasts of Shaolin Kungfu both in China and abroad practiced here, up to now, more than 20,000 students from over 100 countries and regions have been trained in this center. Tens of millions of visitors have enjoyed the consummate Kungfu shows since the establishment of the Wushu Training Center. Meanwhile professional coaches from this center have been invited to visit over 80 countries and regions to teach and impart Shaolin skills.

The Shaolin Temple Wushu Training Center is just located in the birthplace of Shaolin martial arts and the "Hometown of Chinese Kungfu", so numerous Kungfu masters gathered in this Training Center to study and practice. After cou-

---

[1] Jiao Hongbo: Director, Chief Coach of Shaolin Temple Wushu Training Center, Mt. Songshan, Henan Province.

ple of years of in-depth research, exploration and collecting, the Training Center composed a number of representative books which played an important role in promotion and popularity of Shaolin martial arts.

Systematic, standard and practical textbook is needed in order to avoid the phenomenon of misunderstanding and misinterpreting the discipline of Kungfu practices. As the state-level teaching base, the Shaolin Temple Wushu Training Center has the responsibility to compile this authoritative book to provide standard practices.

This Shaolin martial arts textbook consists of three parts: Introduction to Shaolin Martial Arts, Basic Shaolin Boxing Routines, and Basic Skills and Movements of Shaolin Martial Arts. The book, indispensable for studying Shaolin martial arts, describes systematically the theory and methods of Shaolin martial arts. Based on the requirements of Chinese martial arts Duan Ranking System from 1 to 9, the book describes selected Shaolin 18 Forms, Shaolin Shaohuo Stick, Shaolin Long Boxing, Shaolin Seven-star Boxing, Eight-sectioned Exercise (Baduanjin) and Channel-changing Scriptures (Yijinjing) as primary, middle and higher Dan (Rank) practicing routines, to make people who want to get higher grading in the examination have efficient way. It is necessary to be pointed out additionally that some parts of the textbook were completed with the cooperation of the martial arts research and exploration group of National Sports Commission and Professor Men Huifeng of Beijing Sports University in the early 1980s. The parts had produced notable effect by over years teaching practice.

Shaolin martial arts has a long history, consummate techniques, rich content which must be continually explored and studied. We have tried our best to finish this book, but we are still afraid there are some places that need to be perfected, so comments and suggestions will be greatly appreciated.

August 20th, 2016

目 录
Content

第一章　少林六合拳
Chapter 1　Shaolin Liuhe Boxing(Six-Harmony Boxing) ·················· 1
　　第一节　套路动作名称
　　Quarter 1　Routine Names ·················· 1
　　第二节　套路动作图解
　　Quarter 2　Figures of Routine Movements ·················· 4

第二章　少林炮拳
Chapter 2　Shaolin Cannon Boxing ·················· 37
　　第一节　套路动作名称
　　Quarter 1　Routine Names ·················· 37
　　第二节　套路动作图解
　　Quarter 2　Figures of Routine Movements ·················· 40

第三章　少林长护心意门拳
Chapter 3　Shaolin Changhuxinyimen Boxing(Mid-and-will Boxing) ···
·················· 93
　　第一节　套路动作名称
　　Quarter 1　Routine Names ·················· 93
　　第二节　套路动作图解
　　Quarter 2　Figures of Routine Movements ·················· 100

第四章　少林达摩剑
Chapter 4　Shaolin Dharma Sword ·················· 183
　　第一节　套路动作名称
　　Quarter 1　Routine Names ·················· 183

第二节　套路动作图解
Quarter 2　Figures of Routine Movements ……………………… 186

第五章　少林春秋大刀
Chapter 5　Shaolin Chunqiu Broadsword (Spring and Autumn Broadsword) …………………………………………………………… 255

第一节　套路动作名称
Quarter 1　Routine Names ……………………………………… 255

第二节　套路动作图解
Quarter 2　Figures of Routine Movements ……………………… 257

第六章　八段锦
Chapter 6　Baduanjin (Eight-sectioned Exercise) ……………… 310

第一节　【健身气功·八段锦】功法特点
Quarter 1　Features of Fitness Vital Energy—Baduanjin ………… 310

第二节　【健身气功·八段锦】习练要领
Quarter 2　Practicing Essentials of Fitness Vital Energy—Baduanjin … 313

第三节　【健身气功·八段锦】动作说明
Quarter 3　Movements Descriptions of Fitness Vital Energy—Baduanjin … 317

第七章　易筋经
Chapter 7　Yijinjing (Channel-changing Exercise) …………… 357

第一节　【健身气功·易筋经】功法特点
Quarter 1　Features of Fitness Vital Energy—Yijinjing ………… 357

第二节　【健身气功·易筋经】习练要领
Quarter 2　Practicing Essentials of Fitness Vital Energy—Yijinjing …… 360

第三节　【健身气功·易筋经】动作说明
Quarter 3　Movements Descriptions of Fitness Vital Energy—Yijinjing … 364

第一章 少林六合拳

Chapter 1 Shaolin Liuhe Boxing

(Six-Harmony Boxing)

第一节 套路动作名称

Quarter 1 Routine Names

第一段

Section 1

1.预备势

1. Preparation

2.抱拳势

2. Holding fists

3.虚步架打

3. Empty stance parrying

4.左弓步下冲拳

4. Left bow stance punching

5.右弓步下冲拳

5. Right bow stance punching

6.迎面掌

6. Head-on palm

7.左弹腿迎击

7. Left toe kicking

8.右弹腿迎击

8. Right toe kicking

9.迎面掌

9. Head-on palm

10. 左弹腿迎击

10. Left toe kicking

11. 右弹腿迎击

11. Right toe kicking

12. 左弹腿迎击

12. Left toe kicking

13. 迎面掌

13. Head-on palm

14. 缠腕藏身

14. Wrist winding and hiding

15. 劈掌架打

15. Shopping and parrying

16. 搅绕缠手

16. Stirring and winding

17. 迎面抢手

17. Hand-on grabbing

18. 缠手架打

18. Winding and parrying

19. 罗汉担山

19. Arhat shouldering

20. 双折肘

20. Double elbowing

21. 马步截手

21. Horse-riding intercepting

22. 左摇山

22. Left shaking

23. 右摇山

23. Right shaking

24. 仙童献桃

24. Fairchild peach offering

25. 飞身迎面脚

25. Flying hand-on kicking

26. 震脚双砸拳

26. Stamping and punching

第二段

Section 2

27.顺手小牵羊

27. Picking up in passing

28.迎面双推掌

28. Hand-on palm pushing

29.撤步架打

29. Withdrawing and parrying

30.弓步双架打

30. Bow stance double parrying

31.缠腕藏身

31. Wrist winding and hiding

32.马步撞心肘

32. Horse-riding stance elbowing

33.左摇山

33. Left shaking

34.右摇山

34. Right shaking

35.仙童献桃

35. Fairchild peach offering

36.弹腿拍脚

36. Spring kicking

37.摆尾藏身势

37. Swinging and hiding

38.弹腿拍脚

38. Spring kicking

39.震脚劈拳

39. Stamping and intercepting

40.缠腕藏身

40. Wrist winding and hiding

41.转身截掌

41. Turning and intercepting

42.耳把迎击

42. Resisting and striking

43.虚步架打

43. Empty stance parrying

44.收势

44. Closing

第二节　套路动作图解
Quarter 2　Figures of Routine Movements

第一段

Section 1

1.预备势

(甲穿对襟和尚服,没有腰带;乙穿斜襟和尚服,有腰带)(图 1-1)。

1. Preparation

(A dressed in double-breasted gowns without waist belt, B dressed in slant opening gowns with waist belt)(Figure 1-1).

甲、乙并步站立,相距约 4 步,两手五指并拢,两臂垂于身体两侧。目视前方。

A and B stance touch stand, 4 stances apart, close fingers, arms hang naturally. Look straight ahead.

图 1-1(Figure 1-1)

2.抱拳势(图1-2)

甲、乙两掌变拳,两臂屈肘上提抱拳于腰间。目视前方。

2. Holding fists (Figure 1-2)

Both A and B change palms into fists, bend and lift elbows into holding fists against the waist. Look straight ahead.

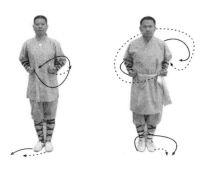

图1-2(Figure 1-2)

3.虚步架打(图1-3)

甲:上体左转退右步成左虚步;右拳由下向前、向上、向腹前摆拳,拳心向上;同时,左拳由下向前、向上摆拳,拳心向上。目视对方。

3. Empty stance parrying (Figure 1-3)

A:Turn left and retreat right stance into the left empty stance, swing right fist forward, upward and to the front of abdomen, fist center upward, at the same time, swing left fist forward and upward, fist center upward. Look at B.

乙:上体右转退右步成左虚步;右拳由下向前、向上、向腹前摆拳,拳心向上;同时,左拳由下向前、向上摆拳,拳心向上。目视对方。

B:Turn right and retreat right stance into the left empty stance, swing right fist forward, upward and to the front of abdomen, fist center upward, at the same time, swing left fist forward and upward, fist center upward. Look at A.

5

图1-3（Figure 1-3）

4.左弓步下冲拳（图1-4）

甲、乙同时向前击步成左弓步；左臂内旋，向前下碰击对方小臂外侧，拳心向下；右拳抱于腰间，拳心向上。目视左拳。

4. Left bow stance punching（Figure 1-4）

Both A and B strike forward into the left bow stance, turn left arm inward, impact forward and downward to B's forearm outward, fist center downward, hold right fist against the waist, fist center upward. Look at left fist.

图1-4（Figure 1-4）

5.右弓步下冲拳（图1-5）

甲：左拳收抱腰间，右脚向前一步成右弓步；右臂内旋向前下方碰击对方小臂外侧，拳心向下。目视对方。

5. Right bow stance punching（Figure 1-5）

A：Close left fist against waist, right foot strides one step into the right bow stance, turn right arm inward, impact forward and downward to B's forearm outward, fist center downward. Look at B.

乙：左拳收抱腰间，左脚向后退一步成右弓步；右臂内旋，向前下方碰击对方小臂外侧，拳心向下。目视对方。

B：Close left fist against waist, left foot retreats one step into the right bow stance, turn right arm inward, impact forward and downward to A's forearm outward, fist center downward. Look at A.

图 1-5（Figure 1-5）

6.迎面掌（图 1-6）

乙：左拳变掌由腰间向甲面部推掌，右拳抱于腰间。目视对方。

6. Head-on palm（Figure 1-6）

B：Change left fist into palm and push to A's face from the waist, hold right fist against the waist. Look at B.

甲：左拳变掌由腰间向前架掌，右拳抱于腰间。目视对方。

A：Change left fist into palm and parry it forward from the waist, hold right fist against the waist. Look straight ahead.

图 1-6（Figure 1-6）

7.左弹腿迎击(图1-7)

乙:左掌变拳抱于腰间;左腿屈膝向前上方弹踢,脚面绷平。目视对方。

7. Left toe kicking (Figure 1-7)

B：Change left palm into fist against the waist, bend left knee and kick forward and upward, instep stretches tight. Look at A.

甲:右腿向后退一步成马步,左掌向下拍击乙脚面;右拳抱于腰间。目视对方脚面。

A：Right leg retreats one step into the horse-riding stance, left palm pats downward to B's instep, hold right fist against the waist. Look at B's instep.

图1-7(Figure 1-7)

8.右弹腿迎击(图1-8)

乙:左脚落地;右腿随即向前上方弹踢,脚面绷平,双拳抱于腰间。目视对方。

8. Right toe kicking (Figure 1-8)

B：Left foot falls, right leg kicks forward and upward, instep stretches tight, hold fists against the waist. Look at A.

甲:左掌变拳收于腰侧,左脚向后退一步成马步;右拳变掌向下方拨击乙脚。目视对方脚面。

A：Change left palm into fist, close it against the waist, left foot retreats one step into the horse-riding stance, change right fist into palm and make it strike downward to B's feet. Look at B's instep.

图 1-8(Figure 1-8)

9.迎面掌(图 1-9)

乙:右脚下落成右弓步;同时,左拳变掌向甲前上方劈掌。目视对方。

9. Head-on palm (Figure 1-9)

B: Right foot falls into the right bow stance, at the same time, change left fist into palm and make it push upward to A. Look at A.

甲:身体右转成弓步;同时,左拳变掌向体前架掌,右掌变拳收抱腰间。目视对方。

A: Turn right into the bow stance, at the same time, change left fist into palm and parry it, change right palm to fist against waist. Look at B.

图 1-9(Figure 1-9)

10.左弹腿迎击(图 1-10)

甲:左掌变拳收抱腰间;同时,左腿向前上方弹踢,脚面绷平。目视对方。

9

10. Left toe kicking (Figure 1-10)

A: Change left palm into fist against waist, at the same time, left leg kicks forward and upward, instep stretches tight. Look at B.

乙：右腿向后退一步成弓步；同时，左掌拨击甲左脚。目视对方脚面。

B: Right leg retreats one step into the bow stance, at the same time, left palm strikes A's left foot. Look at A's instep.

图 1-10 (Figure 1-10)

11.右弹腿迎击(图1-11)

甲：左脚落地，右腿随即向前上方弹踢，脚面绷平；双手抱拳于腰侧。目视对方。

11. Right toe kicking (Figure 1-11)

A: Left foot falls, right leg kicks forward and upward, instep stretches tight, hold fists against the waist. Look at B.

乙：左脚向后退一步成弓步；同时，左掌变拳收抱于腰间；右拳变掌拨击甲脚。目视对方脚面。

B: Left foot retreats one step into the bow stance, at the same time, change left palm into fist against waist, change right fist into palm and make it strike A's feet. Look at A's instep.

第一章　少林六合拳

图 1-11（Figure 1-11）

12.左弹腿迎击(图 1-12)

甲：右脚落地，左腿随即向前上方弹踢，脚面绷平；双手抱于腰间。目视对方。

12. Left toe kicking（Figure 1-12）

A：Right foot falls, left leg kicks forward and upward, instep stretches tight, hold hands against the waist. Look at B.

乙：右掌变拳抱于腰间，左拳变掌拨击甲脚；同时，两腿下蹲成马步。目视对方脚面。

B：Change right palm into fist against the waist, change left fist into palm and make it strike A's feet, at the same time, squat into the horse-riding stance. Look at A's instep.

图 1-12（Figure 1-12）

13.迎面掌(图 1-13)

甲：左脚落地；左拳变掌，小臂内旋向乙胸前推击。目视对方。

11

13. Head-on palm (Figure 1-13)

A: Left foot falls, change left fist into palm, swing forearm inward and push it to B's chest. Look at B.

乙:身体左转成弓步;同时,左掌向身体前上方架掌迎击甲左掌;右拳抱于腰间。目视对方。

B: Turn left into the bow stance, at the same time, left palm forward and upward and parries A's left palm, hold right fist against the waist. Look at A.

图 1-13（Figure 1-13）

14.缠腕藏身(图 1-14)

乙:左手外旋握住甲左手臂向下转腕;右拳抱于腰侧。目视对方。

14. Wrist winding and hiding (Figure 1-14)

B: Hold A's left arm with left hand and swing it downward, hold right fist against the waist. Look at A.

甲:上体随乙转腕的同时右转,左臂下转落于腰后;右拳抱于腰侧。目视对方。

A: Correspondingly turn right, turn left arm behind waist, hold right fist against the waist. Look at B.

图 1-14（Figure 1-14）

15.劈掌架打（图 1-15）

乙：上右步；同时，右掌从腰间向头上方劈掌。目视对方。

15. Chopping and parrying (Figure 1-15)

B：Stride rightward, at the same time, right palm strikes upward from the waist. Look at A.

甲：上体右转，右拳变掌向上架掌。目视对方。

A：Turn right, change right fist into palm and swing it upward. Look at B.

图 1-15（Figure 1-15）

16.搅绕缠手（图 1-16 和图 1-17）

(1)甲：左拳收于腰侧。目视对方。

乙：左手变掌向甲面前抢手插掌。目视对方（图 1-16）。

16. Stirring and winding (Figures 1-16 and 1-17)

(1)A：Close left fist against the waist. Look at B.

B：Change left hand into palm and make it grab. Look at A (Figure 1-16).

13

图 1-16（Figure 1-16）

（2）甲：右臂外旋格住乙左抢手；左拳抱于腰侧。目视右手腕。

乙：左臂内旋搅甲右臂，由上向外划弧至腰外侧；右手抱拳于腰侧。目视左手腕（图 1-17）。

（2）A：Swing right arm outward to resist B's left arm, hold left fist against the waist. Look at right wrist.

B：Twist left arm inward to resist A's right arm, draw curve from upward to outward and against the waist, hold right fist against the waist. Look at left wrist (Figure 1-17).

图 1-17（Figure 1-17）

17. 迎面抢手（图 1-18）

乙：左掌变拳收于腰侧；同时，右拳变掌，向甲面部抢手插掌。目视前方。

17. Hand-on grabbing (Figure 1-18)

B：Change left palm into fist and close it against the waist, at the same time, change right fist into palm, grab A's face. Look straight ahead.

甲:身体后倾,右掌回收,掌臂内旋架掌至脸前;左拳抱于腰侧。目视对方。

A: Lean backward, close right palm backward, turn palm inward and make it grab forward, hold left fist against the waist. Look at B.

图 1-18(Figure 1-18)

18.缠手架打(图 1-19)

甲:右臂外旋向外划弧至脸前,掌心向上下旋时抓对方手腕;左拳抱于腰侧。目视对方。

18. Winding and parrying (Figure 1-19)

A: Swing right arm outward and draw curve to the face, palm center upward and make it grasp B's wrist, hold left fist against the waist. Look at B.

乙:右臂内旋向外划弧至脸前,掌心向下抓对方手腕;左拳抱于腰侧。目视对方。

B: Swing right arm outward and draw curve to the face, palm center downward and make it grab A's wrist, hold left fist against the waist. Look at A.

图 1-19（Figure 1-19）

19.罗汉担山（图 1-20）

乙：左脚向前一步,身体右转,两腿下蹲成马步。左拳向甲胸前冲击；同时,右手上旋,右拉使甲右臂置于肩,肘关节向下。目视对方。

19. Arhat shouldering（Figure 1-20）

B：Left foot strides one step forward, turn right, squat into the horse-riding stance. Left fist impacts A's chest, at the same time, swing right hand upward, pull A's right arm on the shoulder, elbow joints downward. Look at A.

甲：双脚向后跳一步,身体下蹲成马步；同时,右拳变掌向下旋握住乙方左手腕,使左臂肘关节向下。目视对方。

A：Jump one step backward, squat into the horse-riding stance, at the same time, change right fist into palm and make it turn downward and hold B's left wrist, make left arm elbow joint downward. Look at B.

图 1-20（Figure 1-20）

20.双折肘(图1-21)

乙:身体上起,右手握住甲右臂向下拉,肘关节向下折。目视对方。

20. Double elbowing (Figure 1-21)

B: Arise, make right hand pull A's right arm downward, elbow joints downward. Look at A.

甲:左手握乙左臂随乙向下拉的力量挺胸,身体上起,将乙左肘关节向下折。目视对方。

A: Make left hand hold B's left arm and throw out chest, arise, fold B's left elbow joint downward. Look at B.

正(Front)

反(Back)

图 1-21(Figure 1-21)

21.马步截手(图1-22 和图1-23)

(1)甲:双脚跳起离地,身体右转;同时,右臂内旋从对方头上绕过拉对方手腕至腹前。目视对方。

乙:双脚跳起离地,身体左转;同时,左臂内旋,拉对方左手腕至胸前。目视对方(图1-22)。

21. Horse-riding intercepting (Figures 1-22 and 1-23)

(1) A: Jump, turn right, at the same time, make right arm swing inward and across B's head and pull B's wrist to the abdomen. Look at B.

B: Jump, turn left, at the same time, make left arm swing inward, pull A's left wrist to the chest. Look at A (Figure 1-22).

图1-22(Figure 1-22)

（2）甲、乙双脚落地成马步,乙右脚在甲左脚前,两臂和上体不变。目视对方(图1-23)。

(2) Both A and B fall into the horse-riding stance, B's right foot in front of A's left foot, keep arms still. Look at each other (Figure 1-23).

图1-23(Figure 1-23)

22. 左摇山(图1-24)

乙：双手拉住甲手臂向前、向左、向里划弧。目视对方。

22. Left shaking (Figure 1-24)

B: Use hands to make A's arms draw curve forward, leftward and inward. Look at A.

甲：身体随乙的拉力向左前挤靠。目视对方。

A: Lean forward following B's drawing. Look at B.

图 1-24（Figure 1-24）

23.右摇山（图 1-25）

甲：双臂向前、向右、向里划弧。目视对方。

23. Right shaking（Figure 1-25）

A：Make arms draw curve forward, rightward and inward. Look at B.

乙：身体随甲的拉力向右前挤靠。目视对方。

B：Lean rightward and forward following A's drawing. Look at A.

图 1-25（Figure 1-25）

24.仙童献桃（图 1-26 和图 1-27）

甲：右掌外旋置乙方左小臂外侧；同时，向乙方胸前发力推出。目视对方（图 1-26）。

24. Fairchild peach offering（Figure 1-26 and 1-27）

A：Swing right palm forward to B's left forearm forward, at the same time, push B's chest. Look at B（Figure 1-26）.

图 1-26（Figure 1-26）

乙：随甲的推力向后跳步。目视对方（图1-27）。

B：Jump backward following A's pushing. Look at A（Figure 1-27）.

图 1-27（Figure 1-27）

25.飞身迎面脚（图1-28）

甲：双手变拳抱至腰侧；上左步跟右步，左脚踏跳，右腿向前上方弹踢至乙腹前，脚面绷平。目视对方。

25. Flying hand-on kicking（Figure 1-28）

A：Change hands into fists and hold them against the waist, stride leftward and rightward, left foot jumps and right leg kicks forward and upward to B's abdomen, instep stretches tight. Look at B.

乙：向后跳步左脚落地，右腿提膝，双手由上向下拍击甲脚面。目视对方。

B：Jump backward and left foot falls, lift right knee, hands pat A's instep downward. Look at A.

图 1-28（Figure 1-28）

26.震脚双砸拳（图 1-29）

乙：右脚下落震脚发力；同时，左脚向前落脚成弓步；双手变拳由上向下砸至甲头顶上方。目视对方。

26. Stamping and punching（Figure 1-29）

B：Right foot falls and stamps, at the same time, left foot falls forward into the bow stance, change hands into fists and make them hit A's head downward. Look at A.

甲：右脚下落震脚发力；同时，左脚向前落脚成弓步；双手变掌，由下向上架握乙双拳。目视对方。

A：Right foot falls and stamps, at the same time, left foot falls forward into the bow stance, change hands into palms, parry B's fists upward. Look at B.

图 1-29（Figure 1-29）

第二段

Section 2

27.顺手小牵羊(图1-30和图1-31)

(1)甲:两掌向上推乙双臂。目视对方。

乙:顺甲上推之势下拉,向两侧分甲双臂。目视对方(图1-30)。

27. Picking up in passing (Figures 1-30 and 1-31)

(1) A: Palms upward and push B's arms. Look at B.

B: Pulling downward following A's pushing, separate A's arms at both sides. Look at A (Figure 1-30)

图1-30(Figure 1-30)

(2)甲:借乙下拉的同时向乙腹前下插掌。目视对方。

乙:借势将甲两臂向体侧分拨。目视对方(图1-31)。

(2) A: Push to B's abdomen following B's pulling downward. Look at B.
B: Separate A's arms at both sides. Look at A (Figure 1-31).

图1-31(Figure 1-31)

28.迎面双推掌(图1-32和图1-33)

乙:顺势双掌向上扣于甲双臂,推甲胸向前发力。目视对方(图1-32)。

28. Hand-on palm pushing (Figures 1-32 and 1-33)

B：Palm buckle A's arms, push A's chest. Look at A (Figure 1-32).

图1-32(Figure 1-32)

甲:随乙推力向后跳步。目视对方(图1-33)。

A：Jump backward following B's pushing. Look at B (Figure 1-33).

图1-33(Figure 1-33)

29.撤步架打(图1-34)

乙:双脚离地向前跳出,左脚在前成弓步;左臂向甲头前上方劈掌,右拳握于腰侧。目视对方。

29. Withdrawing and parrying (Figure 1-34)

B：Jump forward, left foot in the front into the bow stance, left arm chops overhead of A, right fist against the waist. Look at A.

甲:双脚离地向后跳出,身体重心后移成弓步;左臂内旋屈肘架掌,右拳抱于腰侧。目视对方。

A: Jump backward, shift gravity center backward into the bow stance, twist left arm inward and parry, hold right fist against the waist. Look at B.

图 1-34(Figure 1-34)

30.马步双架打(图 1-35 和图 1-36)

(1)乙:左掌变拳向甲左肋下方击打,右拳收抱腰间。目视对方。

甲:身体左转成马步,左掌变拳向下格挡乙左拳,右拳收抱腰间。目视对方(图 1-35)。

30. Horse-riding stance double parrying (Figure 1-35 and 1-36)

(1) B: Change left palm into fist to hit A's left ribs, close right fist against waist. Look at A.

A: Turn left into the horse-riding stance, change left palm into fist downward to block B's left fist, close right fist against waist. Look at B (Figure 1-35).

图 1-35(Figure 1-35)

(2)乙:收拳向甲头顶上方摆击。目视对方。

甲:收拳向上格挡。目视对方(图1-36)。

(2) B:Swing fists to hit overhead of A. Look at A.

A:Close fists upward to parry. Look at B (Figure 1-36).

图1-36(Figure 1-36)

31.缠腕藏身(图1-37和图1-38)

(1)乙:身体左转成弓步,左拳变掌外旋缠抓甲手腕。

甲:顺势身体右转成弓步,左臂内旋。目视对方(图1-37)。

31. Wrist winding and hiding (Figures 1-37 and 1-38)

(1) B:Turn left into the bow stance, change left fist into palm outward to grab A's wrist.

A:Turn right into the bow stance, twist left arm inward. Look at B (Figure 1-37).

图1-37(Figure 1-37)

(2)乙:向前上一步,右拳由腰间向甲头部摆拳,拳心向下。

甲:屈身低头。目视对方(图1-38)。

(2) B:Stride one step forward,swing right fist to A's head from the waist, palm center downward.

A:Bend.Look at B(Figure 1-38).

图1-38(Figure 1-38)

32.马步撞心肘(图1-39)

乙:摆拳划弧收于胸前后再曲肘向前顶击甲胸部位;同时,身体下蹲变成马步。

32. Horse-riding stance elbowing (Figure 1-39)

B:Swing fists to draw curve against the chest, squat into the horse-riding stance, bend elbow forward to butting A's chest.

甲:起身,右拳变掌迎击乙肘尖。目视对方。

A:Stand, change right fist into palm to resist B's elbow tip. Look at B.

图1-39(Figure 1-39)

33.左摇山(图1-40)

甲:右掌推乙右肘关节,向前推乙。目视对方。

33.Left shaking (Figure 1-40)

A:Right palm pushes B's right elbow joint forward. Look at B.

乙:顺势回拉,双臂由内向外划弧。目视对方。

B:Pull back, arms draw curve outward. Look at A.

图1-40(Figure 1-40)

34.右摇山(图1-41)

乙:身体和双臂向前挤靠甲。目视对方。

34. Right shaking (Figure 1-41)

B:Squeeze A. Look at A.

甲:向回撤身,顺势重心后移。目视对方。

A:Retreat, shift gravity center backward. Look at B.

图1-41(Figure 1-41)

35.仙童献桃(图1-42~图1-44)

(1)甲:右手顺势向下扣住乙方右手腕向怀中下拉,左臂外旋下压对方右臂。目视对方。

35. Fairchild peach offering(Figure 1-42~ Figure 1-44)

(1) A: Naturally buckle down the B's right hand wrist to your bosom and drop down with your right hand, make left arm swing outward and press downward B's right arm. Look at B.

乙:顺甲下压之势,身体向前下方倾伏,左臂随身体下伏时向后摆臂。目视下方(图1-42)。

B: Following A's pressing downward, make the body lean to forward and downward, following the body's underlying and swing the left arm to backward. Look at downward.(Figure 1-42)

图 1-42(Figure 1-42)

(2)甲:右手后收至膝前,左臂外展,左掌向对方腰侧推掌;同时,左脚后撤扣于对方腿后。目视对方。

(2) A: Close your right hand from the backward to the front of knee, make the left arm outreach, pushing palm to B's waist by left palm; at the same time, make the left foot back and buckle behind B's legs. Look at B.

乙:右臂随对方外展之力向体侧绕摆。目视对方(图1-43)。

B: Following A's strength of outreach, make the right arm swing around the body. look at A.(Figure 1-43)

图 1-43(Figure 1-43)

(3)甲:身体上起左转,两掌推至对方腹部。目视对方。

(3) A: Arise and turn left, push to B's stomach by two hands. Look at B.

乙:身体随对方推力向后倾,重心移至左腿。目视对方(图 1-44)。

B: Follow the A's pushing, make the body lean backward, shift gravity center to the left leg. look at A(Figure 1-44)。

图 1-44(Figure 1-44)

36.弹腿拍脚(图 1-45 和图 1-46)

(1)甲:双掌用力向后、向上推击对方腹部。

36. Spring kicking (Figure1-45 and Figure1-46)

(1) A: Double palm forced backward and push B's abdomen to upward.

乙:借对方向后的推力向后腾空撤步。目视对方(图 1-45)。

B: Jump into the air to back by borrowing A's pushing backward. Look at A. (Figure 1-45)。

图 1-45(Figure 1-45)

(2)甲:双掌变拳收抱腰间,左脚向前上一步,右脚随即向前挤步并起脚向对方胸前摆踢。目视对方。

(2) A:Turn two palms to fist and close at the waist, left foot strides one step, move right foot forward, lift the foot and swing it to kick B's chest. Look at B.

乙:右脚落地,左脚向后收步;左掌变拳收抱腰间,左掌拍击对方右脚面。目视左掌(图 1-46)。

B:Let right foot on the ground, move left foot backward and close; change left palm into fist and close at against the waist, slap A's left instep by left palm. Look at the left palm(Figure 1-46).

图 1-46(Figure 1-46)

37.摆尾藏身势(图 1-47)

甲:右脚落地,身体向左后方转身360°;同时,左脚后摆腿扫击乙躯干,双手抱拳于腰侧。目视对方。

37. Swinging and hiding (Figure 1-47)

A: Right foot falls, turn leftward and backward 360°, at the the same time, swing left foot backward to kick B, hold fists against the waist. Look at B.

乙：身体下潜成仆步；双手抱拳于腰侧。目视对方。

B：Bend into the drop stance, hold fists against the waist. Look at A.

图 1-47（Figure 1-47）

38.弹腿拍脚（图 1-48 和图 1-49）

（1）甲：左脚后摆后自然下落，右脚在前。目视对方。

乙：身体上起，重心前移至左腿，双手抱拳。目视对方（图 1-48）。

38. Spring kicking (Figure 1-48 and 1-48)

（1）A：Left foot swings backward and naturally falls, right foot in the front. Look at B.

B：Arise, shift gravity center forward to the left leg, holding fists. Look at A (Figure 1-48).

图 1-48（Figure 1-48）

（2）乙：迅速起腿，摆击甲腹部。目视对方。

甲：右脚后退一步，左拳变掌拍击乙右脚面，右拳抱于腰间。目视对方（图 1-49）。

（2）B：Lift leg rapidly, swing it to kick A's abdomen. Look at A.

A：Right foot retreats one step, change left fist into palm to pat B's right instep, hold right fist against the waist. Look at B (Figure 1-49).

图1-49(Figure 1-49)

39.震脚劈拳(图1-50)

乙:右腿落地震脚,左腿提膝下落成左弓步;左拳击打甲脸部;右拳抱于腰侧。目视对方。

39. Stamping and chopping (Figure 1-50)

B: Right leg falls and stamps, lift left knee into the left bow stance, left fist hits A's face, hold right fist against the waist. Look at A.

甲:左掌内旋由下向上屈肘上架乙拳;右拳抱于腰侧。目视对方。

A: Twist left palm inward and bend elbow upward to parry B's fist, hold right fist against the waist. Look at B.

图1-50(Figure 1-50)

40.缠腕藏身(图1-51)

甲:左掌反抓乙手腕,左臂外旋至乙腰侧。目视对方。

40. Wrist winding and hiding (Figure 1-51)

A: Left palm grabs B's wrist, twist left arm outward to B's waist. Look at B.

乙:上体右转成右弓步,左臂内旋;右手抱拳于腰侧。目视对方。

B: Turn right into the bow stance, twist left arm inward, hold right fist against the waist. Look at A.

图 1-51（Figure 1-51）

41.转身截掌(图 1-52)

甲：上右步成弓步；右拳变掌向前推击乙腰侧。目视对方。

41. Turning and intercepting (Figure 1-52)

A: Stride rightward into the bow stance, change right fist into palm to putt B's waist. Look at B.

乙：上前一步成左弓步；右拳变掌，向右后方下摆击压至甲右掌腕上。目视对方。

B: Stride one step forward into the left bow stance, change right fist into palm, swing rightward and backward to press A's right wrist. Look at A.

图 1-52（Figure 1-52）

42.耳把迎击(图 1-53)

乙：左拳变掌，上体右转，左拳由背后向体前划弧，屈肘拍击甲脸部；右掌握住甲手臂。目视对方。

33

42. Resisting and striking (Figure 1-53)

B: Change left fist into palm, turn right, left fist draws curve forward, bend elbow to pat A's face, right palm holds A's arm. Look at A.

甲:左手变掌由下向上屈肘至脸侧,挡乙左掌。目视对方。

A: Change left hand into palm and bend elbow upward to to face, block B's left palm. Look at B.

图 1-53(Figure 1-53)

43.虚步架打(图 1-54 和图 1-55)

(1)甲、乙双手分开,右脚蹬地跳起,身体右转,左脚先落地成站立势;两臂随身体转动收于体前。目视对方(图 1-54)。

43. Empty stance parrying (Figure 1-54 and 1-55)

(1) Both A and B hands apart, right foot jumps, turn right, left foot falls and stand, close arms in the front. Look at each other (Figure 1-54).

图 1-54(Figure 1-54)

(2)甲、乙同时右拳向上、向前冲至体前,向回收拉于胸前,左拳向下、向上冲拳收于体前;两腿下蹲成虚步。目视对方(图1-55)。

（2）Both A and B punch right fists upward and forward, close them to the chest, punch left fists downward and upward, squat into the empty stance. Look at each other (Figure 1-55).

图1-55(Figure 1-55)

44.收势(图1-56和图1-57)

(1)甲:上右步并左步,双拳抱于腰侧。目视前方。

44. Closing (Figure 1-56 and 1-57)

(1) A：Stride rightward and leftward, hold fists against the waist. Look straight ahead.

乙:上左步并右步,双拳抱于腰侧。目视前方(图1-56)。

B：Stride leftward and rightward, hold fists against the waist. Look straight ahead (Figure 1-56).

图1-56(Figure 1-56)

35

(2)甲、乙双拳变掌,屈肘伸直,五指并拢,两臂垂于身体两侧。目视前方(图1-57)。

(2) Both A and B change fists into palms, bend elbow straight, close fingers, arms fall at both sides. Look straight ahead (Figure 1-57).

图1-57(Figure 1-57)

第二章　少林炮拳
Chapter 2　Shaolin Cannon Boxing

第一节　套路动作名称
Quarter 1　Routine Names

第一段
Section 1

1.预备势

1. Preparation

2.撩手摘心捶

2. Thrust-pick fist

3.转身窝心炮

3. Turning centroid cannon

4.倒步连砸拳

4. Retreat and smash fist

5.马步冲天捶

5. Horse-riding stance pounding upward

6.舞花虎抱头

6. Waving and holding

7.转身云顶七星

7. Turning and waving

8.弓步单鞭

8. Bow stance single whip

9.舞花虎抱头

9. Waving and holding

10. 上步左斜形

10. Stepping obliquely leftward

11. 劈腿右斜形

11. Stretching obliquely rightward

12. 十字踩脚

12. Cross stamping

13. 转身窝心捶

13. Turning centroid fist

14. 倒步连砸拳

14. Retreat and smash fist

15. 马步冲天捶

15. Horse-riding stance pounding upward

第二段

Section 2

16. 拦腰双绝手

16. Blocking palms

17. 抬腿小提鞋

17. Lifting and swinging

18. 蹁腿撞肘

18. Bumping and kicking

19. 转身双撅拳

19. Turning and thrusting

20. 起身双风灌耳

20. Rising and swinging

21. 劈腿右斜形

21. Stretching obliquely rightward

22. 撩手迎面捶

22. Hand-on thrusting

23. 转身云顶七星

23. Turning and waving

24. 马步单鞭

24. Horse-riding stance single whip

25. 舞花虎抱头

25. Waving and holding

26.摇身三卧枕

26. Turning and punching

27.转身一捶

27. Turning and striking

28.倒步连砸捶

28. Retreat and smash fist

29.马步冲天捶

29. Horse-riding stance pounding upward

第三段

Section 3

30.转身仆步

30. Turning for the drop stance

31.起身撞肘

31. Rising and elbowing

32.转身双撅捶

32. Turning and thrusting

33.起身双风灌耳

33. Rising and swinging

34.劈腿斜形

34. Stretching obliquely

35.马步挎毛篮

35. Horse-riding stance swinging

36.震脚海底炮

36. Kicking upward

37.右斜形

37. Turning obliquely rightward

38.原地一掌

38. Palming in situ

39.弓步撞肘

39. Bow stance elbowing

40.转身双撅手

40. Turning and double thrusting

41.起身双风灌耳

41. Rising and swinging

第四段
Section 4

42.跌跃单叉步

42. Jumping and hooking

43.起身冲天炮

43. Rising and pounding upward

44.束身下按掌

44. Bending and palming

45.起身五指朝凤

45. Rising and hooking

46.转身云顶七星

46. Turning and waving

47.坐山单鞭

47. Bend for single whip

48.舞花坐山

48. Swinging and bending

49.并步抱拳

49. Closing and holding

50.收势

50. Closing

第二节 套路动作图解
Quarter 2　Figures of Routine Movements

第一段
Section 1

1.预备势

(1)两脚并立,两臂自然下垂于身体两侧,挺胸收腹,成立正姿势。目视前方(图2-1)。

第二章 少林炮拳

1. Preparation

(1) Feet parallel, arms fall naturally, throw out chest and withdraw abdomen, stand at attention. Look straight ahead (Figure 2-1).

图 2-1(Figure 2-1)

(2)两臂屈肘向上提,两掌变拳抱于腰间;同时,左脚向左一步,与肩同宽。目视前方(图2-2)。

(2) Bend arms and lift elbows, change palms into fists against the waist, at the same time, left foot strides a step leftward, the same wide as shoulders. Look straight ahead (Figure 2-2).

图 2-2(Figure 2-2)

2.撩手摘心捶

(1)左脚向左跨一步,成左弓步;同时,左拳变掌由腰间向左搂手。目视左掌(图2-3)。

2. Thrust-pick fist

(1) Left foot strides a step leftward into the left bow stance, at the same time, change left fist into palm and make it rake leftward against the waist. Look

41

at left palm (Figure 2-3).

图 2-3(Figure 2-3)

(2)接上势,左掌外旋向下缠掌变拳,拳心向里。目视左拳(图2-4)。

(2) Keep moving, swing left palm outward and downward and change it into fist, fist center inward. Look at left fist (Figure 2-4).

图 2-4(Figure 2-4)

3.转身窝心炮

(1)右腿向前提膝;同时,右拳由腰间向上方摆击,置于右胸前,拳心向里,拳眼向上,左拳随身体上起时,向下栽于右膝前,拳心向里,拳眼向上。目视右拳(图2-5)。

3. Turning centroid cannon

(1) Lift right knee forward, at the same time, swing right fist upward against the waist to the right chest, fist center inward, fist eye upward, rise and make left fist downward to the front of the right knee, fist center inward, fist eye upward. Look at right fist (Figure 2-5).

第二章 少林炮拳

图 2-5(Figure 2-5)

（2）上动不停，右腿下落成弓步；同时，左右两拳向体前砸拳，拳心向里，拳眼向上。目视右拳（图 2-6）。

(2) Keep moving, right leg falls into the bow stance, at the same time, fists smash forward, fist center inward, fist eye upward. Look at right fist (Figure 2-6).

图 2-6(Figure 2-6)

（3）上动不停，两脚向左碾地，身体左转 180°成左弓步，右拳随身体左转，向上抄拳，拳面向上，左拳变掌，掌心向下置于右小臂上。目视右拳（图 2-7）。

(3) Keep moving, feet grind leftward, turn leftward 180°into the left bow stance, swing right fist leftward and upward, fist face upward, change left fist into palm and press it against right forearm. Look at right fist (Figure 2-7).

图 2-7(Figure 2-7)

43

4.倒步连砸拳

(1)右脚向左脚后插步成歇步;同时,右拳向上经头顶向右下方摆击,拳心向上,左掌变拳收抱腰间。目视右拳(图2-8)。

4. Retreat and smash fist

(1) Right foot strides behind left foot into the sitting stance, at the same time, swing right fist upward, and rightward and downward, fist center upward, change left palm into fist against the waist. Look at right fist (Figure 2-8).

图 2-8(Figure 2-8)

(2)左脚向左一步;同时,左拳由腰间向上经头顶向右下砸拳,拳眼向上,右拳收抱腰间。目视左拳(图2-9)。

(2) Left foot strides a step leftward, at the same time, smash left fist upward from the waist, rightward and downward, fist eye upward, close right fist against the waist. Look at left fist (Figure 2-9).

图 2-9(Figure 2-9)

第二章 少林炮拳

5.马步冲天捶

身体左转,重心移至两腿中间屈膝下蹲成马步;同时,两拳由下向身体左前上方冲击,拳心向里。目视右前方(图2-10)。

5. Horse-riding stance pounding upward

Turn left, shift gravity center to the crotch, squat into the horse riding stance, at the same time, fists pounce leftward and forward, fist center inward. Look rightward and forward (Figure 2-10).

图 2-10(Figure 2-10)

6.舞花虎抱头

身体重心左移,右脚收到左脚脚腰处,两腿屈膝下蹲成丁步;同时,左拳向下经腹前向头顶右上方摆击,右拳向下置于右腿内侧,拳心向里。目视右前方(图2-11)。

6. Waving and holding

Shift gravity center to left leg, close right foot to left foot into T step, at the same time, swing left fist downward in front of the abdomen, rightward and upward, swing right fist downward to right leg inward, fist center inward. Look rightward and forward (Figure 2-11).

图 2-11（Figure 2-11）

7.转身云顶七星

(1)右脚向左脚后插步,左脚掌向右碾地,身体右转 270°,右脚尖点地;同时,两拳变掌,左掌在上,右掌在下,两掌心相对,在头顶向右摆臂旋转一周变拳收抱腰间。目视前方(图 2-12)。

7. Turning and waving

(1) Right foot strides behind left foot, left sole grinds rightward, turn right 270°, right tiptoes touchdown, at the same time, change fists into palms, left palm above and right palm below, palm centers against each other, swing a circle overhead change them into fists against the waist. Look straight ahead (Figure 2-12).

图 2-12（Figure 2-12）

(2)上动不停,右脚向前一步,左脚向前跟进置于右脚内侧,两腿屈膝下蹲成丁步;同时,左拳置于右小臂内侧手腕处,两臂向前冲击。目视前方(图 2-13)。

(2) Keep moving, right foot strides a step forward, left foot strides forward to right foot inward, squat into T step, at the same time, punch left fist forward

from right forearm inward. Look straight ahead (Figure 2-13).

图 2-13(Figure 2-13)

8.马步单鞭

(1)身体左转,左脚向后一步,两腿屈膝下蹲成马步;同时,两臂屈肘内收置胸前,拳心向里。目视前方(图2-14)。

8. Bow stance single whip

(1) Turn left, left foot retreats a step, squat into the horse-riding stance, at the same time, bend arms against the chest, fist center inward. Look straight ahead (Figure 2-14).

图 2-14(Figure 2-14)

(2)上动不停,两拳同时向身体两侧冲击,拳心向下。目视左前方(图2-15)。

(2) Keep moving, pounce fists at the same time, fist center downward. Look leftward and forward (Figure 2-15).

47

图 2-15(Figure 2-15)

9.舞花虎抱头

身体重心右移,左脚向右脚内侧收步,两腿屈膝下蹲,左脚脚尖点地成丁步;同时,右拳向下经腹前向头顶上方摆击,拳心向上;左拳向下摆击于腹前,拳心向里。目视左前方(图 2-16)。

9. Waving and holding

Shift gravity center rightward, close left foot to right foot inward, tiptoes touchdown into T step, at the same time, swing right fist downward against the abdomen and upward, fist center upward, swing left fist downward in front of abdomen, fist center inward. Look leftward and forward (Figure 2-16).

图 2-16(Figure 2-16)

10.上步左斜形

(1)身体左转,左脚尖点地成左虚步;同时,左拳由里向外摆击,右拳向下摆击收于体前,左拳在前,右拳在后,两拳心向上。目视前方(图 2-17)。

10. Stepping obliquely leftward

(1) Turn left, left tiptoes touchdown into the left empty stance, at the

same time, swing left fist forward, swing right fist downward, left fist in front, right fist behind, fist centers upward. Look straight ahead (Figure 2-17).

图 2-17(Figure 2-17)

(2)右脚向前一步,左脚向前弹踢,两拳收抱腰间。目视左脚(图 2-18)。

(2) Right foot strides a step forward, left foot kicks forward, close fists against the waist. Look at left foot (Figure 2-18).

图 2-18(Figure 2-18)

(3)左腿下落屈膝前弓成弓步;同时,右拳由腰间向前冲击,左拳由腰间向后冲击,两拳心向下成左斜型势。目视前方(图 2-19)。

(3) Bend left knee into the front bow stance, at the same time, pounce right fist forward from the waist, pounce left fist backward from the waist, fist centers downward. Look straight ahead (Figure 2-19).

图 2-19(Figure 2-19)

11.劈腿右斜形

(1)左拳收抱腰间,右脚向上勾踢;同时,右拳回收向下劈拳,拳心向上。目视前方(图 2-20)。

11. Stretching obliquely rightward

(1) Close left fist against the waist, right foot hooks and kicks upward, at the same time, close right fist downward to chop, fist center upward. Look straight ahead (Figure 2-20).

图 2-20(Figure 2-20)

(2)右腿下落屈膝前弓成弓步;同时,右拳向上收至胸前再向后摆击,拳心向下,左拳从腰间向前冲击,拳心向下,两拳眼相对成右斜型势。目视前方(图 2-21)。

(2) Bend right knee into the front bow stance, at the same time, close right fist upward to the front of the chest and make it swing backward, fist center downward, left fist pounces forward from the waist, fist centers downward, fist eyes against each other. Look straight ahead (Figure 2-21).

图 2-21(Figure 2-21)

第二章 少林炮拳

12.十字踩脚

(1)左脚向上弹踢,左拳收抱腰间;同时,右拳变掌拍击左脚面。目视右掌(图2-22)。

12. Cross stamping

(1) Left foot kicks upward, close left fist against the waist, at the same time, change right fist into palm to pat left instep. Look at right palm (Figure 2-22).

图2-22(Figure 2-22)

(2)上动不停,左脚下落,脚尖着地;同时,右掌变拳收抱腰间。目视前方(图2-23)。

(2) Keep moving, left foot falls, tiptoes touchdown, at the same time, change right palm into fist against the waist. Look straight ahead (Figure 2-23).

图2-23(Figure 2-23)

(3)右脚向上弹踢,左拳变掌拍击右脚面。目视左掌(图2-24)。

(3) Right foot kicks upward, change left fist into palm to pat right instep. Look at left palm (Figure 2-24).

图 2-24（Figure 2-24）

（4）上动不停，右脚下落置于左脚前方，脚尖着地；同时，左掌变拳收抱腰间。目视前方（图 2-25）。

（4）Keep moving, right foot falls in front of left foot, tiptoes touchdown, at the same time, change left palm into fist against the waist. Look straight ahead (Figure 2-25).

图 2-25（Figure 2-25）

（5）左脚向上弹踢，右拳变掌拍击左脚面。目视右掌（图 2-26）。

（5）Left foot kicks upward, change right fist into palm to pat left instep. Look at right palm (Figure 2-26).

图 2-26（Figure 2-26）

第二章 少林炮拳

13.转身窝心捶

（1）上动不停,身体左转180°,左腿随身体左转的力量向下外旋勾踢,成蝎子尾勾踢式后向上左提膝;同时,右掌变拳收抱腰间。目视左前方(图2-27)。

13. Turning centroid fist

(1) Keep moving, left foot falls, at the same time turn leftward 180°, left leg hooks and kicks backward like scorpion tail, lift left knee, at the same time, change right palm into fist against the waist. Look leftward and forward (Figure 2-27).

图 2-27（Figure 2-27）

（2）左脚落地成左弓步,右拳向斜上方抄拳,拳心向上;同时,左拳变掌向下按击在右小臂上。目视前方(图2-28)。

(2) Left foot falls into the left bow stance, right fist swings obliquely upward, fist center upward, at the same time, change left fist into palm downward on the right forearm. Look straight ahead (Figure 2-28).

图 2-28（Figure 2-28）

14.倒步连砸拳

(1)右脚向左脚后插步屈膝下蹲成歇步;同时,右拳向上经头顶向右下方摆击,拳心向上,左掌变拳收抱于腰间。目视右拳(图2-29)。

14. Retreat and smash fist

(1) Right foot strides behind left foot into the sitting stance, at the same time, swing right fist upward, rightward and downward, fist center upward, change left palm into fist against the waist. Look at right fist (Figure 2-29).

图2-29(Figure 2-29)

(2)左脚向左一步,脚尖着地;同时,左拳由腰间向上经头顶向身体右下方砸拳,拳眼向上;右拳收抱腰间。目视左拳(图2-30)。

(2) Left foot strides a step leftward, tiptoes touchdown, at the same time, swing left fist upward, rightward and downward, fist eye upward, close right fist against the waist. Look at left fist (Figure 2-30).

图2-30(Figure 2-30)

15.马步冲天捶

身体左转,重心移至两腿中间,两腿屈膝下蹲成马步;同时,两拳由下向身体左上方冲击,拳心向里。目视右前方(图2-31)。

15. Horse-riding stance pounding upward

Turn left, shift gravity center to the crotch, squat into the horse-riding stance, at the same time, swing fist in front of the leftt chest, fist center inward. Look rightward and forward (Figure 2-31).

图 2-31(Figure 2-31)

第二段

Section 2

16.拦腰双绝手

(1)身体右转,两拳变掌向右前方双搂手,右掌在上,左掌在下,掌心向右后方。目视两手(图 2-32)。

16. Blocking palms

(1) Turn right, change fists into palms to rake rightward and forward, right palm above and left palm below, palm centers rightward and upward. Look at hands (Figure 2-32).

图 2-32(Figure 2-32)

(2)上动不停,两掌向后收拉至胸前后变拳,右拳在上,左拳在下,两拳眼相照;同时,身体后穹,右腿提膝。目视右前方(图2-33)。

(2) Keep moving, change palms into fists and close them to the front of the chest, right fist above, left fist below, fist eyes against each other, at the same time, the body back uplift, lift right knee. Look rightward and forward (Figure 2-33).

图 2-34(Figure 2-33)

(3)上动不停,右腿向前落步,左脚向前跟进成右弓步;同时,两拳由腰间向前冲击,两拳眼相对。目视两拳(图2-34)。

(3) Keep moving, right leg falls forward, left foot strides forward into the right bow stance, at the same time, swing fists forward from the waist, fist eyes against each other. Look at fists (Figure 2-34).

图 2-34(Figure 2-34)

17.抬腿小提鞋

身体右转,左腿提膝;同时,两拳变掌内旋,置于左脚跟处,右掌掌心向上,左掌掌心向下。目视左前方(图2-35)。

17. Lifting and swinging

Turn right, lift left knee, at the same time, change fists into palms to turn inward and left heel, right palm center upward, left palm center downward. Look leftward and forward (Figure 2-35).

图 2-35(Figure 2-35)

18.踹脚撞肘

(1)两掌变拳收抱腰间,左腿向前踹击。目视前方(图2-36)。

18. Bumping and kicking

(1) Change palms into fists against the waist, left leg kicks forward. Look straight ahead (Figure 2-36).

图 2-36(Figure 2-36)

(2)上动不停,左腿下落成左弓步;同时,身体前俯,右肘向前横击,左拳变掌按在右肘臂上。目视前方(图2-37)。

(2) Keep moving, left leg falls into the left bow stance, at the same time, bend, swing right elbow forward, change left fist into palm against right elbow. Look straight ahead (Figure 2-37).

图 2-37（Figure 2-37）

19.转身双撇拳

（1）身体向右转180°，身体向前下方俯身前穹，两拳变掌经头顶向体前下方伏抓后随身体后仰的同时再向腹前收拉抱拳至腰间；同时，右腿随身体上起的力量向上提膝。目视前方（图2-38）。

19. Turning and thrusting

(1) Turn rightward 180°, change fists into palms, swing them upward to grab downward and close them against abdomen, change them into fists against the waist, at the same time, lift right leg. Look straight ahead (Figure 2-38).

图 2-38（Figure 2-38）

（2）右脚向前屈膝落步，左腿随即屈膝跟进，脚掌着地成跪步；同时，两拳由腰间向前发力冲击随弹力向后收于胸前，两拳心向里。目视前方（图2-39）。

(2) Right foot strides forward, bend knee and fall, bend left knee, sole touchdown into the kneeling stance, at the same time, swing fists forward from

the waist and close them against the chest, fist centers inward. Look straight ahead (Figure 2-39).

图 2-39(Figure 2-39)

20.起身双风灌耳

右脚先向前一步,左脚随即跟进,两腿上起成并步站立;同时,两拳由体前向下、向两侧摆拳至体前上方时再向胸前合肘摆击,两拳与下额同高,拳心向里。目视前方(图 2-40)。

20. Rising and swinging

Right foot strides a step forward, left foot follows up, lift legs into the waiting stance, at the same time, swing fists downward and sideward, close elbow and swing forward and upward, keep fists at the lower jaw's level, fist center inward. Look straight ahead (Figure 2-40).

图 2-40(Figure 2-40)

21.劈腿右斜形

(1)左脚向前一步,脚尖点地,身体重心在右腿;同时,左拳收抱腰间,右拳向上抄拳。目视前方(图 2-41)。

21. Stretching obliquely rightward

(1) Left foot strides a step forward, tiptoe touchdown, at the same time, close left fist against the waist, swing right fist upward. Look straight ahead (Figure 2-41).

图 2-41（Figure 2-41）

（2）上动不停,身体重心向前移至左腿,右脚向前上方摆踢,右拳向下劈拳,拳心向上。目视前方(图 2-42)。

(2) Keep moving, right foot licks forward and upward, right fist chops downward, fist center upward. Look straight ahead (Figure 2-42).

图 2-42（Figure 2-42）

（3）右腿下落,身体左转下蹲成马步;同时,两臂屈肘抱于胸前,拳心向里。目视前方(图 2-43)。

(3) Right leg falls, turn left and squat into the horse-riding stance, at the same time, bend elbow against the chest, fist center inward, Look straight ahead (Figure 2-43).

第二章 少林炮拳

图 2-43（Figure 2-43）

（4）上动不停，两脚向右碾地，身体右转成右弓步；同时，两臂内旋，左拳向前摆击，右拳向后摆击，两拳眼相对成右斜型势。目视前方（图 2-44）。

（4）Keep moving, feet grind rightward, turn right into the right bow stance, at the same time, turn arms inward, swing left fist forward, swing right fist backward, fist eyes against each other. Look straight ahead (Figure 2-44).

图 2-44（Figure 2-44）

22.撩手迎面捶

（1）左拳变掌，手腕放松由下向上内旋一周，指尖斜向上。目视左掌（图 2-45）。

22 Hand-on thrusting

（1）Change left fist into palm, turn inward and upward, fingertips obliquely upward. Look at left palm (Figure 2-45).

图 2-45（Figure 2-45）

61

（2）上动不停，左脚向前一步成左弓步；同时，右拳向前冲击，迎击在左拳心内。目视左掌（图2-46）。

(2) Keep moving, left foot strides a step forward into the left bow stance, at the same time, swing right fist forward, swing left palm backward to resist right fist. Look at left palm (Figure 2-46).

图2-46（Figure 2-46）

23.转身云顶七星

（1）上动不停，身体右转，左掌向上，右拳变掌。目视右掌（图2-47）。

23. Turning and waving

(1) Keep moving, turn right, left palm upward, change right fist into palm. Look at right palm (Figure 2-47).

图2-47（Figure 2-47）

（2）上动不停，展臂扭腰，两掌由左向右绕头一周后变拳收抱腰间。目视前方（图2-48）。

(2) Keep moving, swing palms around the head from left to right and

change them into fists against the waist. Look straight ahead (Figure 2-48).

图 2-48(Figure 2-48)

(3)右脚向前一步,左脚跟进,脚尖点地置于右脚内侧,两腿屈膝半蹲成左丁步,左拳置于右臂内侧,两拳同时向前冲击,拳心向下。目视右拳(图 2-49)。

(3) Right foot strides a step forward, left heel follows up, tiptoes touchdown and in right foot inward, partly squat into the left T step, left fist in right arm inward, at the same time swing outward, fist center downward. Look at right fist (Figure 2-49).

图 2-49(Figure 2-49)

24.马步单鞭

(1)身体左转,左脚向后一步两腿屈膝下蹲成马步;同时,两臂屈肘回收至胸前,拳心向里。目视前方(图 2-50)。

24. Horse-riding stance single whip

(1) Turn left, left foot retreats a step into the horse-riding stance, at the

same time, bend arms against the chest, fist center inward. Look straight ahead (Figure 2-50).

图 2-50(Figure 2-50)

（2）上动不停,两拳分别向身体两侧冲击,拳心向下。目视左前方(图2-51)。

（2） Keep moving, swing fists sideward, fist center downward. Look leftward and forward (Figure 2-51).

图 2-51(Figure 2-51)

25.舞花虎抱头

身体重心右移,左脚向右脚内侧收步两腿屈膝下蹲成左丁步;同时,右拳向下经腹前向头顶上方摆击,拳心向上,左拳向下摆击于腹前。目视左前方(图 2-52)。

25. Waving and holding

Shift gravity center rightward, close left foot to right foot inward into the left T step, at the same time, swing right fist downward against the abdomen and upward, fist center upward, swing left fist downward against the abdomen. Look leftward and forward (Figure 2-52).

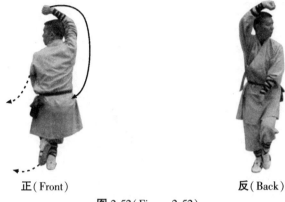

正(Front)　　　　　反(Back)

图 2-52(Figure 2-52)

26.摇身三卧枕

(1)左脚向左一步,脚尖点地;同时,右拳收抱腰间,左拳向左下方摆击。目视左拳(图 2-53)。

26. Turning and punching

(1) Left foot strides a step leftward, tiptoes touchdown, at the same time, close right fist against the waist, swing left fist leftward and downward. Look at left fist (Figure 2-53).

图 2-53(Figure 2-53)

(2)上动不停,左脚向前一步成左弓步;同时,左拳向下、向右经腹前向上摆击,右拳向右下方摆击。目视左前方(图 2-54)。

(2) Keep moving, left foot strides a step forward into the left bow stance,

at the same time, swing left fist downward, rightward and upward against the abdomen, swing right fist rightward and downward. Look leftward and forward (Figure 2-54).

图 2-54(Figure 2-54)

(3)右脚向前上一步身体左转成右弓步；同时，右拳向上、向下摆击置于右胸前，拳心向里，左拳向下外旋划弧置于腹前，拳心向后成右卧枕势。目视后方(图 2-55)。

(3) Right foot strides a step into the right bow stance, at the same time, swing right fist upward and downward against the chest, fist center inward, left fist turns outward and draw curve in front of the abdomen, fist center backward. Look backward (Figure 2-55).

图 2-55(Figure 2-55)

(4)身体向左微转，重心移至左腿，右脚尖点地；同时，左拳收抱腰间，右拳向前冲击，拳心向后。目视右拳(图 2-56)。

(4) Turn slightly leftward, shift gravity center to the left leg, right tiptoes touchdown, at the same time, close left fist against the waist, swing right fist forward, fist center downward. Look at right fist (Figure 2-56).

图 2-56（Figure 2-56）

（5）上动不停,右臂向左下方经腹前向上,经头顶向身体右侧摆击,拳心向里;同时,右脚向右碾脚,身体右转 180°,左脚向上提起,左拳向上经头顶向下摆击,拳心向里。目视右下方(图 2-57)。

(5) Keep moving, swing right arm leftward and downward in front of the abdomen, upward and rightward, fist center inward, at the same time, turn rightward 180°, lift left foot upward, swing left fist upward, overhead and downward, fist center inward. Look rightward and downward (Figure 2-57).

图 2-57（Figure 2-57）

（6）上动不停,左脚下落成弓步;同时,左拳向下经腹前向左上方冲击,拳心向里,右拳向上经头顶向腹前冲击,拳心向后成左卧枕势。目视右后方(图 2-58)。

(6) Keep moving, left foot falls into the bow stance, at the same time, swing left fist downward, against the abdomen, and leftward and upward, fist center inward, swing right fist upward, overhead and in front of abdomen, fist center backward. Look rightward and backward (Figure 2-58).

图 2-58（Figure 2-58）

（7）紧接上动,身体上起,重心移至右腿,左脚尖点地;同时,左臂向前摆击,右拳收抱腰间。目视左拳(图 2-59)。

（7）Keep moving, rise, shift gravity center to the right leg, left tiptoes touchdown, at the same time, swing left arm forward, close right fist against the waist. Look at left fist (Figure 2-59).

图 2-59（Figure 2-59）

（8）上动不停,左脚向左碾脚,身体左转180°,右脚向左前上方上提;同时,左拳向下经腹前向上至头顶后向下摆击于体侧,拳心向后;右拳向右、向上经头顶向身体右侧肩前摆击,拳心向后。目视左拳(图 2-60)。

（8）Keep moving, turn leftward 180°, lift right knee, at the same time, swing left fist downward in front of the abdomen, and upward and downward, fist center backward, swing right fist rightward, upward, overhead, rightward and downward, fist center backward. Look at left fist (Figure 2-60).

图 2-60(Figure 2-60)

(9)上动不停,右腿下落成弓步;同时,左拳向上,向下经腹前向身体左下方冲击,拳心向后,右拳向下、向上屈肘冲拳,肘关节贴紧身体,拳心向里成右卧枕势。目视左后方(图 2-61)。

(9) Keep moving, right leg falls into the bow stance, at the same time, swing left fist upward, downward and in front of the abdomen, and leftward and downward, fist center backward, right fist downward, swing upward, close the elbow, fist center inward. Look leftward and backward (Figure 2-61).

图 2-61(Figure 2-61)

27.转身一捶

双脚向左碾转,身体左转;同时,右拳由下向上冲击,拳心向上,左拳变掌置于右小臂内侧。目视右拳(图 2-62)。

27. Turning and striking

Turn left, at the same time, swing right fist upward, fist center upward, change left fist into palm to right forearm inward. Look at right fist (Figure 2-62).

图 2-62（Figure 2-62）

28.倒步连砸捶

（1）右脚向左脚后插步,两腿屈膝下蹲成歇步;同时,右拳向上经头顶向右下方摆击,拳心向上,左拳变掌收抱腰间。目视右拳(图2-63)。

28. Retreat and smash fist

（1）Right foot strides behind the left foot into the sitting stance, at the same time, swing right fist upward, overhead, rightward and downward, fist center upward, change left fist into palm against the waist. Look at right fist (Figure 2-63).

图 2-63（Figure 2-63）

（2）上动不停,左脚向左一步;同时,右拳收抱腰间,左拳由腰间向上经头顶向身体右前方摆击,拳心向上。目视左拳(图2-64)。

（2）Keep moving, left foot strides a step leftward, at the same time, close right fist against the waist, swing left fist upward, overhead, and rightward and forward, fist center upward. Look at left fist (Figure 2-64).

图 2-64（Figure 2-64）

29.马步冲天捶

（1）身体左转；同时，两腿直立站起，两拳随身体的摆动向左、向上冲击。目视前方（图 2-65）。

29. Horse-riding stance pounding upward

(1) Turn left, at the same time, stand, and swing fists leftward and upward. Look straight ahead (Figure 2-65).

图 2-65（Figure 2-65）

（2）上动不停，两腿屈膝下蹲成马步；同时，两肘弯曲，两拳向下收置于左胸前，拳心向里。目视右前方（图 2-66）。

(2) Keep moving, squat into the horse-riding stance, at the same time, and bend elbows, close fists against the left chest, fist center inward. Look rightward and forward (Figure 2-66).

图 2-66(Figure 2-66)

第三段

Section 3

30.转身仆步

(1)两腿前弓成右弓步;同时,两拳变掌向右前方搂手。目视前方(图2-67)。

30. Turning for the drop stance

(1) Bend legs forward into the right bow stance, at the same time, change fists into palms to rake rightward and forward. Look straight ahead (Figure 2-67).

图 2-67(Figure 2-67)

(2)上动不停,两掌向后搂手,回拉变拳收抱至腰间;同时,身体重心后移至左腿,右脚提起。目视前方(图 2-68)。

(2) Keep moving, close palms against the waist and change them into fists, at the same time, shift the gravity center backward to the left leg, lift right foot. Look straight ahead (Figure 2-68).

第二章 少林炮拳

图 2-68（Figure 2-68）

（3）上动不停,左脚蹬地跳起;同时,身体右转,左拳向头顶上方摆击,右拳抱置腰间。目视前方（图 2-69）。

(3) Keep moving, left foot stamps and jumps, at the same time, turn right, swing left fist overhead, close right fist against the waist. Look straight ahead (Figure 2-69).

图 2-69（Figure 2-69）

（4）上动不停,右脚自然下落,屈膝下蹲,左脚向前落步成仆步;同时,左拳变掌由头顶向下经腹前向左前下方切掌,右拳抱置腰间。目视左掌（图 2-70）。

(4) Keep moving, right foot falls naturally, squat, left foot falls forward into the drop stance, at the same time, change left fist into palm and swing leftward and forward in front of the abdomen, close right fist against the waist. Look at left palm (Figure 2-70).

图2-70(Figure 2-70)

31.起身撞肘

身体上起,两腿前弓成弓步;同时,右臂屈肘向前横击肘,肘尖向前,左掌向后迎击右臂。目视肘尖(图2-71)。

31. Rising and elbowing

Rise, bend into the bow stance, at the same time, swing right elbow forward, elbow tip forward, left palm backward to resist right arm. Look at elbow tip (Figure 2-71).

图2-71(Figure 2-71)

32.转身双撅捶

(1)身体右转180°;同时,两臂伸直,两掌架于头顶,掌心向上。目视两掌(图2-72)。

32. Turning and thrusting

(1) Turn rightward 180°, at the same time, arms straight, close palms overhead, palm centers upward. Look at palms (Figure 2-72).

第二章　少林炮拳

图 2-72（Figure 2-72）

（2）上动不停,身体前伏,右腿向前屈膝成弓步;同时,两掌向下按掌,掌心向下。目视两掌(图 2-73)。

（2）Keep moving, bend, bend right knee forward into the bow stance, at the same time, press palms downward, palm centers downward. Look at palms (Figure 2-73).

图 2-73（Figure 2-73）

（3）上动不停,身体向后起身;重心移至右腿;左脚上提;同时,两掌变拳屈臂向后撞击,拳心向上。目视前方(图 2-74)。

（3）Keep moving, lean backward and rise, shift gravity center to the right leg, lift left foot, at the same time, change palms into fists and bend them backward to strike, fist centers upward. Look straight ahead (Figure 2-74).

图 2-74（Figure 2-74）

（4）左脚向前一步，右脚随即紧跟成左跪步；同时，两拳由腰间向前冲击，两拳心相照。目视两拳（图 2-75）。

(4) Left foot strides a step forward, right foot follows up into the left kneeling stance, at the same time, swing fists forward from the waist, fist centers against each other. Look at fists (Figure 2-75).

图 2-75（Figure 2-75）

33. 起身双风灌耳

右脚向前半步，左脚向前跟进一步，身体上起，两腿直立成并步；同时，两拳向两侧下方摆拳，再向胸前合肘摆击，拳心向里。目视前方（图 2-76）。

33. Rising and swinging

Right foot strides half a step forward, left foot follows up, rise, stand upright into the waiting stance, at the same time, swing fists sideward and downward, close elbow and swing it in front of the chest, fist center inward. Look straight ahead (Figure 2-76).

图 2-76（Figure 2-76）

34. 劈腿斜形

（1）左脚上前半步，脚尖点地；同时，左拳收抱腰间，右臂向前摆击与肩同高,拳心向里。目视右拳(图 2-77)。

34. Stretching obliquely

(1) Left foot strides half a step forward, tiptoes touchdown, at the same time, close left fist against the waist, swing right arm forward. Look at right fist (Figure 2-77).

图 2-77(Figure 2-77)

(2)上动不停,右腿向上勾踢,右拳向身后劈击。目视前方(图 2-78)。

(2) Keep moving, right leg hooks and kicks upward, swing right fist backward. Look straight ahead (Figure 2-78)

图 2-78(Figure 2-78)

(3)上动不停,右腿向前下落,身体左转 90°,两腿屈膝下蹲成弓步;同时,两臂屈肘向胸前收摆,两拳收至下额前,拳心向里。目视两拳(图 2-79)。

(3) Keep moving, right leg falls forward, turn leftward 90°, squat into the bow stance, at the same time, bend and close elbows to the front of the chest, close fists to lower jaw, fist centers inward. Look at fists (Figure 2-79).

图 2-79(Figure 2-79)

(4)接上动,身体右转,重心前移成弓步;同时,两拳由胸前向身体两侧冲击,两拳心向下,拳眼相照,两臂微屈成右斜型势。目视左拳(图 2-80)。

(4) Keep moving, turn right, shift gravity center forward into the bow stance, at the same time, swing fists sideward from the chest, fist centers downward and against each other, bend arms slightly. Look at left fist (Figure 2-80).

图 2-80(Figure 2-80)

35.马步挎毛篮

身体左转,两腿屈膝下蹲成马步;同时,左拳收抱腰间,右拳随身体左转的力量向下、向上弧形摆击,拳心向上。目视右拳(图 2-81)。

35. Horse-riding stance swinging

Turn left, squat, at the same time, close left fist against the waist, swing right fist downward and upward, fist center upward. Look at right fist (Figure 2-81).

第二章 少林炮拳

图 2-81（Figure 2-81）

36.震脚海底炮

（1）身体重心移置左脚，右脚提膝，右拳向上置右胸前，拳心向上，左拳变掌下按，拳心向下。目视左掌（图 2-82）。

36. Kicking upward

(1) Shift gravity center to left foot, lift right knee, close right fist against the chest, fist center upward, change left fist into palm and press it downward, fist center downward. Look at left palm (Figure 2-82).

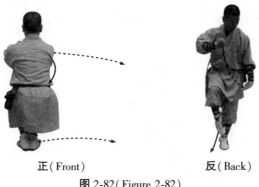

正(Front)　　　反(Back)

图 2-82（Figure 2-82）

（2）右脚向下震脚，两腿屈膝下蹲成并步；同时，右拳向下砸拳，左掌向上迎击，右拳在上，左掌在下。目视右拳发"咦"声（图 2-83）。注：震脚、砸拳的同时发"咦"声。

(2) Right foot stamps, squat into the waiting stance, at the same time, right fist smashes downward, left palm upward to resist, right fist above, left palm below. Look at right fist and cry "Hey" (Figure 2-83). Note：Stamp, smash and at the same time cry "Hey".

79

正(Front)　　　　　　反(Back)

图 2-83(Figure 2-83)

37.右斜形

（1）身体右转90°，左脚向前一步成弓步；同时，左掌变拳向前冲击，拳心向下，右拳收抱腰间。目视前方（图2-84）。

37. Turning obliquely rightward

（1）Turn rightward 90°, left foot strides a step forward into the bow stance, at the same time, swing left fist forward, fist center downward. Look straight ahead (Figure 2-84).

图 2-84(Figure 2-84)

（2）上动不停，身体右转180°；同时，右脚向左腿后插步，左腿前弓成弓步；同时，两拳收抱体前。目视两拳（图2-85）。

（2）Keep moving, turn rightward 180°, right foot retreats a step, bend left leg into the bow stance, at the same time, close fists against the chest. Look at fists (Figure 2-85).

正(Front)　　　　　反(Back)

图 2-85(Figure 2-85)

(3)上动不停,两拳由胸前同时向前、后冲击,两拳心向下,拳眼相照成左斜型势。目视右拳(图 2-86)。

(3) Keep moving, swing fists forward and backward front the chest, fist centers downward, fist eyes against each other. Look at right fist (Figure 2-86).

图 2-86(Figure 2-86)

38.原地一掌

(1)左拳变掌向下收抱腰间,右拳变掌向胸前按掌;同时,左腿提膝。目视右掌(图 2-87)。

38. Palming in situ

(1) Change left fist into palm and close it against the waist, change right fist into palm against the chest, at the same time, lift left knee. Look at right palm (Figure 2-87).

图 2-87(Figure 2-87)

（2）上动不停,左脚下落成左弓步,右掌向下收抱腰间,左掌由胸前向前推出,掌指向上。目视左掌(图 2-88)。

（2）Keep moving, left foot falls into the left bow stance, close right palm against the waist, push left palm forward from the chest, fingers upward. Look at left palm (Figure 2-88).

图 2-88(Figure 2-88)

39.弓步撞肘

上动不停,右臂屈肘上提向左前方撞击,力达肘尖;同时,左掌收回迎击在右肘上。目视肘尖(图 2-89)。

39. Bow stance elbowing

Keep moving, lift right elbow and make it swing forward, at the same time, close left palm to resist on the right arm. Look at elbow tip (Figure 2-89).

图 2-89(Figure 2-89)

40.转身双搬手

(1)身体右转180°,两腿前弓成右弓步;同时,身体前穷,双掌外旋向右前方搂手。目视双掌(图 2-90)。

40. Turning and double thrusting

(1) Turn rightward 180°, bend legs forward into the right bow stance, at the same time, lean forward, hands rotate outward and rake rightward and forward. Look at palms (Figure 2-90).

图 2-90(Figure 2-90)

(2)接上动,身体重心后移,身体后穷,双掌向胸前回拉变掌,两拳眼相照;同时,右腿提膝。目视前方(图 2-91)。

(2) Keep moving, shift the gravity center backward, pull palms to the front of the chest, fist eyes against each other, at the same time, lift right knee. Look straight ahead (Figure 2-91).

图 2-91（Figure 2-91）

（3）紧接上动,右脚向前下落,左脚随即跟进;同时,两拳向前方冲击,拳心向下,右拳在上,左拳在下,两拳眼相对。目视右拳(图 2-92)。

(3) Keep moving, right foot falls forward and downward, left foot follows up, at the same time, swing fists rightward and forward, fist centers downward, right fist above, left fist below, fist eyes against each other. Look at right fist (Figure 2-92).

图 2-92（Figure 2-92）

（4）上动不停,右脚向前一步,屈膝下蹲,左脚随即向前跟步下蹲成右跪步;同时,两拳向下,分别向身体两侧摆击,拳心向上。目视前下方(图2-93)。

(4) Keep moving, right foot strides a step forward, squat, left foot strides forward, squat into the right kneeling stance, at the same time, swing fists downward and sideward, and fist centers upward. Look forward and downward (Figure 2-93).

图 2-93（Figure 2-93）

41.起身双风灌耳

身体上起,右脚向前半步,左脚向前跟进一步,两腿直立成并步,身体左转 90°,两拳向两侧下方摆拳再向胸前合肘摆击,拳心向里。目视左前方（图 2-94）。

41. Rising and swinging

Right foot strides half a step, left foot follows up, rise, stand into the waiting stance, swing fists sideward and downward, close elbows to the front of the chest, fist center inward, at the same time, turn leftward 90°. Look leftward and forward (Figure 2-94).

正（Front）

反（Back）

图 2-94（Figure 2-94）

第四段

Section 4

42.跌跃单叉步

（1）左脚向左前方上步,右拳变掌,左拳向上,右掌向下,在体前迎击,两手心向下。目视右掌(图 2-95)。

42. Jumping and hooking

(1) Left foot strides leftward and forward, change right fist into palm, left fist above, right palm below to resist in front of the chest, hand centers downward. Look at right palm (Figure 2-95).

图 2-95(Figure 2-95)

(2)上动不停,两脚腾空跳起;同时,两掌向上摆击,置于头顶。目视左前下方(图 2-96)。

(2) Keep moving, jump, at the same time, swing palms upward and overhead. Look leftward, forward and downward (Figure 2-96).

图 2-96(Figure 2-96)

(3)右脚落地屈膝,左脚向前方下落成仆步;同时,右掌收抱腰间,左掌由上向下经体前向左下前方切掌,置于左小腿内侧。目视左掌(图 2-97)。

(3) Right foot falls and bend, left foot falls forward into the drop stance, at the same time, right palm against the waist, swing left palm leftward, downward and forward, to left shank inward. Look at left palm (Figure 2-97).

第二章 少林炮拳

图 2-97（Figure 2-97）

43.起身冲天炮

右腿向前提膝,身体上起,左腿弯曲;同时,右掌由腰间经胸前向上插掌,左掌向后经胸前收于右肘下方,掌心向下。目视前方(图 2-98)。

43. Rising and pounding upward

Lift right knee forward, rise, bend left knee, at the same time, swing right palm upward against the waist, close left palm to right elbow downward via the front of the chest, palm center downward. Look straight ahead (Figure 2-98).

图 2-98（Figure 2-98）

44.束身下按掌

右脚向后下方落步,两腿屈膝下蹲,左脚收在右脚内侧,脚尖点地成丁字步;同时,右掌向小腿外侧摆击,掌心向下,左掌收置右胸前,掌心向右。目视左掌(图 2-99)。

44. Bending and palming

Right foot falls backward, squat, close left foot to right foot inward, tiptoes touchdown into T step, at the same time, swing right palm outside the shank, palm center downward, close left palm above the right chest, palm center rightward. Look at left palm (Figure 2-99).

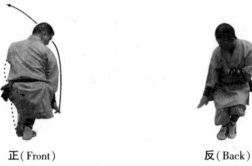

正(Front)　　　　　　　反(Back)

图 2-99(Figure 2-99)

45.起身五指朝凤

右腿弯曲上起，左腿提膝脚尖向下成左提膝；同时，右掌向头顶上方变勾手摆击，勾尖向后下方，左掌向左下方变勾手摆击，勾尖向上。目视左前方(图 2-100)。

45 Rising and hooking

Bend and lift right knee, lift left knee, tiptoes downward, lift left knee, at the same time, change right palm into hook and swing it overhead, hook tip downward, change left palm into hook and swing it leftward and downward, hook tip upward. Look leftward and forward (Figure 2-100).

图 2-100(Figure 2-100)

46.转身云顶七星

(1)左脚向左前方落步成左弓步；同时，左勾手变掌向头顶上方摆掌，掌心向上，右手向下经胸前向左前方摆掌，掌心向上。目视前方(图2-101)。

46. Turning and waving

(1) Left foot falls leftward into the left bow stance, at the same time, change left hand into palm and swing it overhead, palm center upward, swing right palm leftward and forward via the front of the chest, palm center upward. Look straight ahead (Figure 2-101).

图 2-101（Figure 2-101）

（2）身体右转360°,两脚向右碾成右偷步;同时,左掌向下,右掌向上逆时针方向在头顶上方绕转一周后收于体前,右掌在上,左掌在下,两掌心相照。目视右前方(图2-102)。

(2) Turn rightward 360°, feet grind rightward into the right false stance, at the same time, swing palms a circle anticlockwise overhead, close them against the chest, right palm above and left palm below, palm centers against each other. Look rightward and forward (Figure 2-102).

图 2-102（Figure 2-102）

（3）右脚向右上一步,左脚随即跟上,置于右脚内侧成丁字步;同时,两掌变拳收抱腰间后,向前方冲击,左臂屈肘,左拳置于右小臂内侧。目视前方(图2-103)。

（3）Right foot strides a step rightward, left foot follows up to right foot inward into T step, at the same time, change palms into fists against the waist, make them swing forward, bend left elbow, close left fist to right forearm inward. Look straight ahead (Figure 2-103).

图 2-103（Figure 2-103）

47.坐山单鞭

（1）身体左转 90°，左脚向左一步，两腿屈膝下蹲成马步；同时，两臂屈肘，两拳收抱于胸前，拳心向里。目视正前方（图 2-104）。

47. Bend for single whip

（1）Turn leftward 90°, left foot strides a step leftward, squat into the horse-riding stance, at the same time, bend elbows, close fists against the chest, fist center inward. Look straight ahead (Figure 2-104).

图 2-104（Figure 2-104）

（2）上动不停，两拳同时向身体两侧冲击，拳心向下。目视左拳（图2-105）。

（2）Keep moving, swing fists sideward, fist centers downward. Look at left fist (Figure 2-105).

第二章 少林炮拳

图 2-105（Figure 2-105）

48.舞花坐山

（1）身体上起，右脚向前上半步向下震脚，左腿提膝，同时，右拳经胸前向体侧摆击，左拳向上、向下、向左胸前摆击。目视右拳（图2-106）。

48. Swinging and bending

（1）Rise, right foot stride half a step forward, stamp, lift left knee, at the same time, swing right fist sideward via the front of the chest, swing left fist upward, downward and the front of the left chest. Look at right fist (Figure 2-106).

图 2-106（Figure 2-106）

（2）上动不停，左腿向左前方下落成马步；右拳向上、向左摆，架于头右前上方；左拳下栽于左膝上，左臂微屈外展；头随右拳上摆的同时左摆。目视左前方发"威"声（图2-107）。

（2）Keep moving, left leg falls leftward and forward into the horse-riding stance, swing right fist upward and leftward, and rightward and upward, close left fist against left knee, bend left knee slightly and outreach it, right fist upward and turn left. Look leftward and forward, cry "Wei" (Figure 2-107).

图 2-107（Figure 2-107）

49.并步抱拳

接上势，左脚向右成并步；同时，两拳抱于腰间。目视前方（图 2-108）。

49. Closing and holding

Keep moving, left foot strides rightward into the waiting stance, at the same time, close fists against the waist. Look straight ahead (Figure 2-108).

图 2-108（Figure 2-108）

50.收势

接上势，两拳变掌同时自然下垂，至身体两侧。目视前方（图 2-109）。

50. Closing

Keep moving, change fists into palms, at the same time naturally hang against the sides. Look straight ahead (Figure 2-109).

图 2-109（Figure 2-109）

第三章　少林长护心意门拳

Chapter 3　Shaolin Changhuxinyimen Boxing (Mid-and-will Boxing)

第一节　套路动作名称

Quarter 1　Routine Names

第一段

Section 1

1. 预备势
1. Preparation

2. 白蛇吐信
2. Snaking

3. 二龙分水
3. Double snaking

4. 右手摆掌
4. Right palm swinging

5. 天王托塔
5. Swinging and supporting

6. 倒步跨虎
6. Retreating and tiger riding

7. 冲天炮式
7. Upward punching posture

8. 提膝砸拳
8. Knee lifting and fist hammering

9. 转身七星

9. Turning and seven stars

10.二郎担山

10. Mountain shouldering

11.双关铁门

11. Double Closing

12.白猿洗脸

12. Face washing

13.又白猿洗脸

13. Face washing again

14.悬崖勒马

14. Danger avoiding

15.探马捶式

15. Elbow swinging posture

16.千斤砸捶

16. Hammering heavily

17.左翻背捶

17. Left back turning hammering

18.弓步扳掌

18. Bow stance wrestling

19.悬崖勒马

19. Danger avoiding

20.探马捶式

20. Elbow swinging posture

21.倒步跨虎

21. Retreating and tiger riding

22.撩阴手

22. Crotch hand

23.十字通背

23. Cross punching

24.拦腰捶

24. Waist blocking pounding

25.拔步炮

25. Striding cannon

26.悬崖勒马

26. Danger avoiding

27.十字通背

27. Cross punching

28.歇步摆拳

28. Sitting stance swinging

29.提膝抱肘

29. Lift knee and hold elbow

30.武松脱铐

30. Elbows pounding sideward

31.马步单鞭

31. Single horse-riding whipping

第二段

Section 2

32.拧身七星

32. Seven-star twisting

33.弓步双推掌

33. Duoble bow stance pushing

34.右踩脚式

34. Right slapping posture

35.双推掌式

35. Double pushing posture

36.左踩脚式

36. Left slapping posture

37.探马捶

37. Elbow swinging

38.转身推掌

38. Turning and pushing

39.黑虎蹬山

39. Black tiger mountaineering

40.转身扳手

40. Turning and wrestling

41.猿猴束身

41. Monkey closing

42.二起踩脚

42. Jumping and slapping

43.单叉

43. Single fork

44.起身摆腿

44. Arising and leg swinging

45.蝎子摆尾

45. Scorpion tail swinging

46.右摆脚

46. Foot swinging rightward

47.下阴捶

47. Crotch fist

48.反肘一捶

48. Reversing elbow thumping

49.千金砸捶

49. Hammering heavily

50.左翻背捶

50. Left back turning hammering

51.弓步扳掌

51. Bow stance wrestling

52.悬崖勒马

52. Danger avoiding

53.探马捶式

53. Elbow swinging posture

54.倒步跨虎

54. Retreating and tiger riding

55.撩阴手

55. Crotch hand

56.十字通背

56. Cross punching

57.拦腰捶

57. Waist blocking pounding

58.拔步炮

58. Striding cannon

59.悬崖勒马

59. Danger avoiding

60. 十字通背

60. Cross punching

61. 歇步摆拳

61. Sitting stance swinging

62. 提膝抱肘

62. Lift knee and hold elbow

63. 武松脱铐

63. Elbows pounding sideward

64. 马步单鞭

64. Single horse-stance whipping

第三段

Section 3

65. 拧身七星

65. Seven-star twisting

66. 弓步双推掌

66. Double bow stance pushing

67. 下阴腿式

67. Low crotch leg posture

68. 踹腿式

68. Sole kicking posture

69. 弓步双推掌

69. Double bow stance pushing

70. 老牛大摸头

70. Turning and crossed pushing

71. 大跨虎式

71. Tiger riding posture

72. 起身飞脚

72. Arising swinging kick

73. 金鸡独立

73. Standing on one leg

74. 顶心肘

74. Centroid elbowing

75. 翻背捶

75. Back turning punching

76.千斤砸拳

76. Heavily pounding

77.左翻背捶

77. Left back turning hammering

78.转身扳掌

78. Turning and wrestling

79.勒马鞍拳

79. Tightening

80.探马捶式

80. Elbow swinging posture

81.倒步跨虎

81. Retreating and tiger riding

82.撩阴手

82. Crotch hand

83.十字通背

83. Cross punching

84.拦腰捶

84. Waist blocking pounding

85.拔步炮

85. Striding cannon

86.悬崖勒马

86. Danger avoiding

87.十字通背

87. Cross punching

88.霸王观阵

88.Turning and double swinging

第四段

Section 4

89.左游身

89. left leg hitting and fists punching downward

90.双撩阴捶

90. Double crotch fists

91.金鸡独立

91. Standing on one leg

92.右游身

92. Right leg hitting and fists punching downward

93.双撩阴捶

93. Double crotch fists

94.金鸡独立

94. Standing on one leg

95.砸手转身

95. Hand pounding and turning

96.迎门铁扇

96. Head-on iron fan

97.猛虎跳涧

97. Tiger leaping

98.右探马捶

98. Right palm brushing

99.束手阴捶

99. Turning crotch fist

100.古树盘根

100. Ancient tree packs root

101.起身一掌

101. Arising palming

102.古树盘根

102. Ancient tree rooting

103.起身一掌

103. Arising palming

104.双推掌

104. Double pushing

105.倒步右跨虎

105. Retreating swinging rightward

106.倒步左跨虎

106. Retreating swinging leftward

107.双恨脚

107. Double stamping with sword fingers

108.右仙人指路

108. Sword finger thrusting rightward

109.左仙人指路

109. Sword finger thrusting leftward

110.云顶七星

110. Overhead seven stars

111.转身铁扇

111. Turning and iron fan swinging

112.罗汉观阵

112. Arhat-like striking

113.收势

113. Closing form

第二节　套路动作图解
Quarter 2　Figures of Routine Movements

第一段

Section 1

1.预备势

（1）两脚并立，两臂自然下垂于身体两侧，挺胸收腹，成立正姿势。目视前方(图 3-1)。

1. Preparation

(1) Stand with legs together, arms fall naturally, throw out chest and withdraw abdomen, stand at attention. Look straight ahead (Figure 3-1).

图 3-1(Figure 3-1)

(2)两臂屈肘向上提,两掌变拳抱于腰间;同时,左脚向左一步,与肩同宽。目视前方(图3-2)。

(2) Lift arms with bending elbows, change palms into fists against the waist; at the same time, left foot strides leftward a step the same wide as shoulders. Look straight ahead (Figure 3-2).

图3-2(Figure 3-2)

2.白蛇吐信

两拳变掌由腰间向身体前方插掌,掌心向下,指尖向前,两掌与肩同高。目视两掌(图3-3)。

2. Snaking

Change fists into palms to thrust forward from the waist, palm centers downward, fingertips forward at the shoulders' level. Look at palms (Figure 3-3).

图3-3(Figure 3-3)

3.二龙分水

两掌上旋,掌心向上收抱腰间,目视前方(图3-4);上动不停,两掌下旋,掌心向下按掌于身体两侧。目视前方(图3-5)。

3. Double snaking

Rotate palms upward to the waist, palm centers upward, Look straight ahead (Figure 3-4); keep moving, rotate palms downward to press on both sides, palm centers downward. Look straight ahead (Figure 3-5).

图 3-4(Figure 3-4)　　　图 3-5(Figure 3-5)

4.右手摆掌

(1)两掌向腹前上提,右掌在上,左掌在下,两掌心向上。目视右掌(图3-6)。

4. Right palm swinging

(1) Lift palms to the front of the abdomen, right palm above and left palm below, both palm centers upward. Look at right palm (Figure 3-6).

图 3-6(Figure 3-6)

(2)上动不停,右掌向身体右侧扳手击掌,掌心向正前方,掌指向右前方,与肩同高;同时,左掌向下收至腰间。目视右掌(图3-7)。

(2) Keep moving, wrench right palm rightward to clap hands, palm center straight forward, fingers rightward, at the level of shoulders; at the same time,

close left palm downward against the waist. Look at right palm (Figure 3-7).

图 3-7(Figure 3-7)

5.天王托塔

身体向左转180°,右脚不动,左脚向左碾地向后收于右脚内侧成丁字步;同时,右掌向下、向左经体前向左臂下方摆击。掌心向左外侧,掌指尖向上;左掌由腰间屈肘向上摆掌,置于左肩上方。掌心向上,掌指尖向后。目视左前方(图 3-8)。

5.Swinging and supporting

Turn left 180°, keep right foot still, left foot grinds leftward on the floor, and then backward to the inside of the right foot into T-stance; at the same time, swing right palm downward, rightward and then downward below the left arm via the front of the body, palm center outward to the left, fingertips upward; bend left elbow at the waist, swing left palm upward to the position over left shoulder, palm center upward and fingertips backward. Look left forward (Figure 3-8).

正(Front)　　　反(Back)

图 3-8(Figure 3-8)

6.倒步跨虎

(1)右脚向后撤一步,左掌向下按于体前。目视左掌(图3-9)。

6. Retreating and tiger riding

(1) Retreat right foot backward a step, press left palm downward in front of the body. Look at left palm (Figure 3-9).

图3-9(Figure 3-9)

(2)上动不停,左脚向后收半步,脚尖点地,身体重心移向右腿,两脚屈膝下蹲成虚步;同时,左掌向下,向身体左侧弧形摆击于左腿外侧成虎爪掌,掌心向下;右掌变拳向上摆击,收至于右肩上方,拳心向下。目视左前方(图3-10)。

(2) Keep moving, retreat left foot half a step, tiptoe touchdown, shift gravity center to right leg, bend knees to squat into empty stance; at the same time, left palm arcs downward and leftward to the outside of left leg into tiger claw palm, palm center downward; change right palm into fist to swing upward to the position over right shoulder, fist center downward. Look right forward (Figure 3-10).

图3-10(Figure 3-10)

第三章 少林长护心意门拳

7.冲天炮式

（1）左脚向前一步；同时，右拳向下、向上冲击置于腹前；左掌变拳向上冲击，置于右小臂上方，两拳心向上，右拳在前，左拳在后。目视右拳（图3-11）。

7. Upward punching posture

(1) Left foot strides a step forward; at the same time, punch right fist downward, upward to the front of the abdomen; change left palm into fist to punch upward to the position over right forearm, both fist centers upward, right fist in front and left fist behind. Look at right fist (Figure 3-11).

图 3-11(Figure 3-11)

（2）上动不停，右脚向前一步，扣在左脚跟处，成丁字步；同时，右拳向头上方冲出，拳心向左前方；左拳向下收抱腰间。目视左前方（图3-12）。

(2) Keep moving, right foot strides a step forward, buckled at the left heel into T-stance; at the same time, punch right fist upward to the top over the head, fist center left forward; left fist moves downward to the waist. Look left forward (Figure 3-12).

图 3-12(Figure 3-12)

8.提膝砸拳

左脚向前一步,屈膝下蹲,右脚向前提膝上击;同时,右拳向下砸拳,左拳变掌,掌心向上迎击右拳于右膝关节上。目视前方(图 3-13)。

8. Knee lifting and fist hammering

Left foot strides a step forward, bend knee to squat, right foot moves forward with knee lifting; at the same time, right fist hammers downward, change left fist into palm, supinely to resist right fist on the right knee. Look straight ahead (Figure 3-13).

图 3-13(Figure 3-13)

9.转身七星

右脚向后落步,身体右转 180°,左脚随即跟进右脚,脚尖扣在右脚内侧,两腿屈膝下蹲;同时,右拳向前冲出,拳心向下与肩同高,左掌变拳,肘屈向上摆击于右臂肘关节内侧,拳心向下。目视右前方(图 3-14)。

9. Turning and seven stars

Right foot falls backward, turn right 180°, left foot follows at once, buckle tiptoe at the inside of the right foot, bend legs to squat; at the same time, punch right fist forward, fist center downward at the level of shoulders, change left palm into fist, bend elbow to swing to the inside of right elbow joint, fist center downward. Look right forward (Figure 3-14).

图 3-14（Figure 3-14）

10.二郎担山

（1）身体左转,左脚向左后方退一步;同时,右拳向上、向左至左肩前向下摆击于体前,掌心向下;左臂屈肘向上,左拳置于左肩前,拳心向左前下方,两臂交叉,左拳在内,右拳在外。目视左拳(图 3-15)。

10. Mountain shouldering

（1）Turn left, retreat left foot backward to the left, at the same time, right fist moves upward, leftward to the front of the left shoulder, and then swings downward to the front of the body, palm center downward; left arm upward with bending elbow, left fist in front of the left shoulder, fist center left downward, arms crossed, left fist inside and right fist outside. Look at left fist (Figure 3-15).

图 3-15（Figure 3-15）

（2）上动不停,两脚向左碾地,左脚屈膝前弓;同时,左拳向前,右拳向后,两拳同时向身体两侧冲拳,拳心向下,左臂稍高于右臂。目视左前方(图 3-16)。

（2）Keep moving, feet grind leftward on the ground, bend left knee into front bow stance; at the same time, left fist forward and right fist backward, punch fists outside at the same time, fist centers downward, left arm is little higher than right arm. Look left forward (Figure 3-16).

图 3-16(Figure 3-16)

11.双关铁门

左脚向右收脚,脚尖点地,扣在右脚脚腰内,两腿屈膝下蹲;同时,两拳由上向下屈肘向体前摆击,两拳心向下,拳面相对。目视左前方(图 3-17)。

11. Double Closing

Left foot moves rightward, tiptoe touchdown, buckled at the middle of the right sole, bend legs to squat; at the same time, swing fists to the front of the body when bending elbows downward, fist centers downward, fist faces against each other. Look left forward (Figure 3-17).

图 3-17(Figure 3-17)

12.白猿洗脸

左脚向左前上一步,两腿屈膝下蹲;同时,左拳变虎爪掌向身体左下方摆掌,掌心向下,右拳向下收抱腰间。目视左掌(图 3-18)。

12. Face washing

Left foot strides leftward a step, bend legs to squat; at the same time, change left fist into tiger claw palm to swing downward to the left side, palm center downward, close right fist down against the waist. Look at left palm (Figure 3-18).

图 3-18(Figure 3-18)

13.又白猿洗脸

左脚向左碾脚,身体左转 180°,右脚向上勾踢后向下落步,两腿屈膝下蹲;同时,右拳变虎爪掌向身体右侧下方摆掌,掌心向下;左拳收抱腰间。目视右掌(图 3-19)。

13. Face washing again

Left foot grinds leftward on the floor, turn left 180°, right foot hooks and kicks upward, then falls and bend legs to squat; at the same time, change right fist into tiger claw palm to swing downward to the right side, palm center downward; close left fist against the waist. Look at right palm (Figure 3-19).

图 3-19(Figure 3-19)

14.悬崖勒马

身体右转,左腿向前提膝,脚尖向下;同时,右爪变掌收抱腰间,左拳向前冲拳,拳心向上置于左腿上。目视左拳(图3-20)。

14. Danger avoiding

Turn right, lift left knee forward, tiptoe downward; at the same time, change right claw into palm to the waist, punch left fist forward, fist center upward to the left leg. Look at left fist (Figure 3-20).

图 3-20(Figure 3-20)

15.探马捶式

左脚向前下落,屈膝前弓;同时,左臂屈肘向上摆击,置于左肩上方,拳心向下,右拳向前冲击,与肩同高。目视右拳(图3-21)。

15. Elbow swinging posture

Left foot falls forward, bend knee into front bow stance; at the same time, bend left elbow to swing upward to the position over the left shoulder, fist center downward, punch right fist forward at the level of shoulders. Look at right fist (Figure 3-21).

正(Front)   背(Back)

图 3-21(Figure 3-21)

第三章 少林长护心意门拳

16.千斤砸捶

身体右转，两腿屈膝下蹲成马步；同时，右拳向上摆击经头顶向右下方摆拳置于身体右侧。拳心向上；左拳向下收抱腰间。目视右拳(图3-22)。

16. Hammering heavily

Turn right, bend legs to squat into horse riding stance; at the same time, swing right fist upward, then swings right downward via the top of the head to the right side, fist center upward; close left fist downward to the waist. Look at right fist (Figure 3-22).

图 3-22(Figure 3-22)

17.左翻背捶

上动不停，身体上起，右腿向左收步，身体上起两脚并拢；同时，左拳由腰间向右、向上、向身体左侧摆拳，拳眼向前；右拳收抱腰间。目视左前下方(图3-23)。

17. Left back turning hammering

Keep moving, arise, pull right leg leftward, arise to close feet together; at the same time, swing left palm rightward, upward and leftward from the waist, fist eye forward; close right fist to the waist. Look left downward (Figure 3-23).

图 3-23(Figure 3-23)

111

18.弓步扳掌

(1)右脚向右前方上一步,屈膝前弓;同时,左拳变掌,从身体左侧向上经胸前向右下方按于体前,掌心向下;右拳变掌,掌心向上抱于腰间。目视左掌(图 3-24)。

18. Bow stance wrestling

(1) Right foot strides a step forward, bend knee into front bow stance; at the same time, change left fist into palm to move upward from the right side, then to press downward in front of the body via the front of the chest, palm center downward; change right fist into palm to the waist, supinely. Look at left palm (Figure 3-24).

图 3-24(Figure 3-24)

(2)上动不停,右掌经左掌上方向前上方摆击,掌心向里,掌背向前,右掌微高于左肩;左掌向下收至腰间,掌心向上。目视右掌(图 3-25)。

(2) Keep moving, swing right palm upward and forward through over the right palm, palm center inward, palm back forward, right fist is little higher than left shoulder; close left palm downward against the waist, supinely. Look at right palm (Figure 3-25).

图 3-25(Figure 3-25)

19.悬崖勒马

身体右转,左脚向前提膝,脚尖向下;同时,右掌变拳收抱腰间;左掌向体前下方外旋握拳置于左膝前上方;两拳拳心向上。目视前方(图3-26)。

19. Danger avoiding

Turn right, left foot moves forward, lift knee, tiptoe downward; at the same time, close right palm into fist against the waist; rotate left palm inward and downward into fist to the position over left knee; fist centers upward. Look straight ahead (Figure 3-26).

图 3-26(Figure 3-26)

20.探马捶式

左脚向前下落,屈膝前弓;同时,左臂屈肘向上摆拳置于左肩上方,拳心向下;同时,右拳向前冲击,与肩同高。目视右拳(图3-27)。

20. Elbow swinging posture

Left foot falls forward, bend knee into front bow stance; at the same time, bend left elbow to swing upward to the position over the left shoulder, fist center downward; at the same time, punch right fist forward at the level of shoulders. Look at right fist (Figure 3-27).

图 3-27(Figure 3-27)

21.倒步跨虎

(1)左拳变掌向右肩上方插掌,掌心向上(图3-28)。

21. Retreating and tiger riding

(1) Change left fist into palm to thrust upward to the position over right shoulder, supinely (Figure 3-28).

图 3-28(Figure 3-28)

(2)上动不停,左脚向后撤半步,脚尖点地屈膝下蹲成虚步;同时,左掌向下外旋呈虎爪掌向左侧摆击,掌心向下;右拳向上摆击置于右肩上方,拳心向下。目视前方(图3-29)。

(2) Keep moving, retreat left foot half a step, tiptoe touchdown, bend knees to squat into empty stance; at the same time, left palm rotates outward and downward into tiger claw palm to swing leftward, palm center downward; swing right palm upward to the position over right shoulder, fist center downward. Look straight ahead (Figure 3-29).

图 3-29(Figure 3-29)

22.撩阴手

左脚向右腿后侧插一步,两腿屈膝下蹲,成高歇步;同时,左掌向上内旋摆击于腹前,五指分开,掌心向上,右拳在右肩上方不动。目视前方(图 3-30)。

22. Crotch hand

Insert left foot backward behind right leg, bend knees to squat into high sitting stance; at the same time, rotate left palm inward and swing it upward to the front of the abdomen, five fingers apart, supinely, keep right fist still over right shoulder. Look straight ahead (Figure 3-30).

图 3-30(Figure 3-30)

23.十字通背

(1)身体重心移至左腿,右腿提膝身体右转 90°;同时,左掌变拳向上抱于腰间;右拳变掌向下经右膝前向后摆击。目视右后下方(图 3-31)。

23. Cross punching

(1) Shift gravity center to left leg, lift right leg, turn right 90°; at the same time, change left palm into fist upward to the waist; change right fist into palm downward to swing backward via the front of the right knee. Look right backward (Figure 3-31).

图 3-31(Figure 3-31)

（2）上动不停，身体继续右转90°。右脚向右前方落步，屈膝前弓；同时，右掌变拳向身体后侧摆击，拳心向上；左拳向体前冲击，拳心向下与肩同高。目视左拳（图3-32）。

(2) Keep moving, continuously turn right 90°. Right foot falls forward on the floor, bend knee into front bow stance; at the same time, change right palm into fist to swing backward, fist center upward, punch left fist forward, fist center downward at the level of shoulders. Look at left fist (Figure 3-32).

图 3-32（Figure 3-32）

24.拦腰捶

左臂屈肘收于胸前，掌心向下；同时，右拳向前上方由右向左弧形摆击于体前，拳心向下。目视右拳（图3-33）。

24. Waist blocking pounding

(1) Bend left arm to the front of the chest, palm center downward; at the same time, right fist moves upward and forward to arc from right to left to the front of the body, fist center downward. Look at right fist (Figure 3-33).

图 3-33（Figure 3-33）

（2）上动不停，两脚掌碾地，身体左转屈膝下蹲成马步；同时，右拳向下摆击至右腰间后再向前冲出,拳心向下;左拳抱于腰间。目视右拳(图3-34)。

(2) Keep moving, soles grind on the ground, turn left with bending knees to squat into horse riding stance; at the same time, swing right fist downward to the right waist, and then punch it forward, fist center downward; close left fist against the waist. Look at right fist (Figure 3-34).

图 3-34(Figure 3-34)

25.拔步炮

(1)身体重心移至左腿,右腿屈膝上提脚尖向下;同时,右拳变掌向下、向上摆击,置于右肩前,掌心向左外侧,掌指向上,肘与膝相照;左拳变掌,向右肩上方插掌,掌心向右外侧,掌指向上。目视前方(图3-35)。

25. Striding cannon

(1) Shift gravity center to left leg, lift right leg with bending knee, tiptoe downward; at the same time, change right fist into palm to swing downward, and then upward to the front of the right shoulder, palm center outward to the left, fingers upward, elbow and knee face each other; change left fist into palm to thrust upward to the position over right shoulder, palm center outward to the right, fingers upward. Look straight ahead (Figure 3-35).

图 3-35(Figure 3-35)

（2）右脚向左脚前下方震脚，左脚尖扣在右脚内侧，两腿屈膝下蹲；同时，右掌向下摆掌置于右腿前，掌心向左外侧；左掌向上插掌置于右肩前，掌心向右外侧。目视前方（图 3-36）。

（2）Right foot stamps forward in front of the left foot, buckle left tiptoe at the inside of the right foot, bend knees and squat; at the same time, swing right palm downward to the front of the left leg, palm center outward to the left; thrust left palm upward to the front of the right shoulder, palm center outward to the right. Look straight ahead (Figure 3-36).

图 3-36（Figure 3-36）

26. 悬崖勒马

身体右转，左脚向前提起脚尖向下；同时，右掌向上外旋置于体前，左掌向下置于右臂上方，掌心向右外侧。目视右掌（图 3-37）。

26. Danger avoiding

Turn right, lift left foot forward, tiptoe downward; at the same time, right palm moves upward and rotate outward to the front of the body, left palm moves downward to the position over right arm, palm center rightward outside. Look at right palm (Figure 3-37).

图 3-37（Figure 3-37）

27.十字通背

(1)左脚向前落步,屈膝前弓;同时,两掌变拳向下收抱于腰间。目视前方(图 3-38)。

27. Cross punching

(1) Left foot falls forward, bend knee into front bow stance; at the same time, change palms into fists downward to the waist. Look straight ahead (Figure 3-38).

图 3-38(Figure 3-38)

(2)上动不停,身体向左碾腰转臂。右拳向右前方冲击,左拳向左后方冲击。目视右拳(图 3-39)。

(2) Keep moving, turn left with waist grinding and arms rotating. Punch right fist right forward and punch left fist left backward. Look at right fist (Figure 3-39).

图 3-39(Figure 3-39)

28.歇步摆拳

身体右转 90°,右脚向左腿后插步,两腿屈膝下蹲;同时,右拳向右侧下方摆击,拳心向下;左拳抱于腰间。目视右拳(图3-40)。

28.Sitting stance swinging

Turn right 90°, insert right foot to the rear of the left foot, bend legs to squat; at the same time, swing right palm downward to right side, fist center downward; close left fist against the waist. Look at right fist (Figure 3-40).

图 3-40(Figure 3-40)

29.提膝抱肘

身体上起,重心移至右腿,左腿屈膝上提,脚尖向下;同时,两拳变掌经胸前向左右两侧插击,左掌掌心向右外侧,指尖向上置于右臂前,右掌掌心向左外侧。指尖向上置于左臂下方。目视前方(图3-41)。

29. Lift knee and hold elbow

Arise, shift gravity center to the right leg, lift left leg with bending knee, tiptoe downward; at the same time, change fists into palms to thrust sideward via the front of the chest, left palm center rightward outside, fingertip upward to the front of the right arm, right palm center outward to the left, fingertip upward to the position below left arm. Look straight ahead (Figure 3-41).

图 3-41(Figure 3-41)

30.武松脱铐

(1)两臂屈肘向身体两侧击肘(图3-42)。

30. Elbows pounding sideward

(1) Bend arms to pound sideward with elbows (Figure 3-42).

图 3-42(Figure 3-42)

(2)左脚向左侧落步,两脚屈膝下蹲成马步;同时,两肘向下夹击(图3-43)。

(2) Left foot falls leftward, bend knees to squat into horse riding stance; at the same time, elbows clamp downward (Figure 3-43).

图 3-43(Figure 3-43)

31.马步单鞭

两拳同时向身体两侧冲出,拳心向下,与肩同高;两腿下蹲成马步。目视左前方(图3-44)。

31. Single horse-riding whipping

Fists punch sideward at the same time, fist centers downward at the level of shoulders; squat into horse riding stance. Look left forward (Figure 3-44).

图 3-44(Figure 3-44)

第二段

Section 2

32.拧身七星

（1）两脚掌同时向左碾地,左腿屈膝前弓；右拳向下、向前摆击置于左腿前,左拳向前下方摆击于体前；两拳心向里。目视右拳(图 3-45)。

32. Seven-star twisting

(1) Both soles grind leftward on the floor at the same time, bend left knee into the front bow stance; swing right fist downward and forward to the front of left leg, swing left fist forward, downward to the front of the body; fist centers inward. Look at right fist (Figure 3-45).

图 3-45(Figure 3-45)

（2）上动不停,左脚向后撤一步,脚尖点地收于右脚前；同时,左拳向前下方冲击,右拳向后收于腹前,两拳心向里。目视左前下方(图 3-46)。

(2) Keep moving, retreat left foot a step, tiptoe touchdown to the front of the right foot; at the same time, punch left fist forward downward, right fist

moves backward to the front of the abdomen, fist centers inward. Look at left front downward (Figure 3-46).

图 3-46(Figure 3-46)

33.弓步双推掌

左脚向前一步,屈膝前弓;同时,两拳向上收抱于腰间后变掌再向前推出,左掌在前,右掌在后。目视前方(图 3-47)。

33. Duoble bow stance pushing

Left foot strides a step forward, bend knee into front bow stance; at the same time, fists move upward into palms to the waist, and then push forward, left palm in front and right palm behind. Look straight ahead (Figure 3-47).

图 3-47(Figure 3-47)

34.右踩脚式

右脚向前上方弹击,右掌向前下方拍击右脚面;左掌收抱腰间。目视右掌(图 3-48)。

123

34. Right slapping posture

Right foot kicks upward forward, right palm slaps downward against the right instep; close left palm to the waist. Look at right palm (Figure 3-48).

图 3-48（Figure 3-48）

35.双推掌式

右脚向下落步,屈膝前弓;同时,右掌收抱腰间后再同左掌一起向前方推出。右掌在前,左掌在后。目视前方(图 3-49)。

35. Double pushing posture

Right foot falls on the floor, bend knee into front bow stance; at the same time, close right palm to the waist to push forward together with left palm, right palm in front and left palm behind. Look straight ahead (Figure 3-49).

图 3-49（Figure 3-49）

36.左踩脚式

左腿向前上方弹击,左掌拍击左脚面;右掌向下收抱腰间。目视左掌(图 3-50)。

36. Left slapping posture

Left leg kicks upward, left palm slaps against left instep; close right palm downward against the waist. Look at left palm (Figure 3-50).

图 3-50(Figure 3-50)

37.探马捶

(1)左脚向前下落身体右转 90°,两腿屈膝下蹲;同时,左掌变拳向下摆击于身体前方,拳心向上。目视左拳(图 3-51)。

37. Elbow swinging

(1) Left foot falls forward, turn right 90°, bend legs to squat; at the same time, change left palm into fist to swing to the front of the body, fist center upward. Look at left fist (Figure 3-51).

图 3-51(Figure 3-51)

(2)两脚向左碾地,身体上起左腿屈膝前弓;同时,左拳向上摆拳于左肩上方,拳心向下;右拳向前冲出,拳心向下。目视右拳(图 3-52)。

(2) Feet grind leftward on the floor, arise, bend left knee into front bow

stance; at the same time, swing left palm upward to the position over left shoulder, fist center downward; punch right fist forward, fist center downward. Look at right fist (Figure 3-52).

图 3-52(Figure 3-52)

38.转身推掌

(1)左拳变掌向右臂上方插掌,掌心向上,掌指向右外侧(图 3-53)。

38. Turning and pushing

(1) Change left fist into palm to thrust upward to the position over right arm, supinely, fingertips outward to the right (Figure 3-53).

图 3-53(Figure 3-53)

(2)上动不停,左掌向下外旋变勾手,勾尖向上。左臂贴紧身体左侧;同时,身体向右转 180°,右脚抬起向下踩落,屈膝前弓;右拳变掌由胸前向右前方推掌,掌尖与鼻同高。目视右掌(图 3-54)。

(2) Keep moving, rotate left palm outward and downward into hook, hook tip upward. Keep left arm close to the left side; at the same time, turn right 180°, lift right foot to stamp down, bend knee into front bow stance; change right fist into palm to push right forward from the front of the chest, palm tip at

the nose's level. Look at right palm (Figure 3-54).

图 3-54(Figure 3-54)

39.黑虎蹬山

(1)右臂屈肘置于右肩前;同时,重心移至右腿,左腿屈膝上提。脚尖向后。目视左后方(图 3-55)。

39. Black tiger mountaineering

(1) Bend right arm to the front of right shoulder; at the same time, shift gravity center to right leg, lift left leg with bending knee, tiptoes backward. Look left backward (Figure 3-55).

图 3-55(Figure 3-55)

(2)上动不停,左脚向前上步,两腿屈膝下蹲;右脚跟抬起。目视左后方(图 3-56)。

(2) Keep moving, left foot strides forward, bend knees to squat; lift right heel. Look left backward (Figure 3-56).

图 3-56(Figure 3-56)

(3)右脚向前一步(图3-57);右脚蹬地向上跳起,身体向后转180°,右腿屈膝上提,左脚自然下垂;同时,右掌向上摆击,掌心向里;左掌由腰间向上、向下收于右肘下,掌心向下。目视右掌(图3-58)。

(3) Right foot strides a step forward(Figure 3-57); right foot stamps on the floor and jump, turn backward 180°, lift right leg with bending knee, left leg hangs naturally; at the same time, swing right palm upward, palm center inward; left palm moves upward from the waist, then downward under the right elbow, palm center downward. Look at right palm (Figure 3-58).

图 3-57(Figure 3-57)   图 3-58(Figure 3-58)

40.转身扳手

左脚先落地,右脚紧跟落步,屈膝前弓;同时,右掌向前弹击,掌指向上与肩同高,左掌向下收抱于腰间。目视右掌(图3-59)。

40. Turning and wrestling

Left foot falls first and right foot follows, bend knee into front bow stance; at the same time, swing right palm forward, palm fingers upward at the shoulder's level, close left fist downward against the waist. Look at right palm (Figure 3-59).

图 3-59(Figure 3-59)

41.猿猴束身

左脚向前置于右脚前,两腿下蹲;同时,左掌向前下方插掌,掌心向左外侧;右掌向下、向上置于左肩前。目视左前方(图 3-60)。

41. Monkey closing

Left foot moves forward in front of right foot, bend legs to squat; at the same time, thrust left palm forward and downward, palm center to the left outside; swing right palm downward, then upward to the front of the left shoulder. Look left forward (Figure 3-60).

图 3-60(Figure 3-60)

42.二起踩脚

右脚蹬地跳起,向前上方弹击,左腿自然下垂;同时,右掌拍击右脚面;左掌向上变拳收抱腰间。目视前方(图 3-61)。

42. Jumping and slapping

Jump with right foot to kick upward, left leg hangs naturally; at the same time, clap right palm against right instep; left palm moves upward into fist to the waist. Look straight ahead (Figure 3-61).

图 3-61(Figure 3-61)

43.单叉

(1)左脚落地,右脚向左脚后撤步;同时,右掌变剑指向下收于胸前(图3-62)。

43. Single fork

(1) Left foot falls, retreat right foot to the back of the left foot; at the same time, change right palm into sword fingers downward to the front of the chest (Figure 3-62).

图 3-62(Figure 3-62)

(2)上动不停,右腿屈膝下蹲成仆步;同时,左拳变剑指由腰间向体前斜下方插击,掌心向下;右掌向后收拉抱于腰间,掌心向上。目视左前方(图3-63)。

(2) Keep moving, bend right knee to squat into drop stance; at the same time, change left fist into sword finger to thrust downward obliquely from the waist, palm center downward; close right palm backward to the waist, supinely. Look left forward (Figure 3-63).

图 3-63(Figure 3-63)

44.起身摆腿

重心前移至右腿,左脚向外侧碾脚;同时,右脚由右向左(由外向里)向体前下方摆击,身体左转 90°;左掌由左向右(由里向外)拍击右脚脚掌;右掌变拳抱于腰间。目视左掌(图 3-64)。

44. Arising and leg swinging

Shift gravity center to right leg, left foot grinds outside on the floor; at the same time, right foot swings downward from right to left (from outside to inside), turn left 90°; slap left palm against right instep from left to right (from inside to outside); change right palm into fist to the waist. Look at left palm (Figure 3-64).

图 3-64(Figure 3-64)

45.蝎子摆尾

上动不停,身体左转180°,右脚向左脚前方下落;同时,左腿屈膝向右腿后上方摆击,脚掌心向上,右拳变掌向下拍击左脚内侧;左掌向上架于头顶,掌心向上。目视右掌(图3-65)。

45. Scorpion tail swinging

Keep moving, turn left 180°, right foot falls left forward; at the same time, bend left leg to swing upward to the rear of right leg, sole upward, change right fist into palm to slap downward against the inside of left leg, left fist moves upward to parry over the head, supinely. Look at right palm (Figure 3-65).

图 3-65(Figure 3-65)

46.右摆脚

上动不停,左脚向下落步,脚向外碾,身体左转180°。右脚向左摆击于体前;同时,左掌向下拍击右脚掌,右掌变拳抱于腰间。目视左掌(图3-66)。

46. Foot swinging rightward

Keep moving, left foot falls forward, grinds outward, turn left 180°. Swing right foot leftward to the front of the body; at the same time, left palm slaps downward against the right sole, change right palm into fist to the waist. Look at left palm (Figure 3-66).

图 3-66(Figure 3-66)

47.下阴捶

上动不停,左掌变拳屈肘向上冲于左肩前,拳心向后;右拳向上、向下划弧向后下冲拳,拳心向后。目视右下方(图 3-67)。

47. Crotch fist

Keep moving, change left palm into fist, bend elbow to punch upward to the front of right shoulder, fist center backward; right fist draws an arc upward, downward, punch it downward, backward, fist center backward. Look right downward (Figure 3-67).

图 3-67(Figure 3-67)

48.反肘一捶

(1)右脚下落,屈膝前弓;同时,右拳向上收至胸前后再向右前方击肘;左拳向下抱于腰间。目视右肘(图 3-68)。

48. Reversing elbow thumping

(1) Right foot falls, bend knee into front bow stance; at the same time, right fist moves upward to the front of the chest, and then punch elbow forward to the right, close left fist against the waist. Look at right elbow (Figure 3-68).

图 3-68(Figure 3-68)

（2）右拳向右前上方崩拳，拳心向上。目视右拳（图3-69）。

（2）Right fist hits forward to the right, fist center upward. Look at right fist (Figure 3-69).

图 3-69（Figure 3-69）

（3）两脚掌向左碾地，成左弓步；同时，右臂屈肘，右拳收至胸前后再向右下方冲拳，拳心向上，左拳变掌向右肩前插击，掌心向后。目视右后方（图3-70）。

（3）Both soles grind leftward on the floor into left bow stance; at the same time, bend right arm, close right fist to the front of the chest, then to punch downward to the right, fist center upward, change left fist into palm to thrust to the front of right shoulder, palm center backward. Look right backward (Figure 3-70).

图 3-70（Figure 3-70）

49.千斤砸捶

身体右转，两腿屈膝下蹲成弓步；同时，右拳向上摆击经头顶向右下方摆拳置于身体右侧。拳心向上；左拳向下收抱腰间。目视右拳（图3-71）。

49. Hammering heavily

Turn right, bend legs to squat into bow stance; at the same time, swing right palm upward, then swing it right downward, over the head to the right side, fist center upward; close left fist downward to the waist. Look at right fist (Figure 3-71).

图 3-71 (Figure 3-71)

50.左翻背捶

上动不停,身体上起,右腿向左收步,身体上起两脚并拢;同时,左拳由腰间向右、向上、向身体左侧摆拳,拳眼向前;右拳收抱腰间。目视左前下方(图 3-72)。

50. Left back turning hammering

Keep moving, arise, pull right leg leftward, arise to close feet together; at the same time, swing left palm rightward, upward and leftward from the waist, fist eye forward; close right fist against the waist. Look left downward (Figure 3-72).

图 3-72 (Figure 3-72)

51.弓步扳掌

(1)右腿提膝,左拳变掌向身体右侧前方按掌,掌心向下;同时,右拳变掌向上收于胸前,掌心向上,左掌在下,右掌在上。目视右前方(图3-73)。

51. Bow stance wrestling

(1) Lift right knee, change left fist into palm to press forward to the right side of the body, palm center downward; at the same time, change right fist into palm upward to the front of the chest, supinely, right fist above and left fist below. Look right forward (Figure 3-73).

图3-73(Figure 3-73)

(2)上动不停,右脚向前下落,屈膝前弓;右掌向右上方弹击。右掌稍高于肩,掌心向里;同时,左掌下抱腰间。目视右掌(图3-74)。

(2) Keep moving, right foot falls forward, bend knee into front bow stance; swing right palm right upward, right palm is little higher than shoulders, palm centers inward; at the same time, close left palm downward against the waist. Look at right palm (Figure 3-74).

图3-74(Figure 3-74)

52.悬崖勒马

身体右转,左腿向前提膝,脚尖向下;同时,右掌变拳向下抱于腰间,左掌向体前下方外旋抱拳置于左膝上方,两拳心向上。目视前方(图 3-75)。

52. Danger avoiding

Turn right, lift left knee forward, tiptoe downward; at the same time, change right fist into palm downward to the waist, rotate left palm downward to the front of the body into fist over left knee, fist centers upward. Look forward (Figure 3-75).

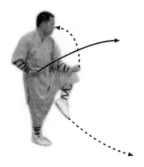

图 3-75(Figure 3-75)

53.探马捶式

左脚向前下落,屈膝前弓;同时,左臂屈肘向上摆击,置于左肩上方,拳心向下;右拳向前冲击,与肩同高。目视右拳(图 3-76)。

53. Elbow swinging posture

Left foot falls forward, bend knee into front bow stance; at the same time, bend left elbow to swing upward to the position over the left shoulder, fist center downward, punch right fist forward at the level of shoulders. Look at right fist (Figure 3-76).

图 3-76(Figure 3-76)

54.倒步跨虎

(1)左拳变掌向右臂上方插掌,掌心向上(图3-77)。

54. Retreating and tiger riding

(1) Change left fist into palm to thrust upward to the position over right shoulder, supinely (Figure 3-77).

图 3-77(Figure 3-77)

(2)上动不停,左脚向后撤半步,脚尖点地,屈膝下蹲成虚步;同时,左掌向下外旋呈虎爪掌向左侧摆击,掌心向下,右拳向上摆击于右肩上方,拳心向下。目视前方(图3-78)。

(2) Keep moving, retreat left foot half a step, tiptoe touchdown, bend knee to squat into empty stance; at the same time, rotate left palm outward and downward into tiger claw palm to swing leftward, palm center downward; swing right palm upward to the position over right shoulder, fist center downward. Look straight ahead (Figure 3-78).

图 3-78(Figure 3-78)

55.撩阴手

左脚向右腿后插一步,两腿屈膝下蹲成高歇步;同时,左掌向上内旋摆击于腹前,五指分开,掌心向上;右拳在右肩上方不动。目视前方(图3-79)。

55. Crotch hand

Insert left foot backward behind right leg, bend knees to squat into high sitting stance; at the same time, rotate left palm inward and swing it upward to the front of the abdomen, five fingers apart, supinely, keep right fist still over the right shoulder. Look straight ahead (Figure 3-79).

图 3-79(Figure 3-79)

56.十字通背

(1)身体重心移至左腿,右腿提膝身体右转90°;同时,左掌变拳向上抱于腰间;右拳变掌向下经右膝前向后摆击。目视右后下方(图 3-80)。

56. Cross punching

(1) Shift gravity center to left leg, lift right leg, turn right 90°; at the same time, change left palm into fist upward to the waist; change right fist into palm downward to swing backward via the front of the right knee. Look right backward (Figure 3-80).

图 3-80(Figure 3-80)

139

（2）上动不停，身体继续右转90°，右脚向右前方落步，屈膝前弓；同时，右掌变拳向身体后侧摆击，拳心向上；左拳向体前冲击，掌心向下与肩同高。目视左拳（图3-81）。

(2) Keep moving, continuously turn right 90°, right foot falls on the floor right forward, bend knee into front bow stance; at the same time, change right palm into fist to swing backward, fist center upward, punch left fist forward, fist center downward at the level of shoulders. Look at left fist (Figure 3-81).

图 3-81（Figure 3-81）

57.拦腰捶

（1）左臂屈肘收于胸前，拳心向下；同时，右拳向前上方由右向左弧形摆击于体前，拳心向下。目视右拳（图3-82）。

57. Waist blocking pounding

(1) Bend left arm to the front of the chest, fist center downward; at the same time, right fist moves upward and forward to arc from right to left to the front of the body, fist center downward. Look at right fist (Figure 3-82).

图 3-82（Figure 3-82）

（2）上动不停，两脚掌碾地，身体左转，屈膝下蹲成马步；同时，右拳向下摆击至右腰间后再向前冲出，拳心向下；左拳抱于腰间。目视右拳

（图3-83）。

（2）Keep moving, soles grind on the ground, turn left with bending knees to squat into horse riding stance; at the same time, swing right fist downward to the right waist, and then punch it forward, fist center downward; close left fist against the waist. Look at right fist (Figure 3-83).

图 3-83（Figure 3-83）

58.拔步炮

（1）身体重心移至左腿,右腿屈膝上提脚尖向下;同时,右拳变掌向下、向上摆击,置于右肩前,掌心向左外侧,掌指向上,肘与膝相对;左拳变掌,向右肩前上方插掌,掌心向右外侧,掌指向上。目视前方(图3-84)。

58. Striding cannon

（1）Shift gravity center to left leg, lift right leg with bending knee, tiptoe downward; at the same time, change right fist into palm to swing downward, and then upward to the front of the right shoulder, palm center outward to the left, fingers upward, elbow and knee face each other; change left fist into palm to thrust upward to the position over right shoulder, palm center rightward outside, fingers upward. Look straight ahead (Figure 3-84).

图 3-84（Figure 3-84）

（2）右脚向左脚前下方震脚,左脚尖扣在右脚内侧,两腿屈膝下蹲;同时,右掌向下摆掌置于右腿前,掌心向左外侧;左掌向上插掌置于右肩前,掌心向右外侧。目视前方(图 3-85)。

(2) Right foot stamps forward in front of the left foot, buckle left tiptoe at the inside of the right foot, bend knees and squat; at the same time, swing right palm downward to the front of the left leg, palm center outward to the left; thrust left palm upward to the front of the right shoulder, palm center outward to the right. Look straight ahead (Figure 3-85).

图 3-85(Figure 3-85)

59.悬崖勒马

身体右转,左脚向前提膝脚尖向下;同时,右掌向上外旋置于体前,左掌向下置于右臂上方,掌心向右外侧。目视右掌(图 3-86)。

59. Danger avoiding

Turn right, lift left foot forward, tiptoe downward; at the same time, right palm moves upward and rotates outward to the front of the body, left palm moves downward to the position over right arm, palm center outward to the right. Look at right palm (Figure 3-86).

图 3-86(Figure 3-86)

60.十字通背

(1)左脚向前落步,屈膝前弓;同时,两拳向下收抱于腰间。目视前方

（图 3-87）。

60. Cross punching

(1) Left foot falls forward, bend knee into front bow stance; at the same time, change palms into fists downward to the waist. Look straight ahead (Figure 3-87).

图 3-87（Figure 3-87）

(2) 上动不停,身体向左碾腰转臂,右拳向右前方冲击,左拳向左后方冲击。目视右拳（图 3-88）。

(2) Keep moving, turn left with waist grinding and arms rotating. Punch right fist right forward and punch left fist left backward. Look at right fist (Figure 3-88).

图 3-88（Figure 3-88）

61. 歇步摆拳

身体右转 90°,右腿向左腿后插步,两腿屈膝下蹲;同时,右拳向右侧下方摆击,拳心向下;左拳抱于腰间。目视右拳（图 3-89）。

61. Sitting stance swinging

Turn right 90°, insert right foot to the rear of the left foot, bend legs to squat; at the same time, swing right palm downward to right side, fist center downward; close left fist against the waist. Look at right fist (Figure 3-89).

图 3-89 (Figure 3-89)

62.提膝抱肘

身体上起,重心移至右腿,左腿屈膝上提,脚尖向下;同时,两拳变掌经胸前向左右两侧插击,左掌掌心向右外侧,指尖向上置于右臂前,右掌掌心向左外侧,指尖向上置于左臂下方。目视前方(图 3-90)。

62. Lift knee and hold elbow

Arise, shift gravity center to the right leg, lift left leg with bending knee, tiptoe downward; at the same time, change fists into palms to thrust sideward via the front of the chest, left palm center rightward outside, fingertip upward to the position in front of the right arm, right palm center leftward outside, fingertip upward to the position below left arm. Look straight ahead (Figure 3-90).

图 3-90 (Figure 3-90)

63.武松脱铐

(1)两臂曲肘向身体两侧击肘(图 3-91)。

63. Elbows pounding sideward

(1) Bend arms to pound sideward with elbows (Figure 3-91).

第三章　少林长护心意门拳

图 3-91（Figure 3-91）

（2）左脚向左侧落步，两腿屈膝下蹲成马步；同时，两肘向下夹击（图3-92）。

（2）Left foot falls leftward, bend knees to squat into horse riding stance; at the same time, elbows clamp downward (Figure 3-92).

图 3-92（Figure 3-92）

64.马步单鞭

两拳同时向身体两侧冲出，拳心向下，与肩同高，两腿下蹲成马步。目视左前方（图 3-93）。

64. Single horse-stance whipping

Fists punch sideward at the same time, fist center downward at the level of shoulders, squat into horse riding stance. Look left forward (Figure 3-93).

图 3-93（Figure 3-93）

第三段
Section 3

65.拧身七星

（1）两脚掌同时向左碾地，左腿屈膝前弓；右拳向下、向前摆击置于左腿前，左拳向前下方摆击于体前；两拳心向里。目视右拳（图3-94）。

65. Seven-star twisting

（1）Both soles grind leftward on the ground at the same time, bend left knee forward into front bow stance; swing right palm downward, forward to the position in front of the left leg, fist centers inward. Look at right fist (Figure 3-94).

图3-94（Figure 3-94）

（2）上动不停，两腿屈膝下蹲，左脚向后撤一步，脚尖点地收于右脚前；同时，左拳向前下方冲击，右拳向后收于腹前；两拳心向里。目视左前下方（图3-95）。

（2）Keep moving, bend legs to squat, retreat left foot a step, tiptoe touchdown in front of right foot; at the same time, punch left fist forward downward, close right fist backward in front of the abdomen; fist centers inward. Look downward at left front (Figure 3-95).

图3-95（Figure 3-95）

第三章 少林长护心意门拳

66.弓步双推掌

左脚向前一步,屈膝前弓;同时,两拳向上收抱腰间后变掌再向前推出,左掌在前,右掌在后。目视前方(图 3-96)。

66. Double bow stance pushing

Left foot strides a step forward, bend knee into front bow stance; at the same time, close fists upward against the waist, change fists into palms to push forward, left palm in front and right palm behind. Look straight ahead (Figure 3-96).

图 3-96(Figure 3-96)

67.下阴腿式

两脚碾地,身体左转;同时,两掌跟相对碾掌。左掌内旋,掌心向下,右掌外旋,掌心向上。目视两掌(图 3-97)。

67. Low crotch leg posture

Feet grind on the floor, turn left; at the same time, rub palm bases against each other. Rotate left palm inward, palm center downward, rotate right palm outward, supinely. Look at palms (Figure 3-97).

图 3-97(Figure 3-97)

68.踹腿式

身体重心移至左腿,右腿向右上方踹腿,脚掌向前;同时,右掌向前击掌,掌心向里,左掌收抱腰间。目视右脚(图3-98)

68. Sole kicking posture

Shift gravity center to left leg, right leg kicks with sole rightward upward, sole forward; at the same time, right palm strikes forward, palm center inward, close left palm against the waist. Look at right foot (Figure 3-98).

图 3-98(Figure 3-98)

69.弓步双推掌

右脚向前落步,身体左转成左弓步;同时,两掌向身体左前方呈十字手向前推出。目视两掌(图3-99)。

69. Double bow stance pushing

Right foot falls forward, turn left into left bow stance; at the same time, change palms into crossed hands to push forward. Look at palms (Figure 3-99).

图 3-99(Figure 3-99)

70.老牛大摸头

(1)身体重心移至右腿,左腿屈膝上提;同时,两掌收于胸前。目视双手(图3-100)。

70. Turning and crossed pushing

(1) Shift gravity center to right leg, lift left leg with bending knee; at the same time, close both palms in front of the chest. Look at hands (Figure 3-100).

图 3-100(Figure 3-100)

(2)上动不停,身体左转180°,左腿向后击脚,两腿屈膝下蹲成仆步;同时,两掌下按至腹前,右掌按在左掌的掌腕上方。目视两掌(图3-101)。

(2) Keep moving, turn left 180°, left leg hits backward, bend legs to squat into drop stance; at the same time, press palms down to the front of the abdomen, press right palm on the left wrist. Look at palms (Figure 3-101).

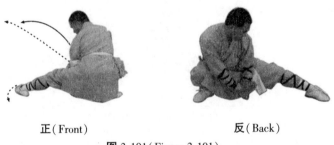

正(Front)　　　　　　反(Back)

图 3-101(Figure 3-101)

(3)左腿向前屈膝前弓成左弓步;同时,两掌成十字手向前推出。目视两掌(图3-102)。

(3) Bent left leg forward with bending knee into front bow stance; at the same time, change palms into crossed hands to push forward. Look at palms (Figure 3-102).

图 3-102（Figure 3-102）

71.大跨虎式

（1）两掌跟相叠，右掌向下外旋，左掌向上内旋，右掌掌心向上。目视两掌（图 3-103）。

71. Tiger riding posture

（1）Both palm bases overlay one another, rotate right palm outward downward, rotate left palm inward upward, right palm center upward. Look at palms（Figure 3-103）

图 3-103（Figure 3-103）

（2）上动不停，左脚向后撤半步，脚尖点地，两腿屈膝下蹲成虚步；同时，左掌呈虎爪掌，向左腿外侧摆击，掌心向下；右掌变拳向右肩上方摆击，拳心向下。目视前方（图 3-104）。

（2）Keep moving, retreat left foot half a step, tiptoe touchdown, bend legs to squat into empty stance; at the same time, change left palm into tiger claw palm to swing to the outside of left leg, palm center downward; change right palm into fist to swing upward above right shoulder, fist center downward. Look straight ahead (Figure 3-104).

图 3-104(Figure 3-104)

72.起身飞脚

(1)接上势,左臂向前摆击,掌心向下(图 3-105)。

72. Arising swinging kick

(1) Continuously, swing left arm forward, palm center downward(Figure 3-105).

图 3-105(Figure 3-105)

(2)上动不停,左脚向前半步右脚向前挤步;同时,左腿向前方踹腿;两掌变拳抱于腰间。目视左脚(图 3-106)。

(2) Keep moving, left foot strides half a step forward and right foot follows; at the same time, kick forward with left sole, close palms into fists against the waist. Look at left foot (Figure 3-106).

图 3-106（Figure 3-106）

73. 金鸡独立

左脚下落,脚掌向左碾地,身体左转180°,身体重心移至左腿,右腿向前屈膝上提;同时,右臂屈肘由外向里横击肘,拳心向里。目视右拳(图3-107)。

73. Standing on one leg

Left foot falls to grind leftward on the floor with the sole, turn left 180°, shift gravity center to left leg, lift right leg forward with bending knee; at the same time, bend right arm to hit inward horizontally from outside with elbow, fist center inward. Look at right fist (Figure 3-107).

图 3-107（Figure 3-107）

74.顶心肘

右脚下落,屈膝前弓;同时,右拳向下摆击至腹前后再向右上方撞肘,肘尖向前;左拳抱于腰间。目视右前方(图3-108)。

74. Centroid elbowing

Right foot fall, bend knee into front bow stance; at the same time, swing right palm downward to the front of the abdomen, then elbow hits left upward, elbow tip forward; close left fist against the waist. Look right forward (Figure 3-108).

图 3-108(Figure 3-108)

75.翻背捶

(1)右拳向右前方崩拳,拳心向上。目视右拳(图 3-109)。

75. Back turning punching

(1) Right fist bursts right forward, fist center upward. Look at right fist (Figure 3-109).

图 3-109(Figure 3-109)

(2)两脚掌向左碾地,成左弓步;同时,右臂屈肘右拳收至胸前后再向右下方冲拳,拳心向上;左拳变掌向右上方插击。目视右后方(图 3-110)。

(2) Both soles grind leftward on the floor into left bow stance; at the same time, bend right arm, close right fist in front of the chest, then to punch right downward, fist center upward; change left fist into palm to thrust right upward. Look right backward (Figure 3-110).

图 3-110(Figure 3-110)

76. 千斤砸拳

两脚向右碾地,屈膝下蹲;同时,右拳向后由腹前向左上方经头顶向右下方砸拳,拳心向上,左拳抱于腰间。目视右拳(图 3-111)。

76. Heavily pounding

Feet grind rightward on the floor, bend knees to squat; at the same time, right fist moves upward from rear via the front of the chest, over the head to pound left downward, fist center upward, close left fist against the waist. Look at right fist (Figure 3-111).

图 3-111(Figure 3-111)

77. 左翻背捶

上动不停,身体上起,右脚向左收步,两脚并拢;同时,左拳由腹前向上至头顶向身体左侧摆击,拳心向里;右拳抱于腰间。目视左前方(图3-112)。

77. Left back turning hammering

Keep moving, arise, pull right leg leftward, feet close together; at the same time, left fist moves upward from the waist to the top of the head, then to swing leftward, fist center inward; close right fist to the waist. Look left downward (Figure 3-112).

图 3-112(Figure 3-112)

78.转身扳掌

（1）右腿向上提膝,左拳变掌向上经头顶向体前按掌;同时,右拳变掌向上摆击。目视右前方(图 3-113)。

78. Turning and wrestling

(1) Lift right knee, change left fist into palm to move upward over the head, then to press to the position in front of the body; at the same time, change right fist into palm to swing upward. Look right forward (Figure 3-113).

图 3-113(Figure 3-113)

（2）上动不停,右脚下落,屈膝前弓;右拳向上弹击,掌心向里;同时,左掌收抱腰间。目视右掌(图 3-114)。

(2) Keep moving, right foot falls, bend knee into front bow stance; swing right palm upward, palm center inward; at the same time, close left palm against the waist. Look at right palm (Figure 3-114).

图 3-114(Figure 3-114)

79. 勒马鞍拳

身体右转,左腿向前提膝脚尖向下;同时,右掌变拳向下抱于腰间,左掌向体前下方外旋握拳,置于左膝上方,两拳心向上。目视前方(图 3-115)。

79. Tightening

Turn right, lift left leg forward, tiptoe downward; at the same time, change right palm into fist downward to the waist, rotate left palm downward into holding fist over left knee, both fist centers upward. Look straight ahead (Figure 3-115).

图 3-115(Figure 3-115)

80. 探马捶式

左脚下落,屈膝前弓;同时,左臂屈肘向左肩上方摆击,拳心向下;右拳向前冲出。目视右拳(图 3-116)。

80. Elbow swinging posture

Left foot falls forward, bend knee into front bow stance; at the same time, bend left elbow to swing upward to the position over the left shoulder, fist center downward; punch right fist forward. Look at right fist (Figure 3-116).

图 3-116(Figure 3-116)

81.倒步跨虎

左脚向后撤半步,脚尖点地,两腿屈膝下蹲成虚步;同时,左拳变掌由右臂上方向下外旋成虎爪掌,掌心向下;右拳收于右肩上方,拳心向下。目视前方(图 3-117)。

81. Retreating and tiger riding

Retreat left foot half a step, tiptoe touchdown, bend knees to squat into empty stance; at the same time, change left fist into palm to rotate outward and downward into tiger claw palm, palm center downward; close right fist to the position over right shoulder, fist center downward. Look straight ahead (Figure 3-117).

图 3-117(Figure 3-117)

82.撩阴手

左脚向右腿后侧插步,两腿屈膝下蹲;同时,左掌由外向里内旋击掌,掌心向上,五指分开,摆击于小腹前;右拳在右肩上方不动。目视前方(图 3-118)。

82. Crotch hand

Insert left foot backward behind the right leg, bend knees to squat; at the same time, rotate left palm inward from outside, supinely, five fingers apart, and swings to the front of the abdomen, keep right fist still over right shoulder. Look straight ahead (Figure 3-118).

图 3-118(Figure 3-118)

83.十字通背

(1)右腿屈膝上提身体右转90°;同时,左掌变拳抱于腰间;右拳变掌向下经右膝前向后摆击。目视右下方(图 3-119)。

83. Cross punching

(1) Lift right leg with bending knee, turn right 90°; at the same time, change left palm into fist to the waist; change right fist into palm downward to swing backward via the front of the right knee. Look right downward (Figure 3-119).

图 3-119(Figure 3-119)

(2)上动不停,身体继续右转90°,右脚向下落步,屈膝前弓;同时,右掌变拳向身体后侧冲击,左拳向身体前方冲击。目视左拳(图 3-120)。

(2) Keep moving, continuously turn right 90°, right foot falls on the floor, bend knee into front bow stance; at the same time, change right palm into fist to swing backward, punch left fist forward. Look at left fist (Figure 3-120).

图 3-120(Figure 3-120)

84.拦腰捶

(1)左臂屈肘收于胸前,拳心向下;同时,右拳向前上方由右向左弧形摆击于体前,拳心向下。目视右拳(图 3-121)。

84. Waist blocking pounding

(1) Bend left arm to the front of the chest, fist center downward; at the same time, right fist moves upward and forward to arc from right to left to the front of the body, fist center downward. Look at right fist (Figure 3-121).

图 3-121(Figure 3-121)

(2)上动不停,两脚掌碾地,身体左转屈膝下蹲成马步;同时,右拳向下摆击至右腰间后再向前冲击;左拳向后收抱腰间。目视右拳(图 3-122)。

(2) Keep moving, soles grind on the ground, turn left with bending knees to squat into horse riding stance; at the same time, swing right palm downward to the right waist, and then to punch it forward; close left fist backward against the waist. Look at right fist (Figure 3-122).

图 3-122（Figure 3-122）

85.拔步炮

（1）身体重心移至左腿,右腿屈膝上提,脚尖向下；同时,右拳变掌向下、向上摆击于右肩前。肘与膝相照；左拳变掌,向右肩前上方插击,掌指向上。目视前方(图 3-123)。

85. Striding cannon

(1) Shift gravity center to left leg, lift right leg with bending knee, tiptoe downward; at the same time, change right fist into palm to swing downward, and then upward to the front of the right shoulder, elbow and knee face each other; change left fist into palm to thrust upward to the position over right shoulder, fingers upward. Look straight ahead (Figure 3-123).

图 3-123（Figure 3-123）

（2）右脚向前下落震脚,左脚尖扣在右脚脚腰内,两腿屈膝下蹲；同时,右掌向下击掌,掌心向左外侧；左掌置于右肩前,掌心向右外侧。目视前方(图 3-124)。

(2) Right foot stamps forward on the floor, buckle left tiptoe at the inside of the right foot, bend knees and squat; at the same time, swing right palm downward, palm center outward to the left; left palm in front of the right

shoulder, palm center outward to the right. Look straight ahead (Figure 3-124).

图 3-124(Figure 3-124)

86.悬崖勒马

身体右转,左腿向前提膝,脚尖向下;同时,右掌向上外旋置于体前,左掌向下置于右臂上方,掌心向右外侧。目视右掌(图 3-125)。

86. Danger avoiding

Turn right, lift left foot forward, tiptoe downward; at the same time, right palm moves upward to rotate outward to the front of the body, left palm moves downward to the position over right arm, palm center outward to the right. Look at right palm (Figure 3-125).

图 3-125(Figure 3-125)

87.十字通背

(1)左脚向前落步,屈膝前弓;同时,两拳向下收抱腰间。目视前方(图 3-126)。

87. Cross punching

(1) Left foot falls forward, bend knee into front bow stance; at the same

time, close fists downward against the waist. Look straight ahead (Figure 3-126).

图 3-126(Figure 3-126)

（2）身体向左碾腰转臂；同时，右拳向右前上方冲击，左拳向左后下方冲击，两拳心向下，拳眼相对。目视右拳（图 3-127）。

(2) Turn left with waist grinding and arms rotating; at the same time, punch right fist right forward and punch left fist left downward, fist centers downward, fist eyes against each other. Look at right fist (Figure 3-127).

图 3-127(Figure 3-127)

88.霸王观阵

右脚向左腿后侧插步，身体右转 90°，两腿屈膝下蹲；同时，右拳由右下方向头顶上方摆拳，拳心向下；左拳由左下方向头顶上方摆击，拳心向下。目视前方（图 3-128）。

88. Turning and double swinging

Insert right foot backward behind left leg, turn right 90°, bend legs to squat; at the same time, swing right palm upward to the position over head from right side, fist center downward; swing left palm upward to the position over head from left side, fist center downward. Look straight ahead (Figure 3-128).

图 3-128(Figure 3-128)

第四段

Section 4

89.左游身

左腿向左前下方击出,屈膝下蹲成仆步;同时,两拳向下冲击,拳心相对,拳眼向上。目视两拳(图 3-129)。

89. left leg hitting and fists punching downward

Left leg hits left downward, bend knees to squat into drop stance; at the same time, punch fists downward, fist centers against each other, fist eyes upward. Look at fists(Figure 3-129).

图 3-129(Figure 3-129)

90.双撩阴捶

身体向上起,左腿屈膝前弓;同时,两拳向左上方摆击,拳心相对,拳眼向上。目视两拳(图 3-130)。

90. Double crotch fists

Arise, bend left knee into front bow stance; at the same time, swing fists left upward, fist centers against each other, fist eyes upward. Look at fists (Figure 3-130).

图 3-130(Figure 3-130)

91.金鸡独立

重心移至左脚,身体右转 90°,右腿屈膝上提,脚尖向下;同时,左拳从身体左侧向头顶上方摆击,拳心向下;右拳收于腹前,拳心向上。目视右前方(图 3-131)。

91. Standing on one leg

Shift gravity center to left foot, turn right 90°, lift right leg with bending knee, tiptoe downward; at the same time, swing left palm to the position over the head from left side, fist center downward; close right fist to the front of the abdomen, fist center upward. Look right forward (Figure 3-131).

图 3-131(Figure 3-131)

92.右游身

右脚向右下方击出,屈膝下蹲成仆步;同时,两拳向下冲击,拳心相对,拳眼向上。目视两拳(图 3-132)。

92. Right leg hitting and fists punching downward

Right foot hits right downward, bend knee to squat into drop stance; at the same time, punch fist downward, fist centers against each other, fist eyes upward. Look at fists (Figure 3-132).

图 3-132(Figure 3-132)

93.双撩阴捶

身体向上起,右腿屈膝前弓;同时,两拳向右上方摆击,拳心相对,拳眼向上。目视两拳(图 3-133)。

93. Double crotch fists

Arise, bend right knee into front bow stance; at the same time, swing fists right upward, fist centers against each other, fist eyes upward. Look at fists (Figure 3-133).

图 3-133(Figure 3-133)

94.金鸡独立

重心移至右脚,身体左转 90°,左腿屈膝上提,脚尖向下;同时,右拳从身体右侧向头顶上方摆击,拳心向下,左拳收至于腹前,拳心向上。目视左前方(图 3-134)。

94. Standing on one leg

Shift gravity center to right foot, turn left 90°, lift left leg with bending knee, tiptoe downward; at the same time, swing right palm to the position over the head from right side, fist center downward; close left fist to the front of the abdomen, fist center upward. Look left forward (Figure 3-134).

图 3-134(Figure 3-134)

95.砸手转身

身体右转 90°；同时，左拳变掌，右拳向下迎击。目视前方（图 3-135）。

95. Hand pounding and turning

Turn right 90°; at the same time, change left fist into palm, right fist downward to resist. Look straight ahead (Figure 3-135).

图 3-135(Figure 3-135)

96.迎门铁扇

（1）右拳变掌向下插击，左掌向上插击在右脸侧。目视前方（图 3-136）。

96. Head-on iron fan

(1) Change right fist into palm to thrust downward, thrust left palm upward by the side of the right face. Look straight ahead (Figure 3-136).

图 3-136（Figure 3-136）

（2）上动不停,左脚向下落步,屈膝前弓。目视前方（图 3-137）。

（2）Keep moving, left foot falls, bend knee into front bow stance. Look straight ahead (Figure 3-137).

图 3-137（Figure 3-137）

97.猛虎跳涧

（1）上动不停,左脚蹬地向前跳步,屈膝上提,脚尖向下,右腿自然下垂,两掌在体侧不动（图 3-138）。

97. Tiger leaping

（1）Keep moving, leap forward with left foot, lift and bend knees, tiptoe downward, right leg hangs naturally, keep palms still by both sides. (Figure 3-138).

图 3-138（Figure 3-138）

（2）右脚先落地，脚尖点地；左脚随即落地屈膝成跪步。目视右掌（图 3-139）。

(2) Right foot falls at first, tiptoe touchdown; left foot follows to fall and bend knee into kneeling stance. Look at right palm (Figure 3-139).

图 3-139（Figure 3-139）

98.右探马捶

（1）身体下蹲右转 90°，左掌置于右肩前不动；右掌随身体右转的同时向下由身体右侧搂击。目视右掌（图 3-140）。

98. Right palm brushing

(1) Squat and turn right 90°, put left palm in front of right shoulder; right palm follows the turning to brush downward from the right side. Look at right palm (Figure 3-140).

第三章 少林长护心意门拳

图 3-140（Figure 3-140）

（2）上动不停，身体继续右转 90°，两脚掌向右碾屈膝前弓；同时，右掌变拳向上搂击于右肩上，拳心向下；左掌变拳向右前冲击，拳心向下。目视左拳（图 3-141）。

（2）Keep moving, continue turning right 90°, soles grind rightward on the floor, bend knee into front bow stance; at the same time, change right palm into fist to bush upward to the position over right shoulder, fist center downward; change left palm into fist to punch right forward, fist center downward. Look at left fist (Figure 3-141).

图 3-141（Figure 3-141）

99.束手阴捶

身体左转 90°，左脚向前一步与右脚并拢，屈膝下蹲；同时，右拳向身体右下侧冲拳，左拳变掌向右肩前上方插掌。目视左掌（图 3-142）。

99. Turning crotch fist

Turn left 90°, left foot strides a step forward close to right foot, bend knees to squat; at the same time, punch right fist rightward and downward, change left fist into palm to thrust upward to the front of right shoulder. Look at left palm (Figure 3-142).

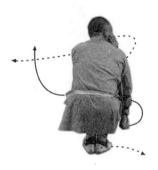

图3-142(Figure 3-142)

100.古树盘根

身体左转90°,左脚向右脚后插一步,脚尖点地,两腿屈膝下蹲;同时,右拳向上变掌与左掌交叉于胸前,再呈叠掌向前推击,左掌在前,右掌在后。目视两掌(图3-143)。

100. Ancient tree rooting

Turn left 90°, left foot inserts behind right foot, tiptoe touchdown, bend legs to squat; at the same time, right fist moves upward into palm to cross with left palm in front of the chest, change then into folded palms to push forward, left palm in front and right palm behind. Look at palms (Figure 3-143).

图3-143(Figure 3-143)

101.起身一掌

身体上起,两掌抱于腹前(图3-144);上动不停,身体右转90°,重心向后移至左腿,右腿屈膝上提;同时,左掌向左前方推出,右掌收于腰间。目视左掌(图3-145)。

第三章 少林长护心意门拳

101. Arising palming

Arise, hold palms in front of the abdomen (Figure 3-144); Keep moving, turn right 90°, shift gravity center backward to left leg, lift right leg with bending knee; at the same time, left palm pushes left forward, close right fist against the waist. Look at left palm (Figure 3-145).

图 3-144(Figure 3-144)

图 3-145(Figure 3-145)

102.古树盘根

（1）右脚向右后下方落步，随即左脚向后撤半步；同时，两掌心向上，用掌背拍击两腿后向身体两侧摆掌(图 3-146)。

102. Ancient tree rooting

(1) Right foot falls right backward, left foot follows to retreat half a step; at the same time, palm centers upward, slap against both legs, swing palms separately to both right and left sides (Figure 3-146).

图 3-146(Figure 3-146)

（2）紧接上动，左脚向右腿后插步，脚尖点地，两腿屈膝下蹲；同时，两掌收至胸前后再呈叠掌向前推击。目视两掌(图 3-147)。

171

（2） Continuously, insert left foot to the rear of the right leg, tiptoe touchdown, bend legs to squat; at the same time, close palms to the front of the chest, change into folded palms to push forward. Look at palms (Figure 3-147).

图 3-147（Figure 3-147）

103.起身一掌

（1）身体上起,重心移至左腿,右腿屈膝上提;同时,两掌内旋,左掌在上,右掌在下,两掌掌心向上收抱于体前(图 3-148)。

103. Arising palming

（1） Arise, shift gravity center to left leg, lift right leg with bending knee; at the same time, rotate palms inward, left palm above and right palm below, supinely, close palms to the front of the body (Figure 3-148).

图 3-148（Figure 3-148）

（2）上动不停,左脚碾地,身体右转 90°;同时,左掌向前推击,右掌收抱于腰间。目视左掌(图 3-149)。

（2） Keep moving, left foot grinds on the floor, turn right 90°; at the same time, push left palm forward, close right palm against the waist. Look at left palm (Figure 3-149).

图 3-149(Figure 3-149)

104.双推掌

身体右转90°,右腿向后下方落步,屈膝前弓;同时,左掌向下收于体前后再呈叠掌向前方推出,右掌在前,左掌在后。目视两掌(图 3-150)。

104. Double pushing

Turn right 90°, right leg falls backward, bend knee into front bow stance; at the same time, close left palm downward to the front of the body, change into folded palm to push forward, right palm in front and left palm behind. Look at palms (Figure 3-150).

图 3-150(Figure 3-150)

105.倒步右跨虎

右脚向后撤半步,脚尖点地;两腿屈膝下蹲成虚步;同时,右掌向下呈虎爪掌向身体下方摆击,掌心向下;左掌变拳向左上方摆击,拳心向下。目视前方(图 3-151)。

105. Retreating swinging rightward

Retreat right foot half a step, tiptoe touchdown; bend legs to squat into empty stance; at the same time, change right palm into tiger claw palm to swing downward, palm center downward; change left palm into fist to swing left upward, fist center downward. Look straight ahead (Figure 3-151).

正(Front)　　　　　　　　反(Back)

图 3-151(Figure 3-151)

106.倒步左跨虎

(1)右脚向后退一步,左腿屈膝前弓;同时,右臂向上摆击,左拳变掌向右臂上方插掌,掌心向上。目视前方(图 3-152)。

106. Retreating swinging leftward

(1) Retreat right foot a step, bend left knee into front bow stance; at the same time, swing right arm upward, change left fist into palm to thrust upward to the position over right arm, supinely. Look straight ahead (Figure 3-152).

图 3-152(Figure 3-152)

(2)上动不停,左脚向后撤半步,脚尖点地成左虚步;同时,左掌向下外旋,呈虎爪掌向身体左下方摆击,掌心向下;右掌变拳向右肩上方摆击,拳心向下。目视前方(图 3-153)。

(2) Keep moving, retreat left foot half a step, tiptoe touchdown into left

empty stance; at the same time, rotate left palm outside upward, change into tiger claw palm to swing leftward downward, palm center downward; change right palm into fist to swing downward to the position below right arm, fist center downward. Look straight ahead (Figure 3-153).

图 3-153(Figure 3-153)

107.双恨脚

身体右转 90°,重心移至左脚,右腿屈膝向下震脚;在右脚落地的同时左腿屈膝向下震脚,两脚并拢;同时,双手变剑指收抱腰间。目视前方(图 3-154)。

107. Double stamping with sword fingers

Turn right 90°, shift gravity center to left foot, bend right leg to stamp; bend left knee to stamp as soon as the right falls, feet close together; at the same time, change hands into sword fingers downward to the waist. Look straight ahead (Figure 3-154).

图 3-154(Figure 3-154)

108.右仙人指路

(1)身体右转 90°,右腿屈膝上提;同时,左掌呈剑指向右膝上方插击,掌心向上；右掌抱在腰间。目视前方（图3-155）。

108. Sword finger thrusting rightward

(1) Turn right 90°, lift right leg with bending knee; at the same time, change left palm into sword finger to thrust upward over right knee, supinely; close right palm against the waist. Look straight ahead (Figure 3-155).

图 3-155（Figure 3-155）

（2）上动不停，右脚向下落步，屈膝前弓；右掌从左掌上方向前剑指插击，掌心向下，指尖向前；左掌从右掌下方收于腰间。目视右掌（图3-156）。

(2) Keep moving, right foot falls on the ground, bend knee into front bow stance; change right palm into sword finger to thrust forward from over left palm, palm center downward, fingertip forward; close left palm from under right palm to the waist. Look at right palm (Figure 3-156).

图 3-156（Figure 3-156）

109. 左仙人指路

（1）身体重心前移至右腿，左腿屈膝上提；同时，右剑指上旋掌心向上。目视前方（图3-157）。

109. Sword finger thrusting leftward

(1) Shift gravity center to right leg, lift left leg with bending knee, at the same time, rotate right sword finger upward, supinely. Look straight ahead (Figure 3-157).

图 3-157（Figure 3-157）

（2）上动不停,左脚向下落步,屈膝前弓,左掌从右掌上方向前剑指插击,掌心向下,指尖向前;右掌从左掌下方收于腰间。目视左掌(图 3-158)。

(2) Keep moving, left foot falls on the floor, bend knee into front bow stance, change left palm into sward finger to thrusts forward from above the right palm, palm center downward, fingertip forward; close right palm from under left palm to the waist. Look at left palm (Figure 3-158).

图 3-158（Figure 3-158）

110.云顶七星

（1）右脚从左腿后侧向前插步,两腿屈膝下蹲,左掌向头顶上前方摆掌,掌心向下;右掌向身体左上方插掌,掌心向上,两掌心相对。目随手走(图 3-159)。

110. Overhead seven stars

(1) Insert right foot forward from the back of left leg, bend legs to squat, swing left palm forward overhead, palm center downward; thrust right palm left forward, supinely, palm centers against each other. Eyes sight follows the hand (Figure 3-159).

图 3-159(Figure 3-159)

(2)上动不停,两脚掌碾地身体右转360°,两掌从头顶上方旋转一周置体前,右掌在上,左掌在下,两掌心相对。目视右掌(图3-160)。

(2) Keep moving, both soles grind on the floor, turn right 360°, rotate palm a circle overhead to the front of the body, right palm above and left palm below, palm centers against each other. Look at right palm (Figure 3-160).

图 3-160(Figure 3-160)

(3)上动不停,右脚向右前方上一步,两掌变拳向下抱至腰间。目视前方(图3-161)。

(3) Keep moving, right foot strides a step forward, change palms into fists

downward to the waist. Look straight ahead (Figure 3-161).

图 3-161(Figure 3-161)

（4）紧接上动,左脚向前一步扣在右脚腰内侧,两腿屈膝下蹲；同时,右拳向前方冲去,左拳向上摆击置于右肘关节内侧,两拳心向下。目视右拳（图 3-162）。

(4) Continuously, left foot strides a step forward to buckle at the inside of the right foot, bend legs to squat; at the same time, punch right fist forward, swing left fist upward to the inside of right elbow, fist centers downward. Look at right fist (Figure 3-162).

图 3-162(Figure 3-162)

111.转身铁扇

右脚掌碾地身体向左转 180°,左腿屈膝上提；同时,右拳变掌向下、向上摆击于身体右侧前方,掌心向左外侧,左拳置于右肘关节内侧,拳心向里。目视前方(图 3-163)。

111. Turning and iron fan swinging

Right sole grinds on the floor, turn left 180°, lift left leg with bending knee; at the same time, change right fist into palm to move downward, upward to the right front of the body, palm center left outside, left fist at the inside of left elbow joint, fist center inward. Look straight ahead (Figure 3-163).

图 3-163(Figure 3-163)

112.罗汉观阵

(1)上动不停,左脚向前下方落步;同时,右掌向下,左拳收抱腰间。目视右掌(图 3-164)。

112. Arhat-like striking

(1) Keep moving, left foot falls forward on the floor; at the same time, right palm moves downward, close left fist against the waist. Look at right palm (Figure 3-164).

图 3-164(Figure 3-164)

(2)上动不停,右脚蹬地向前跳步下落至左脚前,左脚向上提起;同时,右掌变拳向下、向后摆击,拳心向前;左拳由腰间向身体上方摆击。目视右拳(图 3-165)。

(2) Keep moving, leap with right foot forward in front of left foot, lift left foot; at the same time, change right palm into fist to swing downward and backward, fist center forward; swing left palm downward from the waist. Look at right fist (Figure 3-165).

第三章 少林长护心意门拳

图 3-165（Figure 3-165）

（3）上动不停,左脚向前落步,屈膝前弓成左弓步；同时,左拳向下栽拳置于左膝上方,拳心向左外侧；右拳向右肩上方摆击,拳心向下；同时发出"威"的声音。目视左前方（图 3-166）。

(3) Keep moving, left foot falls forward on the floor, bend knee forward into left bow stance; at the same time, pound left fist downward over left knee, fist center leftward outward; swing right palm upward to the position over right shoulder, fist center downward; make a sound of "wei" at the same time. Look left forward (Figure 3-166).

图 3-166（Figure 3-166）

113.收势

（1）身体右转 90°,左脚向后收步,与右脚并拢；同时,两拳收抱腰间。目视前方（图 3-167）。

113. Closing form

(1) Turn right 90°, retreat left foot close together to right foot; at the same

181

time, close fists against the waist. Look straight ahead (Figure 3-167).

图 3-167(Figure 3-167)

（2）紧接上动，两拳变掌向下收于身体两侧，两掌心向内。目视前方，成立正姿势(图 3-168)。

(2) Continuously, change fists into palms downward against both sides, palm centers inward. Look straight ahead, stand at attention (Figure 3-168).

图 3-168(Figure 3-168)

第四章　少林达摩剑
Chapter 4　Shaolin Dharma Sword

第一节　套路动作名称
Quarter 1　Routine Names

第一段
Section 1

1. 预备势
1. Preparation

2. 仙人掌
2. Immortal palm

3. 回头望月
3. Back leg kicking

4. 仙人指路
4. Immortal guiding

5. 弓步下刺
5. Bow stance downward stabbing

6. 云剑前刺
6. Cloud sword forward stabbing

7. 古树盘根
7. Sword winding

8. 削如松林
8. Sword cutting

9. 仙人指路

9. Immortal guiding

10.前劈剑

10. Forward chopping

11.后点剑

11. Backward sword pointing

12.龙摆尾

12. Tail wagging

13.败势观剑

13. Twisting

14.独立点剑

14. Stand on one leg sword pointing

第二段

Section 2

15.仙人指路

15. Immortal guiding

16.玉女穿梭

16. Shuttling

17.三起剑

17. Three thrusting

18.霸王观阵

18. Mighty punching

19.咽喉剑

19. Throat thrusting

20.劈膀剑

20. Shoulder chopping

21.虚步挑剑

21. Empty stance picking

22.弹步磨剑

22. Moving and grinding

第三段

Section 3

23.藏花剑

23. Flowering

24.前劈剑

24. Forward chopping

25.削膝剑

25. Knee cutting

26.观阵剑

26. Arraying

27.穿针引线

27. Threading

28.游龙剑

28. Snaking

29.童子拜观音

29. Boy worshipping Goddess of Mercy

30.咽喉剑

30. Throat thrusting

31.二龙须

31. Double twisting

32.挑踢剑

32. Picking and kicking

33.挂腿前刺

33. Forward stabbing

第四段

Section 4

34.托塔

34. Supporting

35.左右劈剑

35. Left and right chopping

36.探海势

36. Creeping

37.指星势

37. Star pointing

38.怀里藏针

38. Needling

39.朝天一柱香

39. Erecting

40.童子拜佛

40. Boy worshipping the Buddha

41.收势

41. Closing

第二节　套路动作图解

Quarter 2　Figures of Routine Movements

第一段

Section 1

1.预备势

两脚开立,与肩同宽;左手反握剑柄,剑尖向上;右臂自然下垂,右手为掌,轻贴于右腿外侧。目视前方(图4-1)。

1. Preparation

Feet stride standing, the same wide as the shoulders, and left hand reversely grabs sword handle, sword tip upward, right arm falls, and right palm against right leg outward. Look straight ahead (Figure 4-1).

图 4-1(Figure 4-1)

2.仙人掌

(1)右臂由下向右上方举起,掌心向左;左手持剑,肘微屈上提。目视前方(图 4-2)。

2. Immortal palm

(1) Raise right arm rightward and upward, palm center leftward, left hand holds sword, bend and slightly lift the elbow. Look straight ahead (Figure 4-2).

图 4-2(Figure 4-2)

(2)右掌由右向左、向下落于左肩前;同时,左臂向左微展,自然伸直。目视前方(图 4-3)。

(2) Right palm falls in front of left shoulder from right to left, at the same time, left arm slightly extends leftward, straight. Look straight ahead (Figure 4-3).

图 4-3(Figure 4-3)

(3)右手向下落于右腿侧;同时,左脚向左横跨半步,左手握剑向左上方举起。目视前方(图 4-4)。

(3) Right hand falls against right leg, at the same time, left foot strides half a step leftward, left hand raises sword. Look straight ahead (Figure 4-4).

图 4-4(Figure 4-4)

(4)左手握剑向右、向下、向左划弧置于左胯侧;同时,右腿向左腿后插步,右手向右上方举起,掌心向左。目视前方(图4-5)。

(4) Left hand holds sword and draws curve rightward, downward and leftward and against left hip, at the same time, right leg strides to left leg backward, raise right hand rightward and inward, palm center leftward. Look straight ahead (Figure 4-5).

图 4-5(Figure 4-5)

(5)右掌从头前上方向胸前下落,掌心向左;同时,两腿屈膝下蹲,臀部坐于小腿上成歇步。目视掌指(图4-6)。

(5) Right palm falls against the chest from overhead, palm center leftward, at the same time, bend knees and squat, buttocks on the forelegs into the sitting stance. Look at fingers (Figure 4-6).

图 4-6(Figure 4-6)

3.回头望月

(1)身体上起,右脚提起,置于左膝后;同时,两臂向左右两侧摆击,两掌心向下,右掌变剑指。目视前方(图 4-7)。

3. Back leg kicking

(1) Arise, lift right foot against left knee backward, at the same time, swing arms leftward and rightward, palm center downward, change right palm into finger pointing. Look straight ahead (Figure 4-7).

图 4-7(Figure 4-7)

(2)两臂向下,屈肘交叉于胸前,剑身贴于左小臂下方,剑尖向左,右剑指在外,手心向下。目视左前方(图 4-8)。

(2) Arms downward, and cross elbows in front of the chest, sword against left forearm, sword tip leftward, right finger pointing outward, palm center downward. Look left forward(Figure 4-8).

图 4-8(Figure 4-8)

（3）右腿向右跨一步，身体重心移向右腿；同时，两臂向两侧分开，右手臂成平举，左手持剑略低于肩，剑贴臂后。目视左手（图4-9）。

(3) Right leg strides one step rightward, shift gravity center to the right leg, at the same time, arms apart, right arm straight, and left hand holds sword slightly lower than the shoulders, sword against arm. Look at left hand(Figure 4-9).

图 4-9(Figure 4-9)

（4）右腿屈膝，身体重心继续向右移，成弓步；同时，右手抖腕，剑指架于头上方，手心向上；左手持剑向体侧收剑。目视左方（图4-10）。

(4) Bend right knee, shift gravity center rightward into the bow stance, at the same time, shake right wrist, finger pointing overhead, hand center upward, left hand closes sword inward. Look leftward (Figure 4-10).

图 4-10(Figure 4-10)

第四章 少林达摩剑

4.仙人指路

左手持剑向胸前屈肘,剑贴于小臂下方,剑尖向左下方,手心向外;右剑指变掌贴于剑柄下,左右两肘与剑成一直线;同时,左腿屈膝上提扣于右腿膝关节后。目视剑尖(图4-11)。

4. Immortal guiding

Left hand holds sword and bend elbow to the chest, sword against the forearm, sword tip leftward and downward, hand center outward, change right finger pointing into palm against sword handle, left and right elbows and sword in a straight line, at the same time, bend and lift left knee against right knee joints. Look at sword tip (Figure 4-11).

图 4-11(Figure 4-11)

5.弓步下刺

左脚向前落步,屈膝成弓步,右手接剑屈肘从腰侧向左前方下刺,手心向内;左手剑指,从胸前向左斜上方摆击,两臂与剑成一条直线。目视剑尖(图4-12)。

5. Bow stance downward stabbing

Left foot falls forward, bend elbow into the bow stance, right hand picks sword, bend elbow and stab leftward and forward from the waist, hand center inward, left finger pointing, swinging leftward and obliquely upward from the chest, arms and sword in the straight line. Look at sword tip (Figure 4-12).

图 4-12（Figure 4-12）

6.云剑前刺

（1）右腿屈膝向前半步；右臂屈肘抱剑于胸前，手心向上；左剑指向下附于右腕内侧。目视剑尖（图4-13）。

6. Cloud sword forward stabbing

(1) Bend right knee forward half a step, bend right elbow and hold sword in front of the chest, hand center upward, left finger pointing downward against right wrist inward. Look at sword tip (Figure 4-13).

图 4-13（Figure 4-13）

（2）上动不停，左脚蹬地跳起，右腿向前跨步，支撑重心。左腿屈膝，左脚面扣于右膝后；同时，右手握剑，使剑尖向左、向上、向后，经头上向右、向前、向左，环绕一周。右臂屈肘，右手收于右腰间，剑尖向左前方，剑指附于右小臂上。目视剑尖方向（图4-14）。

(2) Keep moving, left foot falls and jumps, right leg stride forward to support gravity center. Bend left knee, buckle left instep behind right knee, at the same time, right hand holds sword, swing sword tip leftward, upward,

backward, overhead, and rightward, forward, leftward a circle. Bend right elbow, close right hand against right waist, sword tip leftward and forward, finger pointing against right forearm. Look at sword tip (Figure 4-14).

图 4-14(Figure 4-14)

（3）左脚向左前方落步成弓步；在身体左转的同时，剑从腰间向前立剑刺出；左手剑指由腰间向头上架起，手心向上。目视剑尖方向(图 4-15)。

(3) Left foot strides leftward and forward into the bow stance, turn left, at the same time, stab sword forward from the waist, parry left finger pointing against the waist and overhead, hand center upward. Look at sword tip (Figure 4-15).

图 4-15(Figure 4-15)

7.古树盘根

（1）右脚向前半步，身体向左转 90°，两腿交叉，左脚在前，右脚在后；右手持剑外旋向上翻腕举剑，掌心向内，剑尖向前；左剑指向下附于右腕内侧。目视剑尖(图 4-16)。

7. Sword winding

(1) Right foot strides half a step, turn leftward 90°, legs cross, left foot in

193

the front, right foot behind, right hand turns outward and lift sword, palm center inward, sword tip forward, left finger pointing downward and against right wrist inward. Look at sword tip (Figure 4-16).

图4-16(Figure 4-16)

（2）上动不停,两腿屈膝下蹲成歇步；右手握剑向胸前收剑,手心向里,剑尖向左上方,左手指不动。目视右前方(图4-17)。

(2) Keep moving, bend knees and squat into the sitting stance, right hand holds sword to the front chest, hand center inward, sword tip leftward and upward, keep left fingers still. Look right forward (Figure 4-17).

图4-17(Figure 4-17)

8.削如松林

向右转身180°,由歇步变为马步；右手持剑随转体使剑在膝下平扫至身体右侧,手心向下；左手剑指向上架于头顶上方。上身保持挺直。目视剑尖(图4-18)。

8. Sword cutting

Turn right 180°, change the sitting stance into the horse-riding stance, right hand swings sword rightward, hand center downward, left finger pointing upward and overhead. Keep straight. Look at sword tip (Figure 4-18).

图 4-18(Figure 4-18)

9.仙人指路

(1)身体重心左移,右腿挺膝伸直成弓步;右手持剑向上翻腕,经头上方向左带剑;左手剑指附于右手腕。目视剑尖方向(图 4-19)。

9. Immortal guiding

(1) Shift gravity center leftward, right knee straight into the bow stance, right hand holds sword and turn wrist upward, swing sword overhead, left finger pointing against right wrist. Look at sword tip (Figure 4-19).

图 4-19(Figure 4-19)

(2)上动不停,身体重心左移;右手持剑向左下劈落;左手剑指附于右腕处。目视剑尖(图 4-20)。

(2) Keep moving, shift gravity center leftward, right hand holds sword and chop sword downward, left finger pointing against right wrist. Look at sword tip (Figure 4-20).

图4-20(Figure 4-20)

（3）上动不停,身体右转,左膝全蹲成右仆步;右手持剑从左膝下向右带剑,手心向里;左手剑指附于右手前。目视剑尖(图4-21)。

(3) Keep moving, turn right, left knee spring sitting into the drop stance, right hand holds sword and swings rightward against left knee, hand center inward, left finger pointing against right hand. Look at sword tip (Figure 4-21).

图4-21(Figure 4-21)

（4）上动不停,身体上起;右脚向前上一步,身体先向左再向右转身;同时,右手持剑由下向上挑剑至体前,向左下方划弧再向右上方挑剑,剑尖向左下方,左手剑指附于右腕。目视剑尖(图4-22)。

(4) Keep moving, arise, outreach right tiptoes, right hand lifts sword rightward and upward to forehead, sword tip downward and leftward, left finger pointing against right wrist. Look at sword tip (Figure 4-22).

图 4-22（Figure 4-22）

（5）上动不停,右手持剑向右抽剑,手心向外,剑尖指向左方;左手剑指附于右腕;同时,左腿屈膝提起,脚尖向下,脚掌贴靠右膝。目视剑尖(图 4-23)。

(5) Keep moving, right hand thrusts sword rightward, palm outward, sword tip leftward, left finger pointing against right wrist, at the same time, bend and lift left knee, tiptoes downward, sole against right knee. Look at sword tip (Figure 4-23).

图 4-23（Figure 4-23）

10.前劈剑

（1）左脚向前落步成弓步;同时,右手持剑从左向上、向后、向右使剑尖划弧在头上云剑,举至右肩上,剑尖向右后上方;左手剑指附于右腕。目视前下方(图 4-24)。

10. Forward chopping

(1) Left foot falls forward into the bow stance, at the same time, right hand holds sword and draw curve upward, backward and rightward, make sword tip cloud sword overhead, lift it to right shoulder, sword tip rightward and backward, left finger pointing against right wrist. Look forward and downward (Figure 4-24).

图 4-24(Figure 4-24)

(2)上动不停,右手持剑,从上向前下劈,剑尖向斜前下方;随即左手剑指向下、向左、向上架于头上方。目视剑尖(图 4-25)。

(2) Keep moving, right hand holds sword, chop it downward and forward, sword tip obliquely forward and downward, and left finger pointing downward and leftward, parry it overhead. Look at sword tip (Figure 4-25)

图 4-25(Figure 4-25)

11.后点剑

重心前移,左腿用力蹬地向上跳起,身体右转;左脚向上提起,随之右手握剑向上、向右下挥落点剑,左手剑指在体前向下、向左架于头上方。手心向上。目视剑尖(图 4-26)。

11. Backward sword pointing

Shift gravity center to left leg, jump, and turn right, left foot upward, right hand wave sword upward and rightward, left finger pointing parries downward and overhead. Hand center upward. Look at sword tip (Figure 4-26).

图 4-26(Figure 4-26)

12.龙摆尾

(1)左脚向左落步,身体重心左移;同时,右手持剑以腕为轴,剑尖从左向上、向右、向下、向左绕环绞剑至右前方,剑尖向斜下,手心斜向上。目视剑尖(图 4-27)。

12. Tail wagging

(1) Left foot falls leftward, shift gravity center leftward, at the same time, right hand holds sword and wings sword tip upward, rightward, downward and leftward a circle with the wrist as the axis, sword tip obliquely downward, hand center obliquely upward. Look at sword tip (Figure 4-27).

图 4-27(Figure 4-27)

(2)上动不停,右脚后撤半步成虚步;右手持剑以腕为轴,使剑尖由内向外划圆绞剑,手心仍斜向上。目视剑尖(图 4-28)。

(2) Keep moving, right foot retreats half a step into the empty stance, right hand holds sword and wings sword tip a circle with the wrist as the axis, hand center obliquely upward. Look at sword tip (Figure 4-28).

图4-28（Figure 4-28）

（3）上动不停，右腿屈膝提起；右手持剑抽于右腰间，手心向上，剑尖指向前下方；左手剑指附于右腕内侧。目视剑尖方向（图4-29）。

(3) Keep moving, bend and lift right knee, right hand holds sword against right waist, hand center upward, sword tip forward and downward, left finger pointing against right wrist inward. Look at sword tip (Figure 4-29).

图4-29（Figure 4-29）

（4）上动不停，右脚向前上一步成弓步；同时，右手持剑从腰间向前下方刺出，拇指一侧向上；左手剑指随即屈肘向上横架于头上方，手心向上。目视剑尖（图4-30）。

(4) Keep moving, right foot strides one step into the bow stance, at the same time, right hand holds sword and thrusts it forward and downward from the waist, thumb upward, bend elbow upward and left finger pointing overhead, hand center upward. Look at sword tip (Figure 4-30).

图 4-30（Figure 4-30）

13.败势观剑

重心移向左腿,成左横弓步;同时,右手持剑,沉腕向上成崩剑,剑尖向上。目视剑尖(图 4-31)。

13. Twisting

Shift gravity center to left leg into the left bow stance, at the same time, right hand holds sword, bend and lift elbow into the tilt sword, sword tip upward. Look at sword tip (Figure 4-31).

图 4-31（Figure 4-31）

14.独立点剑

(1)右脚向左脚后插步;右手持剑外旋向上、向下按至左胯侧,手心向里,剑尖向左上方;左手剑指附于右腕。目视剑尖(图 4-32)。

14. Stand on one leg sword pointing

(1) Right foot strides to left foot backward, right hand holds sword and swings it outward, upward, downward and against left hip, hand center inward,

sword tip leftward and upward, left finger pointing against right wrist. Look at sword tip (Figure 4-32).

图 4-32（Figure 4-32）

（2）上动不停，以左脚跟、右脚掌为轴，身体右转180°；右腿支撑身体重心，左脚屈膝上提；同时，右手持剑随转体使剑尖向下、向右、向上、向下方点剑；左手剑指屈肘向上横架于头上，手心向上。上体微右前倾。目视剑尖（图4-33）。

（2）Keep on moving, turn rightward 180° with left heel and right sole as the axis, right leg supports gravity center, bend and lift left knee, at the same time, right hand holds sword with sword tip downward and swings it rightward, upward and downward, bend left elbow and parry upward and overhead, hand center upward. Turn slightly forward. Look at sword tip (Figure 4-33).

图 4-33（Figure 4-33）

第二段

Section 2

15. 仙人指路

（1）左腿向左落步，右腿屈膝向前半步，前脚掌点地，身体左转90°；随之右手持剑从右经上向左下挂剑,剑身立于身体左前,剑尖向下;左手剑指附于右大臂内侧。目视前方(图 4-34)。

15. Immortal guiding

(1) Left leg falls leftward, bend right knee and stride half a step, front sole touchdown, turn leftward 90°, right holds sword and swings it leftward and downward, sword forward and leftward, sword tip downward, left finger pointing against right arm. Look straight ahead (Figure 4-34).

图 4-34(Figure 4-34)

(2)上动不停,左脚向后一步成右弓步;同时,上体微左转,再右转;右手握剑使剑向左、向上,臂外旋翻腕,使剑再向右、向下、向后划弧挂至身体右前方;剑尖向后下方。目视前方(图 4-35)。

(2) Keep moving, left foot retreats one step into the bow stance, at the same time, turn leftward slightly, turn right, right hand holds sword, swings sword leftward and upward, bend elbow outward and turn wrist, make sword draw curve rightward, downward and backward, swing it rightward and forward, sword tip backward and downward. Look straight ahead (Figure 4-35).

图 4-35(Figure 4-35)

(3)上动不停,右脚向后一步成左弓步;右手握剑经右腿侧向上、向前划弧挂劈剑,右臂与剑身保持平直;左手剑指附于右小臂。目视剑尖(图4-36)。

(3) Keep moving, right foot retreats into the left bow stance, right hand holds sword, make sword draw curve upward and forward, right arm and sword straight, left finger pointing against right forearm. Look at sword tip (Figure 4-36).

图4-36(Figure 4-36)

(4)上动不停,右手持剑向后拉平,重心略向后移,左手剑指从后向前慢推,附于剑柄上。目视剑尖(图4-37)。

(4) Keep moving, right hand holds sword backward, shift gravity center slightly backward, left finger pointing slowly pushes forward and against sword handle. Look at sword tip (Figure 4-37).

图4-37(Figure 4-37)

(5)上动不停,身体右转;右手持剑向后平拉,横举于右肩前上方,手心向外,剑尖向左;左手剑指向左平指;同时,身体重心移至右腿,左腿屈膝提起。目视剑指方向(图4-38)。

(5) Keep moving, turn right, right hand pulls sword straight, and lift it above right shoulder, palm outward, sword tip leftward, left finger pointing straight, at the same time, shift gravity center to right leg, bend and lift left knee. Look at finger pointing (Figure 4-38).

第四章　少林达摩剑

图 4-38(Figure 4-38)

16.玉女穿梭

(1)左脚向左落步。目视剑指(图 4-39)。

16. Shuttling

(1) Left foot falls leftward. Look at finger pointing (Figure 4-39).

图 4-39(Figure 4-39)

(2)上动不停,右腿随即向前摆起,左脚蹬地跳起,左腿屈膝,脚背绷直,身体在空中左转 180°;同时,右手持剑从颈部向右平刺,拇指一侧向上,剑指随转体举至左上方。目视剑尖(图 4-40)。

(2) Keep moving, right leg swings forward, left foot falls and jumps, bend left knee, keep instep straight, turn leftward 180° in the air, at the same time, right hand holds sword and stabs it rightward from the neck, thumb upward, at the same time finger pointing leftward and upward. Look at sword tip (Figure 4-40).

图 4-40（Figure 4-40）

（3）上动不停,随即在空中身体速向左转180°,右脚、左脚依次落地;右腿屈膝半蹲,左腿挺膝伸直成右弓步;右手持剑从右经上向下劈剑;左手剑指屈肘横架于头上。手心向上。目视剑尖方向(图4-41)。

(3) Keep moving, turn leftward 180° in the air, right foot and left foot fall, bend right knee on semi-crouch balance, left knee straight into the bow stance, right hand holds sword and chops it downward, bend elbow and parry left finger pointing overhead. Palm center upward. Look at sword tip (Figure 4-41).

图 4-41（Figure 4-41）

17.三起剑

（1）身体重心左移,左腿屈膝,右手持剑,臂向内旋,拇指向下,剑尖指向右前下方,左手剑指向下附于右胸前。目视剑尖方向(图4-42)。

17. Three thrusting

(1) Shift gravity center leftward, bend left knee, right hand holds sword, arm turns inward, thumb downward, sword tip downward, forward and rightward, left finger pointing in front of the right chest. Look at sword tip

(Figure 4-42)。

图 4-42（Figure 4-42）

（2）上动不停,右脚斜向前上一步,屈膝半蹲,大腿接近水平,全脚着地,左腿向后收半步微屈,脚尖点地;同时,右手持剑外旋,从右向左前上挑剑,小指侧刃向上;左手剑指附于右腕内侧。目视剑尖(图 4-43)。

（2）Keep moving, right foot strides one step obliquely forward, bend knees on semi-crouch balance, thigh horizontal, foot touchdown, close left leg half a step backward, slightly bend, tiptoes touchdown, at the same time, right hand holds sword and swing it outward, make it pick forward and leftward, little finger inward, sword blade upward, left finger pointing against right wrist. Look at sword tip (Figure 4-43).

图 4-43（Figure 4-43）

（3）上动不停,起身站立,右小臂外旋,右手持剑,由上向下穿剑,手心向外,剑尖向下,左手剑指附于右腕。目视剑尖(图 4-44)。

（3）Keep moving, stand up, right forearm swings outward, right hand holds sword, thrust it downward, palm outward, sword tip downward, left finger pointing against right wrist. Look at sword tip (Figure 4-44).

图 4-44（Figure 4-44）

（4）上动不停,右脚向前一步,脚尖外展;同时,右手持剑以手腕为轴,使剑向后、向上、向前劈挂剑;左手剑指附于右腕上。目视剑尖(图 4-45)。

(4) Keep moving, right foot strides one step forward, tiptoes outreach, at the same time, right hand holds sword, swing it backward, upward and forward with wrist as the axis, left finger pointing against right wrist. Look at sword tip (Figure 4-45).

图 4-45（Figure 4-45）

（5）上动不停,两脚屈膝下蹲成歇步;右手持剑向右下方直臂戳剑,手心向下;左手剑指向左上方摆击。目视剑尖(图 4-46)。

(5) Keep moving, bend knees and squat into the sitting stance, right hand holds sword and thrusts it rightward and downward, palm center downward, left finger pointing swings leftward and upward. Look at sword tip (Figure 4-46).

图 4-46（Figure 4-46）

第四章 少林达摩剑

（6）身体上起，右手持剑经右腿侧向前下挑剑，手心向里，剑尖指向前下方；左手剑指附于右腕上。目视剑尖（图4-47）。

（6）Arise, right hand holds sword and picks it forward and downward via right leg inward, palm inward, sword tip forward and downward, left finger pointing against right wrist. Look at sword tip（Figure 4-47）.

图 4-47（Figure 4-47）

（7）上动不停，左脚向左上半步，脚尖点地；右手持剑，右小臂外旋，以右腕为轴向上、向后屈臂划弧，手心向内，剑尖向右斜上方；左手剑指附于右腕上。目视剑尖（图4-48）。

（7）Keep moving, left foot strides half a step forward, tiptoes touchdown, right hand holds sword, right forearm swings outward, bend right knee and take it as the axis to draw curve upward and backward, palms inward, sword tip rightward and obliquely upward, left finger pointing against right wrist. Look at sword tip（Figure 4-48）.

图 4-48（Figure 4-48）

（8）上动不停，两腿屈膝下蹲，成虚步；右手持剑向下、向前、向左以剑侧刃为力点向上挑剑，手心向上，剑尖向左前上方；左手剑指附于右腕上。目视剑尖方向（图4-49）。

(8) Keep moving, bend knees and squat into the empty stance, right hand holds sword and picks it downward, forward and leftward with sword blade as force point, palm center upward, sword tip forward and leftward, left finger pointing against the right wrist. Look at sword tip (Figure 4-49).

图 4-49(Figure 4-49)

18.霸王观阵

(1)身体上起,右手持剑外旋翻腕向下、向后,使剑尖由前经右腿侧向后穿剑,手心向外,剑尖向后;左手剑指落于左腿侧。目视剑尖(图 4-50)。

18. Mighty punching

(1) Arise, right hand holds sword and swings it outward, downward and backward, thrust sword tip backward from right leg, palm outward, sword tip backward, left finger pointing against left leg. Look at sword tip (Figure 4-50).

图 4-50(Figure 4-50)

(2)上动不停,右手持剑由后经头顶向前刺剑,手心向外,剑尖向前。目视剑尖(图 4-51)。

(2) Keep moving, right hand holds sword and stabs it overhead and forward, palm outward, and sword tip forward. Look at sword tip (Figure 4-51).

图 4-51(Figure 4-51)

(3)上动不停,右脚向左前上一步,脚尖外摆成盖叉步;右手持剑由上向下穿刺,使剑垂于体前;右臂屈肘,拇指一侧向下;左手屈肘向体侧摆击。目视前方(图 4-52)。

(3) Keep moving, right foot strides one step leftward, outreach tiptoes into the fork stance, right hand holds sword and stabs it downward, make sword fall in front, bend the right arm and lower the elbow, thumb downward, bend left elbow and swing outward. Look straight ahead (Figure 4-52).

图 4-52(Figure 4-52)

19.咽喉剑

(1)两腿不动,上身略向左转,重心在左腿;右手持剑由下向上起;左手剑指由头上落于右腕。目视剑尖(图 4-53)。

19. Throat thrusting

(1) Keep legs still, turn left slightly, shift gravity center to left leg, right hand holds sword and raises it, left finger pointing falls right wrist from overhead. Look at sword tip (Figure 4-53).

图4-53（Figure 4-53）

（2）上动不停，右脚支撑，左腿屈膝提起，脚背扣于右腿膝窝处；同时，右手持剑翻腕下压，屈肘收于腰间，剑身平直，手心向上，剑尖向前；左臂屈肘轻贴剑身上，剑指附于右手拇指上。目视剑尖方向（图4-54）。

(2) Keep moving, with right foot as the support, bend and lift left knee, buckle instep into right knee fossa, at the same time, right hand holds sword and presses wrist, bend elbow against the waist, sword straight, palm center upward, sword tip forward, bend left elbow against sword, finger pointing against right thumb. Look at sword tip (Figure 4-54).

图4-54（Figure 4-54）

（3）左脚向前迈出一步成弓步；同时，右手持剑向前平刺出，左手剑指附于右腕。目视剑尖方向（图4-55）。

(3) Left foot strides one step into the bow stance, at the same time, right hand holds sword and stabs it forward, left finger pointing against right wrist. Look at sword tip (Figure 4-55).

第四章 少林达摩剑

图 4-55(Figure 4-55)

20.劈膀剑

(1)右脚跟半步,右手持剑翻腕向左划弧,手心向下,左手剑指附于右腕。目视剑尖(图 4-56)。

20. Shoulder chopping

(1) Right foot strides half a step, right hand holds sword, bend wrist to draw curve leftward, palm center downward, left finger pointing against right wrist. Look at sword tip (Figure 4-56).

图 4-56(Figure 4-56)

(2)两膝略屈;同时,右手持剑从前向上、向右、向下以小指侧刃为用力点甩臂轮臂,两手收于腰间,右手心向上,剑尖指向前;左手剑指屈肘附于右腕。目视剑尖(图 4-57)。

(2) Bend knees slightly, at the same time, right hand holds sword, swing upward, rightward, downward with little finger as force point, hands against the waist, right palm upward, sword tip forward, left finger pointing against right wrist. Look at sword tip (Figure 4-57).

213

图 4-57（Figure 4-57）

（3）上动不停，左脚蹬地跳起，身体右后转270°，右腿挺膝直立，左腿屈膝上提；同时，右手持剑从腰间向前下方刺出，拇指一侧向上，剑尖指向右侧下方；左手剑指屈肘横架于头上，手心向上。目视剑尖（图4-58）。

(3) Keep moving, left foot falls and jumps, turn rightward and backward 270°, bend and lift right knee, at the same time, right hand holds sword against the waist and thrusts it forward and downward, thumb upward, sword tip rightward and downward, left finger pointing parries overhead, palm center upward. Look at sword tip (Figure 4-58).

图 4-58（Figure 4-58）

21.虚步挑剑

右脚落地屈膝下蹲，左脚随即向下落步，脚尖点地成虚步；同时，身体左转，右手持剑以小拇指侧刃为力点，屈肘使剑向下、向左挑剑，剑尖向左前上方；左手剑指由上向下附于右手腕上。目视剑尖（图4-59）。

21. Empty stance picking

Right foot falls and squat, left foot falls, tiptoes touchdown into the empty stance, at the same time, turn left, right hand holds sword, take little finger inward as force point, bend elbow and make it pick downward and leftward, sword tip forward and leftward, left finger pointing against right wrist. Look at sword tip (Figure 4-59).

图 4-59(Figure 4-59)

22.弹步磨剑

(1)左脚向前半步,重心上起前移,两腿屈膝,右脚前掌趴地,向后撩起;同时,右手持剑,两臂外旋,向左右分开,剑尖剑指均向前。目视前方(图 4-60)。

22. Moving and grinding

(1) Left foot strides half a step forward, shift gravity center forward, bend knees, right sole touchdown, backward and upward, at the same time, right hand holds sword, swing arms outward, leftward and rightward respectively, sword tip and finger pointing forward. Look straight ahead (Figure 4-60).

图 4-60(Figure 4-60)

(2)上动不停,右脚向前,屈膝落步;左腿屈膝,左脚前掌趴地,向后撩起;同时,右手持剑与剑指同时内旋,屈肘向胸前相合,两手心向上,剑尖向前,剑指向上。目视剑尖(图 4-61)。

(2) Keep moving, right foot forward, bend elbow and fall, bend left knee, left sole touchdown and backward, at the same time, right hand holds sword, turn inward, bend elbow to the chest, palm upward, sword tip forward, finger pointing upward. Look at sword tip (Figure 4-61).

图 4-61 (Figure 4-61)

（3）上动不停，左脚向前屈膝落步，右脚前掌趴地，向后撩起；同时，右手持剑，两臂外旋，向左右分开，剑尖剑指均向前。目视前方（图4-62）。

(3) Keep moving, left foot forward and bend knee, right sole touchdown and backward, at the same time, right hand holds sword, swing arms outward, leftward and rightward respectively, sword tip and finger pointing forward. Look straight ahead (Figure 4-62).

图 4-62 (Figure 4-62)

（4）上动不停，右脚向前，屈膝落步，左腿屈膝，左脚前掌趴地，向后撩起；同时，右手持剑与剑指同时内旋，屈肘向胸前相合，两手心向上，剑尖向前，剑指向上。目视剑尖（图4-63）。

(4) Keep moving, right foot forward, bend elbow and fall, bend left knee, left sole touchdown and backward, at the same time, right hand desperately turns inward together with finger pointing, bend elbow to the chest, palms upward,

sword tip forward, finger pointing upward. Look at sword tip (Figure 4-63).

图 4-63(Figure 4-63)

（5）上动不停，左脚向前屈膝落步，右脚前掌趴地，向后撩起；同时，右手持剑，两臂外旋，向左右分开，剑尖剑指均向前。目视前方（图 4-64）。

(5) Keep moving, left foot forward and bend knee, right sole touchdown and backward, at the same time, right hand holds sword, arms swing outward, leftward and rightward respectively, sword tip and finger pointing forward. Look straight ahead (Figure 4-64).

图 4-64(Figure 4-64)

（6）上动不停，右手持剑与左手剑指屈肘同时收于腹前，手心均向上，剑尖指向前，左手剑指附于右手背；同时，右腿屈膝向前提起，左腿挺直。目视剑尖方向（图 4-65）。

(6) Keep moving, right hand holds sword, bend elbow, close left finger pointing against front abdomen, palms upward, sword tip forward, left finger pointing against right hand back, at the same time, bend and lift right knee, left leg straight. Look at sword tip (Figure 4-65).

图 4-65（Figure 4-65）

（7）上动不停，右脚向前落步屈膝半蹲，左腿挺膝伸直，成右弓步；同时，右手持剑从胸前向前上方刺出，剑尖指向前上方；左手剑指附于右腕上，手心向下。目视剑尖（图 4-66）。

（7）Keep moving, right foot falls and bend knees on semi-crouch balance, left leg straight into the right bow stance, at the same time, right hand holds sword, thrusts it forward and upward, sword tip forward, left finger pointing against the right wrist, palm center downward. Look at sword tip（Figure 4-66）.

图 4-66（Figure 4-66）

第三段

Section 3

23. 藏花剑

（1）身体右转；同时，右脚向左脚后退一步成左弓步；右手持剑向下，向右后撩剑，手心向外，剑尖向右方；左手剑指不动。目视剑尖（图 4-67）。

第四章 少林达摩剑

23. Flowering

(1) Turn right, at the same time, right foot retreats a step to left foot into the left bow stance, right hand holds sword and picks it rightward and backward, palm outward, sword tip rightward, and left finger pointing still. Look at sword tip (Figure 4-67).

图 4-67(Figure 4-67)

(2)上动不停,右手持剑使剑尖向上、向左经体前向下、向右后穿,臂内旋,手心向上,身体重心左移;左臂屈肘,剑指落于右肩前。目视剑尖(图 4-68)。

(2) Keep moving, right hand holds sword, make sword tip upward and leftward, thrust forward, rightward and backward, arm turns inward, palm center upward, shift gravity center leftward, bend the right arm and lower the elbow, finger pointing against right shoulder. Look at sword tip (Figure 4-68).

图 4-68(Figure 4-68)

(3)上动不停,左腿屈膝全蹲,右腿挺膝伸直,成右仆步,上体右转;右手持剑臂外旋,使剑继续向右穿出,拇指一侧向上;左手剑指向左上方穿出。目视剑尖(图 4-69)。

219

(3) Keep moving, bend left knee into spring sitting, right leg straight into the drop stance, turn right, right hand holds sword, arm swings outward, make sword thrust rightward, thumb upward, left hand holds sword and make it thrust leftward and upward. Look at sword tip (Figure 4-69).

图 4-69(Figure 4-69)

（4）上动不停，左腿伸直，起身右转成叉步；右手持剑屈肘向胸前收，手心向上，剑尖向左；左手剑指屈肘附于剑柄处。目视剑尖（图 4-70）。

(4) Keep moving, left leg straight, stand and turn right into the fork stance, right hand holds sword and bend elbow to the chest, palm center upward, sword tip leftward, left finger pointing against sword handle. Look at sword tip (Figure 4-70).

图 4-70(Figure 4-70)

（5）上动不停，身体右转，左右两腿屈膝下蹲，成歇步；右手持剑臂内旋，向右拉剑，手心向外，剑身略高于肩，剑尖向左；左手剑指附于右手腕处。目视剑尖（图 4-71）。

(5) Keep moving, turn right, bend knees and squat into the sitting stance, right hand holds sword and swing arm inward, pull sword rightward, palm outward, sword slightly higher than shoulder, sword tip leftward, left

finger pointing against right wrist. Look at sword tip (Figure 4-71).

图 4-71(Figure 4-71)

24.前劈剑

(1)身体立起,左脚向左前一步,右膝略屈;右手持剑向上横架于头上,手心向前,剑尖指向左;左手剑指附于右腕。目视左方(图 4-72)。

24. Forward chopping

(1) Stand up, left foot strides one step forward and leftward, bend right knee slightly, right hand holds sword upward and overhead, palm forward, sword tip leftward, left finger pointing against right wrist. Look leftward (Figure 4-72).

图 4-72(Figure 4-72)

(2)上动不停,左脚向左上半步成弓步;右手持剑向左、向后,向前下方劈剑,右手拇指一侧向上,剑尖向前下方;左手剑指向左后摆臂。目视剑尖(图 4-73)。

(2) Keep moving, left foot strides half a step forward and leftward into the bow stance, right hand holds sword and chops it leftward, backward, forward

and downward, right thumb upward, sword tip forward and downward, and left finger pointing leftward. Look at sword tip (Figure 4-73).

图 4-73（Figure 4-73）

25.削膝剑

(1)右脚向前一步；同时，身体左转180°成弓步；右手持剑屈肘向上、向左划弧，手心向内，剑尖向左上方；左手剑指屈肘附于右腕。目视剑尖（图4-74）。

25. Knee cutting

(1) Right foot strides one step forward, at the same time, turn leftward 180° into the bow stance, right hand holds sword, make elbow draw curve upward and leftward, palm inward, sword tip rightward, left finger pointing against right wrist. Look at sword tip (Figure 4-74).

图 4-74（Figure 4-74）

(2)上动不停，右手持剑向上、向右、向下划弧斩剑，剑尖指向右前下方；左手剑指屈肘横架于头上，手心向上；同时，两腿屈膝身体下蹲成马步。目视剑尖（图4-75）。

第四章　少林达摩剑

（2）Keep moving, right hand holds sword, draw curve upward, rightward and downward, sword tip rightward and downward, left finger pointing overhead, palm center upward, at the same time, bend knees and squat into the horse-riding stance. Look at sword tip (Figure 4-75).

图 4-75（Figure 4-75）

26. 观阵剑

（1）右手持剑臂外旋，使剑由右经上向左、向下划弧压剑，手心向上，剑尖指向左前方；左手剑指向下收于体前，掌心向下；同时，身体重心随压剑移向右腿。目视剑尖方向（图 4-76）。

26. Arraying

（1）Right hand holds sword, arm swings outward, draw curve leftward and downward, palm center upward, sword tip leftward and forward, left finger pointing downward and forward, palm center downward, at the same time, shift gravity center to right leg. Look at sword tip (Figure 4-76).

图 4-76（Figure 4-76）

（2）上动不停，右手持剑下旋由左经前向右划弧平斩剑，手心向下，剑尖指向右前方；左手剑指附于肘内侧。目视剑尖（图 4-77）。

(2) Keep moving, right hand holds sword, draw curve rightward to cut, palm center downward, sword tip rightward and forward, left finger pointing against elbow inward. Look at sword tip (Figure 4-77).

图 4-77(Figure 4-77)

(3)上动不停,左脚经右腿前向右跨一步,两腿屈膝下蹲变成歇步;同时,右手持剑与左手剑指由右经头上向左划弧下按,立剑横于右膝前,剑尖向左前方;剑指指向剑尖方向。目视剑尖(图 4-78)。

(3) Keep moving, left foot strides one step rightward, bend knees and squat into the sitting stance, at the same time, right hand holds sword, draw curve leftward and overhead, sword against right knee, sword tip leftward and forward. Look at sword tip (Figure 4-78).

图 4-78(Figure 4-78)

(4)上动不停,右脚向右一步,两腿屈膝,身体下蹲成弓步;同时,右手持剑向右、向上、向左、向下劈剑于体前,剑尖仍向左;剑指与剑向同一方向。目视剑尖(图 4-79)。

(4) Keep moving, right foot strides one step rightward, bend knees and squat into the bow stance, at the same time, right hand holds sword and chops it rightward, upward, leftward and downward, sword tip leftward, finger pointing

and sword in the same direction. Look at sword tip (Figure 4-79).

图 4-79(Figure 4-79)

（5）上动不停，上身右转，右腿上提；同时，右手持剑由左经体前向右划弧抽剑收于右腰间，手心向下，剑尖向前；左手剑指指向前方。目视剑指方向（图 4-80）。

（5）Keep moving, turn right, lift right leg, at the same time, right hand holds sword, draw curve rightward and against right waist, palm center downward, sword tip forward, left finger pointing forward. Look at finger pointing (Figure 4-80).

图 4-80(Figure 4-80)

（6）上动不停，右腿向下落地，左腿屈膝上提，脚尖向下；同时，右手持剑向上直臂刺出，剑尖向上；左手剑指屈肘收于右肩前。目视左方（图 4-81）。

（6）Keep moving, right leg falls, bend and lift left knee, tiptoes downward, at the same time, right hand holds sword and stabs it upward, sword tip upward, left finger pointing against right shoulder. Look leftward (Figure 4-81).

图 4-81（Figure 4-81）

27.穿针引线

（1）身体左转,右手持剑向左后划弧下劈;同时,左腿上提。目视剑尖（图4-82）。

27. Threading

(1) Turn left, right left hand holds sword, draw curve to chop leftward, backward and downward, at the same time, lift left leg. Look at sword tip (Figure 4-82).

图 4-82（Figure 4-82）

（2）上动不停,左脚向左后落步,右脚略屈膝;同时,右手持剑向前、向后划弧带剑,手心向下,剑尖指向前下方。目视剑尖（图4-83）。

(2) Keep moving, left foot strides one step and falls, bend right knee slightly, at the same time, right hand holds sword, draw curve forward and backward, palm center downward, sword tip forward and downward. Look at sword tip (Figure 4-83).

第四章 少林达摩剑

图 4-83（Figure 4-83）

（3）上动不停，右手持剑向右抽剑收于腰间，剑尖向前下方；同时，右脚向左脚内侧收步，前脚掌着地，两腿略屈膝；左手剑指附于体前下方。目视前下方（图 4-84）。

(3) Keep moving, right hand holds sword rightward, sword against the waist, sword tip forward and downward, at the same time, close right foot to left foot inward, front sole touchdown, bend knees slightly, left finger pointing forward and downward. Look front downward (Figure 4-84).

图 4-84（Figure 4-84）

（4）上动不停，右手持剑从腰间向前直臂刺出。剑尖向前；同时，右脚收于左脚内侧震脚并拢，双腿屈膝半蹲，大腿保持水平，成椅子桩；左手剑指附于右小臂内侧。目视剑尖（图 4-85）。

(4) Keep moving, right hand holds sword, stab it straight from the waist, word tip forward, at the same time, close right foot to left foot inward, bend knees on semi-crouch balance, thigh still into the chair piling, left finger pointing against right forearm inward. Look at sword tip (Figure 4-85).

227

图 4-85（Figure 4-85）

28.游龙剑

（1）右脚向前上一步，上体左转。右手持剑，剑尖经头上方向左划弧，手心向内，剑尖向右上；左手剑指附于右手腕处。目视剑尖（图 4-86）。

28. Snaking

(1) Right foot strides one step, turn left. Right hand holds sword, make it draw curve overhead and leftward, palm inward, sword tip upward, left finger pointing against right wrist. Look at sword tip (Figure 4-86).

图 4-86（Figure 4-86）

（2）上动不停，重心前移，身体左转 180°右脚向前收于左脚内侧，双腿屈膝下蹲，左脚脚尖点地成左丁步；右手持剑向上、向下、向左提膝剑，剑尖向前；左手剑指附于右腕内侧。目视剑尖（图 4-87）。

(2) Keep moving, shift gravity center forward, turn leftward 180°, close right foot to left foot inward, bend knees and squat, tiptoes touchdown into the left T-step, right hand holds sword, swings it upward, downward and leftward, sword tip forward, left finger pointing against right wrist inward. Look at sword tip (Figure 4-87).

第四章　少林达摩剑

图 4-87（Figure 4-87）

（3）上动不停,左脚向前一步成弓步,右手持剑沉腕上挑剑,剑尖向上、向右划弧,剑尖向右上;左手剑指附于右小臂内侧。目视剑尖(图 4-88)。

（3）Keep moving, left foot strides one step into the bow stance, right hand holds sword, draw curve upward and rightward, sword tip rightward, left finger pointing against right forearm inward. Look at sword tip (Figure 4-88).

图 4-88（Figure 4-88）

（4）上动不停,身体左转 90°,右脚向前收于左脚内侧成丁步;同时,右手持剑由胸前向下、向左、向上划弧于右胸前,右臂外旋,剑尖向右;左手剑指附于剑柄处。目视剑尖方向(图 4-89)。

（4）Keep moving, turn rightward 90°, close right foot forward to left foot inward into the T-step, at the same time, right hand holds sword, draw curve downward, leftward and upward, right arm swings outward, sword tip forward, left finger pointing against sword handle. Look at sword tip (Figure 4-89).

229

图 4-89（Figure 4-89）

（5）上动不停,右脚向前一步;同时,右手持剑由左向右划弧横于体前,手心向下,剑尖向左;左手剑指附于右腕处。目视前方(图 4-90)。

(5) Keep moving, right foot strides one step, at the same time, right hand holds sword, draw curve rightward, palm center downward, sword tip leftward, left finger pointing against right wrist place. Look straight ahead (Figure 4-90).

图 4-90（Figure 4-90）

（6）上动不停,重心后移,右腿屈膝上提;同时,右手持剑手臂外旋向上、向右、向下屈肘收于右胸前,剑尖向前;左手剑指附于右腕处。目视剑尖方向(图 4-91)。

(6) Keep moving, shift gravity center backward, bend and lift right knee, at the same time, right hand holds sword, swings it outward, upward, rightward and downward, bend elbow to right chest, sword tip forward, right finger pointing against right wrist. Look at sword tip (Figure 4-91).

第四章　少林达摩剑

图 4-91（Figure 4-91）

（7）上动不停,右脚向下落地震脚,左腿随即屈膝提起,扣于右腿膝窝处,脚尖绷直;同时,身体向右后转,右手持剑以腕为轴从上向下经右腿外侧向上、向前绕腕花收于腰间,手心向上,剑尖向左前;左手剑指附于右手腕处。目视剑尖方向(图 4-92)。

(7) Keep moving, right foot falls and stamps, bend and lift left knee, and buckle it in right knee fossa, tiptoes straight, at the same time, turn right, right hand holds sword , swings it upward and forward with wrist as the axis, palm center upward, sword tip forward and leftward, left finger pointing against right wrist. Look at sword tip (Figure 4-92).

图 4-92（Figure 4-92）

（8）上动不停,左脚向前落步成弓步;同时,右手持剑从腰间向前直臂刺出,剑尖向前;左手剑指附于右手腕处。目视剑尖方向(图 4-93)。

(8) Keep moving, left foot falls forward into the bow stance, at the same time, right hand holds sword, stabs it forward, sword tip forward, left finger pointing against right wrist. Look at sword tip (Figure 4-93).

231

图 4-93(Figure 4-93)

29.童子拜观音

（1）右腿向前提膝,左腿屈膝;同时,右手持剑,臂向外旋,向上撩剑经头顶向后劈剑,剑尖向右后上方,右手至右胯旁,左手剑指附于右手腕上。目视剑尖(图 4-94)。

29. Boy worshipping Goddess of Mercy

(1) Right leg forward and lift knee, bend left knee, at the same time, right hand holds sword, arm outward, swings sword upward and backward, sword tip downward and rightward, right hand against right hip, left finger pointing against right wrist. Look at sword tip (Figure 4-94).

图 4-94(Figure 4-94)

（2）上动不停,右脚向下落步,左腿屈膝;右手持剑向下、向前、向上到头顶后侧,身体左转 180°,再向右转 270°,再向左、向下、向上撩剑,手心向外,剑尖向左前;左手剑指附于右腕。目视剑尖方向(图 4-95)。

(2) Keep moving, right foot falls, bend left knee, right hand holds sword,

swings it downward, forward and upward, turn leftward 180°, and rightward 270°, swings sword leftward, downward and upward, palm outward, sword tip forward and leftward, left finger pointing against right wrist. Look at sword tip (Figure 4-95).

图 4-95(Figure 4-95)

(3)上动不停,身体上起,腰右转,右手持剑向上、向下、向前撩剑至面前时,身体左转180°,剑随身体向上、向下划弧,左手剑指附于右手腕处。目视剑尖方向(图4-96)。

(3) Keep moving, arise, swing waist rightward, right hand holds sword, swing sword upward, downward and forward, turn leftward 180°, draw curve upward and downward, left finger pointing against right wrist. Look at sword tip (Figure 4-96).

图 4-96(Figure 4-96)

(4)上动不停,左腿向前屈膝落步;同时,右手持剑向下、向前、向上撩剑,剑尖向前;左手剑指随右手附于手腕不动。目视剑尖方向(图4-97)。

(4) Keep moving, bend left knee forward, at the same time, right hand holds sword, swings it downward, forward and upward, sword tip forward, left finger pointing against the wrist, right hand still. Look at sword tip (Figure 4-97).

图 4-97 (Figure 4-97)

(5)上动不停,右腿向前上提,身体右转;同时,右手持剑,臂外旋,使剑向上、向下、向后置于体侧,剑尖斜向上,左手剑指随右手附于右手腕处。目视剑尖方向(图 4-98)。

(5) Keep moving, lift right leg, turn right, at the same time, right hand holds sword, arm swings outward, swing sword upward and downward, sword tip obliquely upward, left finger pointing against right wrist. Look at sword tip (Figure 4-98).

图 4-98 (Figure 4-98)

(6)上动不停,右脚向前落步,右手持剑向下、向前、向上撩剑,身体左转 180°;同时,两腿屈膝下蹲成歇步,身体右转 180°,左手剑指随右手附于右手腕处。目视剑尖方向(图 4-99)。

(6) Keep moving, right foot falls, right hand holds sword, swings it downward, forward and upward, turn leftward 180°, at the same time, bend knees and squat into the sitting stance, turn rightward 180°, left finger pointing against right wrist. Look at sword tip (Figure 4-99).

图 4-99(Figure 4-99)

(7)上动不停,右手持剑,向前下方刺剑,剑尖向下,使剑垂于体前;左手剑指指向右侧,上撑架于头顶上方。目视右前方(图 4-100)。

(7) Keep moving, right hand holds sword, stabs it forward and downward, sword tip downward, left finger pointing rightward, parry it overhead. Look rightward and forward (Figure 4-100).

正(Front)　　　　　　反(Back)

图 4-100(Figure 4-100)

30.咽喉剑

(1)身体左转上起,左腿向前提起;同时,右手持剑,臂外旋,手心向上,剑尖向左前方;左手剑指由上向下收于右腕处。目视剑尖方向(图 4-101)。

30. Throat thrusting

(1) Turn left and arise, lift left leg, at the same time, right hand holds

sword, arm swings outward, palm center upward, sword tip leftward and forward, left finger pointing against right wrist. Look at sword tip (Figure 4-101).

图 4-101（Figure 4-101）

（2）上动不停,左脚向前一步成弓步;同时,右手持剑向前直臂刺出,剑尖向前;左手剑指附于右腕处。目视剑尖方向(图 4-102)。

（2）Keep moving, left foot strides one step into the bow stance, at the same time, right hand holds sword, thrusts it forwards, sword tip forward, left finger pointing against right wrist place. Look at sword tip (Figure 4-102).

图 4-102（Figure 4-102）

31.二龙须

（1）右脚经左腿后方,向前插步;同时,身体右转,右手持剑以腕为轴,先外旋,再内旋,使剑向下、向右、向上、向左腕花划弧于体左前,剑尖向左上方;左手剑指关于右腕。目视剑尖方向(图 4-103)。

31. Double twisting

（1）Right foot strides via left leg backward, at the same time, turn right,

right hand holds sword, turn outward and inward with wrist as the axis, make sword draw curve downward, rightward, upward and leftward, sword tip leftward and upward, left finger pointing again at right wrist. Look at sword tip (Figure 4-103).

图 4-103(Figure 4-103)

（2）上动不停,身体右转180°,重心落于右腿成弓步;同时,右手持剑随身体右转的同时向右、向上划弧,右臂外旋,剑尖向上;左手剑指附于右小臂。目视左前方(图4-104)。

(2) Keep moving, turn rightward 180°, shift gravity center to right leg into the bow stance, at the same time, right hand holds sword, make it draw curve rightward and upward, right arm swings outward, sword tip upward, left finger pointing against right forearm. Look left forward (Figure 4-104).

图 4-104(Figure 4-104)

（3）上动不停,身体重心移至右腿,左腿屈膝上提,脚背绷直,脚尖向下,腰随即左拧;同时,右手持剑臂外旋,使剑经右下向后上划弧,剑尖向右前;左手剑指架于头顶上方,掌心向上。目视剑尖(图4-105)。

(3) Keep moving, shift gravity center to right leg, bend and lift left knee,

instep straight, tiptoes downward, twist waist leftward, at the same time, right hand holds sword, arm swings outward, make it draw curve downward and backward, sword tip forward and leftward, left finger pointing overhead, supinely. Look at sword tip (Figure 4-105).

图 4-105（Figure 4-105）

32.挑踢剑

（1）左脚向左前落步，脚尖点地，重心在右脚；同时，右手持剑向左下划弧，手心斜向上，剑尖向下；左手剑指屈肘附于右腕。目视剑尖方向（图 4-106）。

32. Picking and kicking

(1) Left foot strides one step leftward and forward, tiptoes touchdown, shift gravity center to right foot, at the same time, right hand holds sword, make it draw curve leftward and downward, palm center obliquely upward, sword tip downward, left finger pointing against right wrist. Look at sword tip (Figure 4-106).

图 4-106（Figure 4-106）

（2）上动不停，左脚向前一步，右腿屈膝向前弹踢；同时，右手持剑向上挑剑；左手剑指附于右手腕处。目视剑尖方向（图 4-107）。

(2) Keep moving, left foot strides one step forward, bend right knee and

kick forward, at the same time, right hand holds sword, picks it upward, left finger pointing against right wrist. Look at sword tip (Figure 4-107).

图 4-107（Figure 4-107）

33.挂腿前刺

（1）右腿屈膝回收；同时，右手持剑收于腰间；左手剑指附于右腕。目视剑尖方向（图 4-108）。

33. Forward stabbing

(1) Bend and retreat right knee, at the same time, right hand holds sword against the waist, left finger pointing against right wrist. Look at sword tip (Figure 4-108).

图 4-108（Figure 4-108）

（2）上动不停，左脚蹬地上起，右脚向下落地震脚；左腿随即屈膝提起，扣于右腿膝窝；右手持剑以腕为轴，向下、向前腕花收于腰间；左手剑指附于右手腕处。目视剑尖（图 4-109）。

(2) Keep moving, left foot kicks the floor and arise, right foot falls and stamps, bend and lift left knee, buckle it to right poples, right hand holds sword, thrust it downward and forward with wrist as the axis, left finger pointing

against right wrist. Look at sword tip (Figure 4-109).

图 4-109(Figure 4-109)

（3）上动不停，左脚向前落地成弓步；同时，右手持剑从腰间向前直臂刺出；左手剑指屈肘横架于头上。目视剑尖（图 4-110）。

(3) Keep moving, left foot falls forward into the bow stance, at the same time, right hand holds sword, make it thrust straight forward, left finger pointing overhead. Look at sword tip (Figure 4-110).

图 4-110(Figure 4-110)

第四段

Section 4

34.托塔

（1）上体右转，右手持剑，臂外旋，向右后劈剑，剑尖斜向上；左手剑指收于右小臂内侧。目视剑尖（图 4-111）。

34. Supporting

(1) Turn right, right hand holds sword, arm swings outward, chop sword

第四章　少林达摩剑

rightward and backward, sword tip oblique upward, left finger pointing against right forearm. Look at sword tip (Figure 4-111).

图 4-111(Figure 4-111)

（2）上动不停，身体左转，右脚向前上一步，脚尖点地；同时，右手持剑向下、向前、向上屈肘撩剑，手心向内，剑尖向前，左手剑指附于右手腕处。目视剑尖(图 4-112)。

（2）Keep moving, turn left, right foot strides one step forward, tiptoes touchdown, at the same time, right hand holds sword, thrusts it downward, forward and upward, palms inward, sword tip forward, left finger pointing against right wrist. Look at sword tip (Figure 4-112).

图 4-112(Figure 4-112)

（3）上动不停，右脚向前半步，身体右转，左腿向前提起，右手持剑向上、向后经左腿外侧向前撩剑，剑尖向下，左手剑指附于右手腕处。目视剑尖方向(图 4-113)。

（3）Keep moving, right foot strides half a step, turn right, lift left leg, right hand holds sword, thrusts it upward and backward, sword tip downward, left finger pointing against right wrist. Look at sword tip (Figure 4-113).

241

图4-113(Figure 4-113)

(4)上动不停,左脚向前落步,上体微右转,重心移至左腿,右脚尖点起;右手持剑向上、向后屈臂撩剑,剑尖向右后上方;左手剑指屈肘附于右手小臂上。目视剑尖方向(图4-114)。

(4) Keep moving, left foot falls forward, turn right slightly, shift gravity center to left leg, right heel touchdown, and right hand holds sword, thrusts it upward and backward, sword tip rightward, backward and upward, left finger pointing against right forearm. Look at sword tip (Figure 4-114).

图4-114(Figure 4-114)

(5)上动不停,左脚向前上半步,上体左转,右腿提膝;同时,右手持剑向下经右腿外侧向前屈臂向前撩剑,左手剑指附于右手腕处。目视剑指(图4-115)。

(5) Keep moving, left foot strides half a step, turn left, lift right knee, at the same time, right hand holds sword, swings it downward and forward, left finger pointing against right wrist. Look at finger pointing (Figure 4-115).

第四章 少林达摩剑

图 4-115（Figure 4-115）

（6）上动不停,身体左转,右脚向前落步成弓步;同时,右手持剑向上、向左下屈臂划弧劈剑横于胸前,剑尖向左;左手剑指附于右腕。目视剑尖（图 4-116）。

(6) Keep moving, turn left, right foot falls into the bow stance, at the same time, right hand holds sword, make it draw curve upward, downward and leftward, sword tip leftward, left finger pointing against right wrist. Look at sword tip (Figure 4-116).

图 4-116（Figure 4-116）

（7）上动不停,身体左转成左弓步;同时,右手持剑臂内旋,剑尖向右前划弧斩剑,剑尖朝向右上方;左手剑指屈肘收于胸间。目视剑尖方向（图 4-117）。

(7) Keep moving, turn left into the left bow stance, at the same time, right hand holds sword, arm turns inward, make sword draw curve forward and rightward, sword tip rightward and upward, left finger pointing against chest. Look at sword tip (Figure 4-117).

243

图 4-117（Figure 4-117）

35.左右劈剑

（1）身体上起重心收于右腿,左脚向后收半步,上体左转立起,脚尖点地;同时,右手持剑向上、向左、向下、向后划弧,收于右腿外侧,剑尖向左下方;左手剑指由胸前向体前下方摆击。目视左手(图 4-118)。

35. Left and right chopping

(1) Arise and shift gravity center to right leg, left foot retreats half a step, turn left and stand, tiptoes touchdown, at the same time, right hand holds sword, make it draw curve upward, leftward, downward and backward, sword tip leftward and downward, left finger pointing swings forward and downward. Look at left hand (Figure 4-118).

图 4-118（Figure 4-118）

（2）上动不停,左脚向前上一步,脚尖外摆,身体左转,右脚掌右碾,脚尖点地;同时,右手持剑向前、向上、向右、向下划弧穿劈剑。剑尖向后;左手剑指屈肘附于右臂前。目视剑尖(图 4-119)。

(2) Keep moving, left foot strides one step, outreach tiptoes, turn left, right sole grinds rightward, tiptoes touchdown, at the same time, right hand

holds sword, make it draw curve forward, upward, rightward and downward, sword tip backward, left finger pointing against right arm. Look at sword tip (Figure 4-119).

图 4-119(Figure 4-119)

(3)上动不停,右脚向前上一步,脚尖外摆,身体右转,左脚掌左碾,脚尖点地;右手持剑,臂外旋向下、向前、向上、向后劈剑,左手剑指附于右臂内侧。目视剑尖(图 4-120)。

(3) Keep moving, right foot strides one step, outreach tiptoes, turn right, left sole grinds leftward, tiptoes touchdown, right hand holds sword, chops it downward, forward, upward and backward, left finger pointing against right arm. Look at sword tip (Figure 4-120).

图 4-120(Figure 4-120)

(4)上动不停,身体左转,左脚向前一步,两腿屈膝下蹲;同时,右手持剑臂内旋向下、向前、向上刺剑,左手剑指变掌附于右手下方,剑尖斜向上。目视剑尖(图 4-121)。

(4) Keep moving, turn left, left foot strides one step, bend knees and squat, at the same time, right hand holds sword, arm turns inward, stabs sword downward, forward and upward, change left finger pointing into palm against

245

right hand, sword tip obliquely upward. Look at sword tip (Figure 4-121).

图 4-121(Figure 4-121)

36.探海势

(1)身体上起,左腿屈膝上提,两手抱剑向下收剑。目视剑尖(图 4-122)。

36. Creeping

(1) Arise, bend and lift left knee, hold and close sword downward. Look at sword tip (Figure 4-122).

图 4-122(Figure 4-122)

(2)上动不停,左腿向后蹬踢,脚尖绷直,脚掌向上,右腿挺膝直立;同时,右手持剑由胸前向前直臂刺出;左手附于右手上,塌腰仰头。目视剑尖(图 4-123)。

(2) Keep moving, left leg kicks backward, tiptoes straight, sole upward, right knee straight, at the same time, right hand holds sword, stabs it forward, left hand against right hand, waist downward, look up. Look at sword tip (Figure 4-123).

第四章 少林达摩剑

图 4-123（Figure 4-123）

（3）上动不停,保持平衡,双手向左右两边直臂划弧分开,剑尖向前;左手剑指向左。目视前方(图 4-124)。

(3) Keep moving, maintain balance, arms draw curve leftward and rightward, sword tip forward, left finger pointing leftward. Look straight ahead (Figure 4-124).

图 4-124（Figure 4-124）

37.指星势

（1）左脚向前落步,剑尖外摆,右脚碾地,脚尖跷起,身体左转 180°;同时,右手持剑臂外旋随身体左转的力量向左侧劈剑,手心向上,剑尖向左后,左手剑指收附于剑柄内侧。目视剑尖(图 4-125)。

37. Star pointing

(1) Left foot falls, sword tip outreaches, right foot grinds, tiptoes lift, turn leftward 180°, at the same time, right hand holds sword, chops it leftward, palm center upward, sword tip leftward and backward, left finger pointing

against sword handle inward. Look at sword tip (Figure 4-125).

图 4-125(Figure 4-125)

（2）上动不停,身体向右后转360°;右手持剑,以腕为轴,随身体右转的力量向头顶云剑划弧一周,剑尖向左前;左手剑指附于右腕。目视剑尖(图4-126)。

(2) Keep moving, turn rightward 360°, right hand holds sword, make it draw s circle overhead with wrist as the axis, sword tip forward and leftward, left finger pointing against wrist. Look at sword tip (Figure 4-126).

图 4-126(Figure 4-126)

（3）上动不停,身体重心向前下倾,右脚向外碾地,右腿屈膝半蹲;同时,右手持剑,臂内旋向下经右腿外侧向右后上方直臂撩剑,剑尖朝向右后上方;左手剑指向前收于体侧。目视剑尖(图4-127)。

(3) Keep moving, shift gravity center forward and downward, right foot grinds outward, bend right knee on semi-crouch balance, at the same time, right hand holds sword, thrust it rightward and upward, sword tip rightward and upward, left finger pointing inward. Look at sword tip (Figure 4-127).

第四章 少林达摩剑

图 4-127（Figure 4-127）

38.怀里藏针

（1）身体左转180°成弓步，随之右手持剑向下、向左经右腿外侧向上划弧撩剑，左手剑指随身体左转向上摆臂收于体侧。目视剑尖（图 4-128）。

38. Needling

(1) Turn leftward 180° into the bow stance, right hand holds sword, make it draw curve upward against right leg outward, left finger pointing upward and to the side. Look at sword tip (Figure 4-128).

图 4-128（Figure 4-128）

（2）上动不停，身体左转向前下倾；右手持剑向上、向左、向下经腋下腰侧向上穿剑，剑尖指上；左手剑指由上向右脚尖外侧直臂下落。目视左后方（图 4-129）。

(2) Keep moving, turn left and lean downward, right hand holds sword, thrusts it upward, leftward and downward via armpit, sword tip upward, left finger pointing straight and falls to tiptoes outward. Look leftward and backward (Figure 4-129).

249

图 4-129(Figure 4-129)

39.朝天一柱香

(1)身体上起向右后转 180°,右手持剑向下、向右、向上撩剑,手心向前,剑尖指向左前方;左手剑指屈肘附于右腕。目视剑尖(图 4-130)。

39. Erecting

(1) Arise, turn rightward and backward 180°, right hand holds sword, thrusts it downward, rightward and upward, palm forward, sword tip leftward and forward, left finger pointing against right wrist. Look at sword tip (Figure 4-130).

图 4-130(Figure 4-130)

(2)上动不停,上体继续右转 180°,两脚成叉步;同时,右手持剑,随身体右转时由上向下撩剑,左手剑指向左侧摆击。目视剑尖方向(图 4-131)。

(2) Keep moving, turn rightward 180°, feet into the fork stance, at the same time, right hand holds sword, thrusts it downward, left finger pointing leftward. Look at sword tip (Figure 4-131).

第四章 少林达摩剑

图 4-131（Figure 4-131）

（3）上动不停，右手持剑向体前上方撩剑，左手剑指向体前头顶上方同右手合拢，手心向后，剑尖向上。目视前方（图 4-132）。

(3) Keep moving, right hand holds sword and thrusts it forward and upward, left finger pointing overhead and against right hand, palm backward, sword tip upward. Look straight ahead (Figure 4-132).

图 4-132（Figure 4-132）

（4）上动不停，身体下蹲成歇步，两手抱剑从上向下收于体前，剑身竖直。目视前方（图 4-133）。

(4) Keep moving, squat into the sitting stance, hands hold sword, sword upright. Look straight ahead (Figure 4-133).

图 4-133（Figure 4-133）

40.童子拜佛

（1）身体上起，右脚向右后撤一步，身体右转；随之右手持剑臂外旋向下、向后穿剑于体右侧，剑尖斜向上，左手剑指附于右小臂上。目视剑尖（图 4-134）。

40. Boy worshipping the Buddha

（1）Arise, right foot retreats one step rightward and backward, turn right, right hand holds sword, swings it downward and rightward, sword tip obliquely upward, left finger pointing against right forearm. Look at sword tip (Figure 4-134).

图 4-134（Figure 4-134）

（2）上动不停，右手持剑从右后经体前向上划弧穿剑，左手向体前收于右手腕上；同时，左脚向后退一步，上体略左转。目视剑尖（图 4-135）。

（2）Keep moving, right hand holds sword, make it draw curve upward, close left hand to right wrist, at the same time, left foot retreats one step, turn leftward slightly. Look at sword tip (Figure 4-135).

第四章 少林达摩剑

图 4-135（Figure 4-135）

（3）上动不停，右手持剑向左后上方划弧抛剑于肩前，剑尖向上；同时，左手屈肘向上接剑柄。目视剑身（图 4-136）。

(3) Keep moving, right hand holds sword, make it draw curve leftward, backward and upward, sword tip upward, at the same time, bend left elbow upward to pick sword handle. Look at the sword (Figure 4-136).

图 4-136（Figure 4-136）

（4）上动不停，左手反握剑柄接剑，顺势收剑向下、向后、向上使剑身贴靠臂后，手心向后；右手向后直臂划弧变剑指，手心向后收于体侧；同时，身体右转，右脚后退半步与左脚平行，两脚距离与肩同宽。目视右手（图 4-137）。

(4) Keep moving, left hand reversely grabs handle to pick sword, close it downward, backward and upward and make it against arm, palm center backward, right arm straight and draw curve backward, palm backward and inward, at the same time, turn right, right foot retreats half a step and parallel to left foot, feet and shoulders keep the same wide. Look at right hand (Figure 4-137).

253

图 4-137（Figure 4-137）

（5）上动不停,右手剑指向上经头上屈肘落于胸前;左手反握剑,剑柄贴靠左胯侧。目视前方（图 4-138）。

(5) Keep moving, right finger pointing overhead and front chest, left hand reversely grabs sword, sword handle against left hip. Look straight ahead (Figure 4-138).

图 4-138（Figure 4-138）

41.收势

左脚向右脚内侧收步,两腿伸直;同时,右掌从胸前直臂垂于右腿外侧,左手持剑垂臂收于左体侧。目视前方（图 4-139）。

41. Closing

Close left foot to right foot inward, legs straight, at the same time, right palm hangs against right leg, left hand holds sword. Look straight ahead (Figure 4-139).

图 4-139（Figure 4-139）

第五章 少林春秋大刀

Chapter 5 Shaolin Chunqiu Broadsword (Spring and Autumn Broadsword)

第一节 套路动作名称

Quarter 1 Routine Names

第一段

Section 1

1.起势

1. Starting

2.虚步托刀(神出鬼没)

2. Empty stance broadsword supporting (Elusive)

3.并步托刀(严阵以待)

3. Step touch broadsword supporting (Embattled)

4.弓步推带(立斩华雄)

4. Bow stance pushing (Chopping)

5.提膝亮刀(大鹏展翅)

5. Knee lifting broadsword (Winging)

6.翻身劈刀(猛虎翻身)

6. Turning and chopping (Mighty)

7.拨刀下刺(艄公摇橹)

7. Downward stabbing (Swinging)

8.拗步压刀(彼进右顾)

8. Twisting and pressing (Advancing)

9.弓步推带(一推二抹)

9. Bow stance pushing (Wiping)

第二段

Section 2

10.抱刀摆腿(风摆荷叶)

10. Swinging and tackling (Turning)

11.纵步平戳(智斩颜良)

11. Striding and poking (Cutting)

12.云刀下截(拨云见日)

12. Broadsword downward chopping (Stirring)

13.弓步背刀(苏秦背剑)

13. Bow stance broadsword thrusting (Backing)

14.回身后戳(回马刀)

14. Turning and stabbing (Thrusting)

15.提膝举刀(朝天刀)

15. Knee and broadsword lifting (Overturning)

16.上步三撩(三撩刀)

16. Forward triple arc kicking (Arc kicking)

17.弓步上撩(挑帘刀)

17. Bow stance upward arc kicking (Tilting)

18.滚身平错(蹚里藏身)

18. Rolling and rubbing (Kicking and hiding)

19.提膝劈刀(青龙戏水)

19. Knee lifting and chopping (Paddling)

20.翻身劈刀(反败为胜)

20. Turning and chopping (Saving)

21.托刀上架(霸王举鼎)

21. Supporting and parrying (Erecting)

22.插步戳把(回马戳把)

22. Forward stabbing (Poking)

第三段

Section 3

23.背上平扎(担山平扎)

23. Backing and thrusting (Pricking)

24.刀腕平错(揪刀头)

24. Grabbing and rubbing (Seizing)

25.弓步推挡(力挡千军)

25. Bow stance pushing (Stopping)

26.插步反撩(犀牛望月)

26. Forward arc kicking (Back leg)

27.丁步斜架(乌龙戏水)

27. T-step obliquely parrying (Switching)

28.舞花下点(凤凰点头)

28. Downward waving (Spotting)

29.绕肩舞花(绕肩花)

29. Shoulder waving (Flowering)

30.转身云刀(风卷残云)

30. Turning and swinging (Sweeping)

31.弓步提刀(提腰刀)

31. Bow stance lifting (Raising)

32.弓步推刀(智斩葵阳)

32. Bow stance pushing (Beheading)

33.收刀合十(收山势)

33. Closing and palming (Closing)

34.收势

34. Closing

第二节　套路动作图解

Quarter 2　Figures of Routine Movements

第一段

Section 1

1.起势

(1)身体直立,两脚并步;右手紧握大刀护手盘处,使大刀垂直于身体右侧;左手成掌,直臂下垂贴于身体左侧。目视前方(图 5-1)。

1.Starting

(1) Stand upright, feet step touch, right hand clenches broadsword handguard against the right side, change left hand into palm, arm falls against the left side. Look straight ahead (Figure 5-1).

图 5-1(Figure 5-1)

(2)上动不停,左掌由下向上屈肘立于胸前。掌尖向上,高不过下颚。目视前方(图 5-2)。

(2) Keep moving, bend left elbow upward and against the chest. Palm tip upward, lower than lower jaw. Look straight ahead (Figure 5-2).

图 5-2(Figure 5-2)

2.虚步托刀(神出鬼没)

(1)接上势,上体略右转,左脚不变,右腿提膝外展,以脚内侧向前踢击刀把;同时,右手提刀,使刀把向前上方摆起;左手接握把端。虎口向上。目视前方(图 5-3)。

第五章　少林春秋大刀

2. Empty stance broadsword supporting (Elusive)

(1) Keep moving, turn right slightly, left foot unchanged, lift and outreach right knee, kick broadsword handle forward, at the same time, right hand holds broadsword, swing broadsword handle forward and upward, left hand holds broadsword handle end, the part between the thumb and the forefinger upward. Look straight ahead (Figure 5-3).

图 5-3 (Figure 5-3)

(2) 上动不停，右脚随即向前落步，脚尖外展，两手持刀向后下挂刀，刀柄贴身，刀刃向下。目视正前方（图5-4）。

(2) Keep moving, right foot falls forward, tiptoes outreach, hands hangs broadsword downward and backward, broadsword handle against the side, broadsword blade downward. Look straight ahead (Figure 5-4).

图 5-4 (Figure 5-4)

(3) 上动不停，左脚上前一步，脚尖点地，右腿屈膝半蹲成右虚步；同时，两手握刀，使刀由后下向前上撩推；左把贴胯，刀刃向左。目视左方（图5-5）。

(3) Keep moving, left foot strides forward, tiptoes touchdown, bend right

knee on semi-crouch balance into the empty stance, at the same time, hands hold broadsword, push it upward and forward, broadsword handle against the hip, broadsword blade leftward. Look leftward (Figure 5-5).

图 5-5(Figure 5-5)

3.并步托刀(严阵以待)

(1)接上势,身体直起,右腿挺膝直立,左腿屈膝上提,两手不变。目视前方(图 5-6)。

3. Step touch broadsword supporting (Embattled)

(1) Keep moving, stand straight, bend and lift right knee, bend and lift left knee, hands unchanged. Look straight ahead (Figure 5-6).

图 5-6(Figure 5-6)

(2)上动不停,左脚向前落地,接着右脚向前一步,左脚向右脚并拢成并步直立,两手握刀不动。目视左方(图 5-7~图 5-9)。

(2) Keep moving, left foot falls forward, right foot strides one step forward, close left foot to right foot into step touch and upright, hands hold

broadsword still. Look leftward (Figures 5-7 to 5-9).

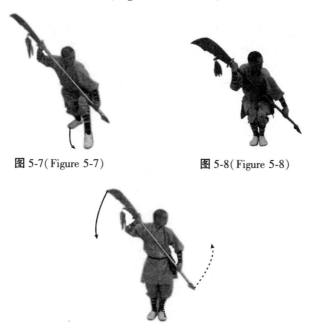

图 5-7(Figure 5-7)　　　图 5-8(Figure 5-8)

图 5-9(Figure 5-9)

4.弓步推带(立斩华雄)

(1)接上势,左腿提膝。右腿直立;右手屈肘带刀于右肩处;同时,左手提推,使把向左击出。目视刀把(图 5-10)。

4. Bow stance pushing (Chopping)

(1) Keep moving, lift left knee, right leg upright, bend right elbow and swing broadsword against right shoulder, at the same time, left hand pushes to hit leftward. Look at broadsword handle (Figure 5-10).

图 5-10(Figure 5-10)

261

（2）上动不停，左脚向左落地，两腿屈膝半蹲成半马步（图5-11）。

（2）Keep moving, left foot falls leftward, bend knees on semi-crouch balance into the bow and horse-riding stance（Figure 5-11）.

图 5-11（Figure 5-11）

（3）上动不停，身体左转90°，右脚蹬地挺直，左腿屈膝，半蹲成左弓步；同时，右手握刀由右后向前上方用力撩刀。刀刃向上；左手握把紧贴左胯。目视前方（图5-12）。

（3）Keep moving, turn leftward 90°, right foot falls straight, and bend left knee and squat into the left bow stance, at the same time, right hand pushes broadsword from rightward and backward, broadsword blade leftward, broadsword tip obliquely downward, close left hand against left hip. Look straight ahead（Figure 5-12）.

图 5-12（Figure 5-12）

（4）上动不停，右手拧把外旋，使刀下劈后向上翻转，刀刃朝上；同时，左手握把屈肘向腰间拉刀。目视刀尖（图5-13）。

（4）Keep moving, screw right hand and turn outward, let the sword down and flip up, make the blade up; at the same time, hold the sword with left hand and bend the elbow then wield the sword to waist. Look at the top of sword.（Figure 5-13）.

第五章 少林春秋大刀

图 5-13(Figure 5-13)

5.提膝亮刀(大鹏展翅)

(1)接上势,左脚收于右脚内侧,前脚掌着地;同时,两手持刀,使刀向右经头上方云刀一周至身体右侧,右手握刀侧上举,刀刃向下;把贴后背;左手脱把变掌附于右肩前,掌指向上,掌心向右。目视刀尖(图 5-14)。

5. Knee lifting broadsword (Winging)

(1) Keep moving, close left foot to right foot inward, front sole touchdown, at the same time, hands hold broadsword, swing broadsword upward and rightward a circle, right hand holds broadsword upward, broadsword blade downward, change left hand into palm against right shoulder, fingers upward, palm rightward. Look at broadsword tip (Figure 5-14).

图 5-14(Figure 5-14)

(2)上动不停,左脚屈膝上提。右腿挺膝直立;左掌向左平推,掌尖向上。目视左掌(图 5-15)。

(2) Keep moving, bend and lift left knee, bend and lift right knee, left palm pushes leftward, palm tip upward. Look at left hand (Figure 5-15).

263

图 5-15（Figure 5-15）

6.翻身劈刀（猛虎翻身）

（1）接上势，身体左转 180°，左脚落地，脚尖外展，两腿微曲交叉站立；同时，右手持刀，以刀背领先向右、向下挂刀；左手屈肘与右腋下接把。目视刀背（图 5-16）。

6. Turning and chopping（Mighty）

（1）Keep moving, turn leftward 180°, left foot falls, tiptoes outreach, slightly cross legs and stand, at the same time, right hand holds broadsword, swing broadsword back rightward and downward, bend elbow to hold broadsword handle in right armpit. Look at broadsword back（Figure 5-16）.

图 5-16（Figure 5-16）

（2）上动不停，右脚向前一步，两腿屈膝下蹲成马步；同时，两手握刀划弧，由下向左、向上、向右下方劈刀，左腿屈膝向左上方摆起。目视右下方（图 5-17）。

（2）Keep moving, right foot strides one step forward, bend knees on semi-crouch balance into the bow and horse-riding stance and lift it leftward, hands hold broadsword, make it leftward, upward, leftward and chopping. Look rightward and downward (Figure 17).

图 5-17(Figure 5-17)

(3)上动不停,右脚蹬地,左腿屈膝向左上方摆起,使身体腾空跃起,左翻转180°;同时,两手持刀随身体翻转撩刀上举。目视右下方(图5-18)。

(3) Keep moving, right foot falls, bend left knee and lift it leftward, backward and upward, jump, turn leftward 180°, at the same time, hands hold broadsword and swing it upward. Look rightward and downward (Figure 5-18).

图 5-18(Figure 5-18)

(4)上动不停,身体继续左转180°,左脚先落地,右脚随即落地成马步,双手持刀由上向右前下方劈刀。目视刀尖(图5-19)。

(4) Keep moving, left foot falls and right foot falls, turn leftward 180°, swing broadsword obliquely rightward and upward. Look at broadsword tip (Figure 5-19).

图 5-19(Figure 5-19)

7.拨刀下刺(艄公摇橹)

（1）接上势,左腿经右腿后插步成右弓步;同时,右手腕外转,手心向上,使刀背向外拦拨。目视刀背(图5-20)。

7. Downward stabbing (Swinging)

(1) Keep moving, left leg closes to right leg backward, at the same time, right wrist turns outward, palm center upward, swing broadsword back outward. Look at broadsword back (Figure 5-20).

图 5-20(Figure 5-20)

（2）上动不停,右脚后退半步,左脚随即也向后退半步成右弓步;同时,右手腕内旋使刀向下扣压。目视刀尖(图5-21)。

(2) Keep moving, right foot strides rightward, at the same time, turn right wrist inward and press broadsword downward. Look at broadsword tip (Figure 5-21).

图 5-21(Figure 5-21)

（3）上动不停,右脚向后退半步,左脚随即也向后退半步成右弓步,随插步向右下方戳刀,刀刃向下。目视刀尖(图5-22)。

(3) Keep moving, left leg closes to right leg backward, hands pull broadsword tip obliquely upward, swing it rightward and downward, broadsword blade downward. Look at broadsword tip (Figure 5-22).

第五章 少林春秋大刀

图 5-22(Figure 5-22)

8.拗步压刀(彼进右顾)

(1)接上势,左脚向左前上步,膝稍曲,脚尖内扣;右手握刀翻腕内旋,使刀背向下。目视刀背(图 5-23)。

8. Twisting and pressing (Advancing)

(1) Keep moving, left foot strides forward and leftward, bend knee slightly, buckle tiptoes inward, right hand holds broadsword, turn wrist inward, broadsword downward. Look at broadsword back (Figure 5-23).

图 5-23(Figure 5-23)

(2)上动不停,右腿向前弧形上步,脚尖外展;两手持刀由后下向前上、向右、向下反压,刀背向后。目视刀背(图 5-24)。

(2) Keep moving, right leg draws curve forward, tiptoes outreach, hands hold broadsword, make it forward, rightward and downward, broadsword backward. Look at broadsword back (Figure 5-24).

图 5-24(Figure 5-24)

9.弓步推带(一推二抹)

(1)接上势,上体右转90°,左脚向前弧形上步,脚尖内扣,两腿微屈稍蹲;右臂屈肘将刀收于右腰间,刀刃斜向外。目视刀刃(图5-25)。

9. Bow stance pushing (Wiping)

(1) Keep moving, turn rightward 90°, left foot draws curve forward, buckle tiptoes inward, bend knees slightly and squat, bend right elbow to close broadsword against right waist, broadsword blade obliquely outward. Look at broadsword blade (Figure 5-25).

图 5-25(Figure 5-25)

(2)上动不停,上体左转90°;右腿蹬直,左腿屈膝,半蹲成左弓步;同时,两手持刀用力向前上方推斩。右臂伸直,左把贴于左胯处。目视刀身(图5-26)。

(2) Keep moving, turn leftward 90°, right leg straight, bend left knee, squat into the left bow stance, at the same time, hands holds broadsword and push it forward, right arm against left hip. Look at broadsword (Figure 5-26).

图 5-26（Figure 5-26）

（3）上动不停,步型不变;左手拧把内旋,右手松握并屈肘收于胸前,使刀刃向外翻转回带,刀刃向右。目视刀刃(图 5-27)。

(3) Keep moving, stances unchanged, left hand twists inward, loosen right hand and bend elbow in front of the chest, turn broadsword blade outward, broadsword blade rightward. Look at broadsword blade (Figure 5-27).

图 5-27（Figure 5-27）

第二段

Section 2

10.抱刀摆腿(风摆荷叶)

（1）接上势,右腿向前,向左由直到屈扣腿提膝,脚面绷直;左腿挺膝立直,双手持刀不变。目视刀刃(图 5-28)。

10. Swinging and tackling (Turning)

(1) Keep moving, right leg forward, bend knee leftward and buckle leg, instep straight, lift left knee, stand, and hands hold broadsword. Look at broadsword blade (Figure 5-28).

图 5-28（Figure 5-28）

（2）上动不停右脚向右蹬出，脚尖勾起，力达脚掌。目视右前方（图 5-29）。

(2) Keep moving, right foot kicks rightward, hook tiptoes, keep at the shoulder's level. Look rightward and forward (Figure 5-29).

图 5-29（Figure 5-29）

（3）上动不停，身体右转 90°；右脚向前落地，脚尖外展；左脚脚跟提起，两膝微屈成交叉步；两手持刀不变随身体右转。目视右方（图 5-30）。

(3) Keep moving, turn rightward 90°, right foot falls forward, tiptoes outreach, lift left heel, bend knees slightly into the cross stance, hands hold broadsword and turn right. Look rightward (Figure 5-30).

图 5-30（Figure 5-30）

11. 纵步平戳(智斩颜良)

(1)接上势,左脚向右前方弧形上步,脚尖内扣;两手持刀于胸前,刀柄贴身。目视刀尖(图5-31)。

11. Striding and poking (Cutting)

(1) Keep moving, left foot draws curve rightward and forward, buckle tiptoes inward, hands hold broadsword in front of the chest, broadsword handle against the chest. Look at broadsword tip (Figure 5-31).

图 5-31(Figure 5-31)

(2)上动不停,身体右转90°;右脚向右前弧形上步;两手持刀不变随身体右转。目视前方(图5-32)。

(2) Keep moving, turn rightward 90°, right foot draws curve rightward and forward, hands hold broadsword, turn right. Look straight ahead (Figure 5-32).

图 5-32(Figure 5-32)

(3)上动不停,右脚蹬地向前垫上一步,前脚掌着地,左腿屈膝上提;上体向前倾探;同时,两手持刀用力向前上方戳击,刀刃向右。目视刀尖(图5-33)。

（3）Keep moving, right foot strides one step forward, front sole touchdown, bend and lift left knee, lean forward, at the same time, hands holds forward and poke it forward and upward, broadsword blade rightward. Look at broadsword tip (Figure 5-33).

图 5-33（Figure 5-33）

12. 云刀下截（拨云见日）

（1）接上势，左脚向前落步，两臂屈肘使刀梢回收。目视前方（图 5-34）。

12. Broadsword downward chopping (Stirring)

（1）Keep moving, left foot falls, and bend elbows, close broadsword tip. Look straight ahead (Figure 5-34).

图 5-34（Figure 5-34）

（2）上动不停，身体稍向左转，右腿向右前上步，脚尖外展，身体重心落于右腿；左腿稍屈离地；两手持刀向右上方举起。目视刀尖（图 5-35）。

（2）Keep moving, turn left slightly, right leg strides forward and rightward, tiptoes outreach, shift gravity center to right leg, bend and lift left knee, hands hold broadsword, swing it rightward and upward. Look at broadsword tip (Figure 5-35).

第五章　少林春秋大刀

图 5-35（Figure 5-35）

（3）上动不停，左腿屈膝上摆。右腿同时蹬地，使身体腾空右转 270°；两手举刀过头沿顺时针方向平云一周。目视右方（图 5-36）。

(3) Keep moving, bend left knee, right leg stamps, jump and turn rightward 270°, hands holds broadsword overhead, swing it clockwise a circle. Look rightward (Figure 5-36).

图 5-36（Figure 5-36）

（4）上动不停，两脚落地屈膝半蹲成弓步；同时，两手持刀出后上向左、向前、向下弧形下截，刀刃向下，左把反贴右腋下。目视刀尖（图 5-37）。

(4) Keep moving, feet fall, bend knees on semi-crouch balance into the bow stance, at the same time, hands hold broadsword, make it draw curve leftward, forward and downward, broadsword blade downward, reversely against the right armpit. Look at broadsword tip (Figure 5-37).

图 5-37（Figure 5-37）

273

13.弓步背刀(苏秦背剑)

(1)接上势,身体直起,右腿向左稍收,膝关节内扣,脚跟微提;上体稍左转,右手带刀,以刀背领先由右下贴身向左挂起。目视刀背(图5-38)。

13. Bow stance broadsword thrusting (Backing)

(1) Keep moving, stand, close right leg leftward, knee joints buckle inward, slightly lift heel, turn left, right hand holds broadsword, swing broadsword back leftward against the chest. Look at broadsword back (Figure 5-38).

图 5-38(Figure 5-38)

(2)上动不停,右腿上提。脚尖外展,左脚脚跟提起,前脚掌碾地,身体右转180°;两手持刀,以刀背领先由左向上,随身体右转向右后下方撩刀后斜举于右肩上方。目视左方(图5-39)。

(2) Keep moving, lift right leg, tiptoes outreach, lift left heel, front sole grinds, turn rightward 180°, hands hold broadsword, swing broadsword back upward, rightward, backward and downward, lift it above right shoulder. Look leftward (Figure 5-39).

图 5-39(Figure 5-39)

(3)上动不停,右脚震脚落地,左腿屈膝后抬,脚尖绷直成独立姿势;同时,右手持刀用力向前、向下、向右后反撩,刀柄贴背;左手助力撩刀后,脱把变掌立于右肩前。目视刀刃(图 5-40)。

(3) Keep moving, right foot stamps, bend and lift left knee, tiptoes straight into the stand on one leg posture, at the same time, right hand holds broadsword, swing it forward, downward and rightward, broadsword handle against the back, left hand helps to swing it, change left hand into palm against right shoulder. Look at broadsword blade (Figure 5-40).

图 5-40(Figure 5-40)

(4)上动不停,左脚向左上步,屈膝半蹲成左弓步;同时,左掌向左平推,掌尖向上,右手持刀,使刀柄紧贴后背,刀刃向上。目视推掌方向(图 5-41)。

(4) Keep moving, left foot strides leftward, bend knees on semi-crouch balance into the left bow stance, at the same time, left palm pushes leftward, palm tip upward, right hand holds broadsword, make broadsword handle against the back, broadsword blade upward. Look at pushing target (Figure 5-41).

图 5-41(Figure 5-41)

14.回身后戳(回马刀)

(1)接上势,身体立起,左脚稍向右回收;右脚向前上步,脚尖内扣,身体左转180°;同时,右手持刀以刀背领先由后向上、向前、向下绕行挂刀;左手置右腋下接握刀柄。目随刀行(图5-42)。

14. Turning and stabbing (Thrusting)

(1) Keep moving, stand up, close left foot rightward, right foot strides one step forward, buckle tiptoes inward, turn leftward 180°, at the same time, right hand holds broadsword back, swing it upward, forward and downward, left hand holds broadsword handle in right armpit. Look at broadsword (Figure 5-42).

图 5-42(Figure 5-42)

(2)上动不停,刀背领先,使刀由下向左、向上绕行挂刀。目随刀行(图5-43)。

(2) Keep moving, swing broadsword back leftward and upward. Look at broadsword (Figure 5-43).

图 5-43(Figure 5-43)

(3)上动不停,左脚向前上步,脚尖稍内扣;右腿向上正踢,上体右转

180°;同时,两手持刀由前向右后平戳,右手松握滑把,两手握刀柄后段使刀放长击远,刀刃向下。目视刀尖(图 5-44)。

(3) Keep moving, left foot strides one step forward, tiptoes slightly buckles inward, right leg kicks upward, turn rightward 180°, at the same time, hands hold broadsword and make it poke rightward and backward, loosen right hand, hands hold the end of broadsword handle, swing broadsword further, broadsword blade downward. Look at broadsword tip (Figure 5-44).

图 5-44(Figure 5-44)

15.提膝举刀(朝天刀)

(1)接上势,上体稍回转,右脚落地,脚尖内扣;左手提拉使刀收于右身后,右身滑至护手盘处,刀刃向下。目视正前方(图 5-45)。

15. Knee and broadsword lifting (Overturning)

(1) Keep moving, slightly turn back, right foot falls, buckle tiptoes inward, left hand pulls broadsword rightward and backward, right hand slips to the guard, broadsword blade downward. Look straight ahead (Figure 5-45).

图 5-45(Figure 5-45)

（2）右脚内扣,身体左转约180°;同时,两手持刀以刀背领先由右后向上、向前、向下、向左立圆划弧形挂刀。目视刀背(图5-46)。

（2）Right foot buckles inward, turn left about 180°, at the same time, hands hold broadsword, make broadsword back draw curve upward, forward and downward. Look at broadsword back (Figure 5-46).

图 5-46(Figure 5-46)

（3）上动不停,继续使刀向上经头前上方向下抱于右臂前,刀刃向上;两腿微屈,身体重心移至左腿(图5-47)。

（3）Keep moving, swing broadsword forward, upward and downward to right arm, broadsword blade upward, bend legs slightly, shift gravity center to left leg (Figure 5-47).

图 5-47(Figure 5-47)

（4）上动不停,左腿屈膝上提,右腿立直成提膝平衡;同时,两手持刀垂直上举,右前臂外旋,使刀刃向左。刀柄紧贴右肋部。目视左方(图5-48)。

（4）Keep moving, bend and lift left knee, right leg straight into knee balance, at the same time, hands hold broadsword, raise it upward, swing right arm outward, broadsword blade leftward, broadsword handle against right ribs. Look leftward (Figure 5-48).

图 5-48(Figure 5-48)

16.上步三撩(三撩刀)

(1)接上势,左脚向左落步,身体左转180°;随即右脚随体转向右上步;同时,两手持刀,刀刃领先由上向下、向前,随右腿上步向右前上方撩起。目视刀身(图5-49)。

16. Forward triple arc kicking (Arc kicking)

(1) Keep moving, left foot falls leftward, turn leftward 180°, right foot strides rightward, at the same time, hands hold broadsword, swing broadsword blade downward, forward, rightward and upward. Look at broadsword (Figure 5-49).

图 5-49(Figure 5-49)

(2)上动不停,左脚经右脚前向右交叉上步,脚尖外撇;两手持刀继续向上、向左、向下划弧劈撩。目视右前方(图5-50)。

（2）Keep moving, left foot strides rightward via right foot, tiptoes outreach, hands hold broadsword, make it draw curve upward, leftward and downward. Look rightward and forward (Figure 5-50).

图 5-50（Figure 5-50）

（3）上动不停,两脚掌碾地,身体右转270°;同时,两手持刀,以刀背领先下挂。目视刀身(图5-51)。

（3）Keep moving, soles grind, turn rightward 270°, at the same time, hands hold broadsword, swing broadsword back downward. Look at broadsword (Figure 5-51).

图 5-51（Figure 5-51）

（4）上动不停,身体右转约180°,右腿向后撤步,脚尖外撇;左腿随即上前一步,脚尖外撇成交叉步;同时,两手持刀以刀刃领先,贴右腿外侧,随撤步转体向后,向上挂刀,然后翻刀用刃向左后下撩刀。目视右前方(图5-52)。

（4）Keep moving, turn right about 180°, right leg retreats, tiptoes outreach, left leg strides one step forward, tiptoes outreach into the cross stance, at the same time, hands hold broadsword, swing broadsword blade against right leg, turn back, swing broadsword upward, swing broadsword blade leftward, backward and downward. Look rightward and forward (Figure 5-52).

图 5-52(Figure 5-52)

（5）上动不停,上体右转90°;两手持刀向前上反撩,右臂伸直上举,刀柄紧贴右肋,刀刃向前;右腿随撩刀上举之势向上正踢,脚尖勾起。目视前方(图 5-53)。

(5) Keep moving, turn rightward 90°, hands hold broadsword, swing it forward, right arm straight and upward, broadsword handle against right ribs, broadsword blade forward, right leg kicks upward, tiptoes hook upward. Look straight ahead (Figure 5-53).

图 5-53(Figure 5-53)

17.弓步上撩(挑帘刀)

（1）接上势,右腿屈膝收提,脚面绷直;左腿支撑站稳;两手持刀,左把上提。右手握护手盘贴右腰间,手心向外,刀刃斜向下。目视刀身（图5-54）。

17. Bow stance upward arc kicking (Tilting)

(1) Keep moving, bend and lift right knee, keep instep straight, left leg

supports, stand, hands hold broadsword, lift it leftward. Right hand holds guard against right waist, palms outward, broadsword blade obliquely downward. Look at broadsword (Figure 5-54).

图 5-54(Figure 5-54)

（2）上动不停,右腿前落屈膝,半蹲成右弓步;同时,两手持刀贴身向前撩起。刀刃向上。目视刀刃（图 5-55）。

(2) Keep moving, right leg falls, bend knees and squat into the right bow stance, at the same time, hands holds broadsword, swing it against the chest, broadsword blade upward. Look at broadsword blade (Figure 5-55).

图 5-55(Figure 5-55)

18.滚身平错(蹬里藏身)

（1）接上势,右脚内扣,左腿屈膝上提并外展;上体左转后仰,仰面向上;同时,两手持刀与胸腹平行（图 5-56）。

18. Rolling and rubbing (Kicking and hiding)

(1) Keep moving, right foot buckles inward, bend left knee and lift and outreach it, turn left and back, overturn, at the same time, hands hold broadsword against the chest (Figure 5-56).

第五章　少林春秋大刀

图 5-56(Figure 5-56)

（2）上动不停,上体继续左转 90°;左腿随转体向左落步,两腿屈膝半蹲成半马步;右手紧握护手盘。将刀按于左肩前,两手屈臂胸前持刀。右小臂在上,左小臂在下,刀刃向外。目视左前方(图 5-57)。

(2) Keep moving, turn leftward 90°, left leg falls leftward, bend knees on semi-crouch balance into the bow and half horse-riding stance, right hand clenches the guard. Press broadsword against left shoulder, hands hold broadsword, right forearm in front, left forearm downward, broadsword blade outward. Look leftward (Figure 5-57).

图 5-57(Figure 5-57)

（3）上动不停,上体左转 90°,右腿挺膝蹬直,左腿屈膝半蹲成左弓步;同时,右手握刀向前平挫,刀刃向外。目视前方(图 5-58)。

(3) Keep moving, turn leftward 90°, right leg kicks straight, and bend left knee and squat into the left bow stance, at the same time, right hand holds broadsword, push it forward, broadsword blade outward. Look straight ahead (Figure 5-58).

283

图 5-58（Figure 5-58）

19.提膝劈刀（青龙戏水）

（1）接上势，两腿立直，右脚稍向左收。左脚碾地，身体右转约180°；同时，两手举刀向上，向右划弧挂刀。目视右前方（图 5-59）。

19. Knee lifting and chopping（Paddling）

（1）Keep moving, stand, slightly close right foot leftward, left foot grinds, turn rightward about 180°, at the same time, hands holds broadsword, make it draw curve upward and rightward. Look rightward and forward（Figure 5-59）.

图 5-59（Figure 5-59）

（2）上动不停，身体重心稍下降，上体右转约 90°；两手持刀向下、向右后、向上划弧挂刀，右臂外旋屈肘将刀举于右臂上方；左手持柄于腹前。目视前方（图 5-60）。

（2）Keep moving, shift gravity center downward slightly, turn rightward about 90°, hands hold broadsword, make it draw curve downward, rightward, and upward, right arm swings outward, bend elbow, swing broadsword above right arm, left hand holds the handle against abdomen. Look straight ahead（Figure 5-60）.

图 5-60（Figure 5-60）

（3）上动不停，右腿直立，左腿屈膝上提，脚面绷直。上体左转 90°；同时，右手直臂压刀向右下斜劈；左手握把上提与肩同高，刀刃向下。目视右下方（图 5-61）。

(3) Keep moving, right leg upright, bend and lift left knee, keep instep straight. Turn leftward 90°, at the same time, right arm presses broadsword and make it cut rightward, left hand makes it at the shoulder's level, broadsword blade downward. Look rightward and downward (Figure 5-61).

图 5-61（Figure 5-61）

20.翻身劈刀（反败为胜）

（1）接上势，左脚向左落步，脚尖外展，身体稍左转，两手持刀，刀尖斜向下（图 5-62）。

20. Turning and chopping (Saving)

(1) Keep moving, left foot falls leftward, tiptoes outreach, turn left slightly, hands hold broadsword, broadsword tip obliquely downward (Figure 5-62).

图 5-62（Figure 5-62）

（2）上动不停,身体左转90°,右脚随体转上前一步;两手提刀随身撩动（图5-63）。

(2) Keep moving, turn leftward 90°, right foot strides one step forward, hands hold broadsword to carry (Figure 5-63).

图 5-63（Figure 5-63）

（3）上动不停,左脚上前一步;两手提刀随身撩动（图5-64）。

(3) Keep moving, left foot strides one step forward, hands hold broadsword to carry (Figure 5-64).

图 5-64（Figure 5-64）

（4）上动不停,右腿向上提起,左脚用力蹬地,使身体腾空向左转体180°;同时,两手持刀向上撩刀举起,上体仰头挺胸（图5-65）。

(4) Keep moving, lift right leg upward, left foot stamps, jump and turn leftward 180°, at the same time, hands hold broadsword and parry it upward, look up and throw out chest (Figure 5-65).

图 5-65(Figure 5-65)

（5）上动不停,身体继续左转180°;两脚右左依次落地;同时,两手持刀由上向下顺势劈刀,右臂伸直,左臂屈肘提把与肩平。目视刀刃(图5-66)。

(5) Keep moving, turn leftward 180°, feet fall, at the same time, hands hold downward and parry it upward, right arm straight, bend left elbow at the shoulder's level. Look at broadsword blade (Figure 5-66).

图 5-66(Figure 5-66)

21.托刀上架(霸王举鼎)

接上势,右脚内扣,两腿立直;两手举刀上架,刀刃向上,挺胸仰头。目视上方(图5-67)。

21. Supporting and parrying (Erecting)

Keep moving, right foot buckles inward, stand, hands hold broadsword, broadsword blade upward, look up and throw out chest. Look upward (Figure 5-67).

图 5-67（Figure 5-67）

22.插步戳把(回马戳把)

(1)接上势,身体右转 90°,右脚尖外展,左脚跟提起;同时,两手持刀,以刀背领先贴身体右侧向下、向后挂刀。目视前方(图 5-68)。

22. Forward stabbing（Poking）

(1) Keep moving, turn rightward 90°, outreach right tiptoes, lift left heel, at the same time, hands hold broadsword, swing broadsword back downwardand backward. Look straight ahead（Figure 5-68）.

图 5-68（Figure 5-68）

(2)上动不停,两手持刀由后向上、向前挂刀。目视刀刃(图 5-69)。

(2) Keep moving, hands hold broadsword, swing it upward and forward. Look at broadsword blade（Figure 5-69）.

第五章　少林春秋大刀

图 5-69（Figure 5-69）

（3）上动不停，身体右转 180°；两手持刀继续向下、向左经左腿外侧向左上方挂刀。目视左方（图 5-70）。

(3) Keep moving, turn rightward 180°, hands hold broadsword, swing it downward, leftward and upward. Look leftward (Figure 5-70).

图 5-70（Figure 5-70）

（4）上动不停，两手持刀继续向上、向右划弧。两臂屈肘平举，使刀身平置与肩同高，刀刃向上。目视右方（图 5-71）。

(4) Keep moving, hands hold broadsword, make it draw curve upward and rightward. Bend and lift elbows, keep broadsword at the shoulder's level, broadsword blade upward. Look rightward (Figure 5-71).

图 5-71（Figure 5-71）

（5）上动不停,右腿经左腿后向左插步,脚跟提起。前脚掌着地。左腿屈膝半蹲成交叉步;同时,两手持刀向左上方戳把,左臂伸直。目视把端（图5-72）。

（5）Keep moving, right leg strides leftward via left leg backward, lift heel. Front sole touchdown. Bend left knee and squat into the cross stance, at the same time, hands hold broadsword, swing it leftward and upward, left arm straight. Look at the broadsword handle end（Figure 5-72）.

图 5-72（Figure 5-72）

第三段

Section 3

23.背上平扎(担山平扎)

（1）接上势,右腿向右上步,身体右转约90°;右臂伸直,左把上举,使刀以刀背领先随上步向右下挂刀(图5-73)。

23. Backing and thrusting（Pricking）

（1）Keep moving, right leg strides one step rightward, turn rightward about 90°, right arm straight, lift broadsword upward, swing broadsword back rightward（Figure 5-73）.

图 5-73（Figure 5-73）

第五章　少林春秋大刀

（2）上动不停，左腿向前上步；两手持刀使刀经右腿外侧向后、向上、向前立圆划弧。目视前方（图5-74）。

（2）Keep moving, left leg strides forward, hands hold broadsword, make it draw curve backward, upward and forward. Look straight ahead (Figure 5-74).

图5-74（Figure 5-74）

（3）上动不停，以左脚为轴，前脚掌碾地，身体右转180°；右脚随转体向右移动收于左脚内侧。脚跟离地；同时，两手持刀以刀刃领先向下、向右上反手撩刀。目视刀刃（图5-75）。

（3）Keep moving, front sole grinds with left foot as the axis, turn rightward 180°, move right foot rightward and close it to left foot inward, heel jumps, at the same time, hands hold broadsword, swing broadsword blade downward, rightward and upward. Look at broadsword blade (Figure 5-75).

图5-75（Figure 5-75）

（4）上动不停，使刀继续向上、向右划弧，当刀绕至头部右侧时，左把上举过头，将刀柄平放于两肩上，如挑担状，刀刃向上。目视右方（图5-76）。

（4）Keep moving, make broadsword draw curve upward and rightward, hold broadsword handle on both shoulders into load carrying, broadsword blade upward. Look rightward (Figure 5-76).

图 5-76（Figure 5-76）

（5）上动不停,右脚向右上步,屈膝半蹲成右弓步;同时,右手持刀向右平扎,刀刃向下;左手脱把变掌侧平举。目视刀身(图5-77)。

(5) Keep moving, right foot strides rightward, bend knees on semi-crouch balance into the bow stance, at the same time, right hand holds broadsword, broadsword blade downward, loosen left hand and change it into palm. Look at broadsword (Figure 5-77).

图 5-77（Figure 5-77）

24.刀腕平挫(揪头刀)

（1）接上势,上体右转180°,左腿向前上步;右手使刀向右,向后运转;同时,左手向前接握刀把(图5-78)。

24. Grabbing and rubbing (Seizing)

(1) Keep moving, turn rightward 180°, left leg strides forward, right hand holds broadsword and swings it rightward and backward, at the same time, left hand holds broadsword handle (Figure 5-78).

第五章　少林春秋大刀

图 5-78（Figure 5-78）

（2）上动不停,右脚向前上步,脚尖外展,身体左转 90°;同时,两手持刀向上、向前弧线下压,刀刃向左。目视前下方(图 5-79)。

(2) Keep moving, right foot strides one step forward, tiptoes outreach, turn leftward 90°, at the same time, hands hold broadsword, make it draw curve upward and forward, broadsword blade leftward. Look forward and downward (Figure 5-79).

图 5-79（Figure 5-79）

（3）上动不停,左腿屈膝上提,脚面绷直,右腿直立;同时,右手持刀乘势置于右胯外侧,左手脱把变掌向前平推,掌尖向上。目视前方(图 5-80)。

(3) Keep moving, bend and lift left knee, keep instep straight, right leg upright, at the same time, right hand holds against right hip outward, change left hand into palm to push forward, palm tip upward. Look straight ahead (Figure 5-80).

293

图5-80(Figure 5-80)

(4)上动不停,左脚向左落步,两腿屈膝半蹲成半马步;同时,右手持刀不变,左掌向外缠腕抓握成拳,拳心向内。目视前方(图5-81)。

(4) Keep moving, and left foot falls leftward, bend knees on semi-crouch balance into the bow and horse-riding stance, at the same time, right hand holds broadsword, change left palm into fist, fist center inside. Look straight ahead (Figure 5-81).

图5-81(Figure 5-81)

(5)上动不停,右腿蹬直,左腿屈膝半蹲成左弓步;同时,右手持刀向前平刺;左拳变掌在右腋下接握刀柄。目视前方(图5-82)。

(5) Keep moving, right leg straight, bend left knee and squat into the left bow stance, at the same time, right hand pushes broadsword forward, change left fist into palm to hold broadsword handle in right armpit. Look straight ahead (Figure 5-82).

图 5-82(Figure 5-82)

25.弓步推挡(力挡千军)

(1)接上势,身体直起,右转 90°,重心移至左腿上,右腿向左稍收;同时,两手持刀向上、向右划弧,刀刃向上。目视右方(图 5-83)。

25. Bow stance pushing (Stopping)

(1) Keep moving, stand, turn rightward 90°, shift gravity center to left leg, close right leg leftward, at the same time, hands hold broadsword, make it draw curve upward and rightward, broadsword blade upward. Look rightward (Figure 5-83).

图 5-83(Figure 5-83)

(2)上动不停,身体右转 180°,左腿微屈支撑,右腿向左腿并拢屈膝提跟;同时,两手持刀由上向下,贴右腿外侧向后、向上划弧,右臂屈肘将刀斜举于右肩侧,刀刃向左。目视右手(图 5-84)。

(2) Keep moving, turn rightward 180°, bend left leg slightly to support, close right leg to left leg, at the same time, hands hold broadsword, make it draw curve upward and rightward, bend right elbow and lift broadsword against right shoulder, broadsword blade leftward. Look at right hand (Figure 5-84).

图 5-84（Figure 5-84）

（3）上动不停，右腿震脚落步，左腿屈膝后抬；接着上体左转约 45°，左脚向左前落步，屈膝成左弓步；同时，两手持刀向上步方向立刀猛推，两臂伸直，刀尖向上，刀刃向前。目视前方（图 5-85 和图 5-86）。

(3) Keep moving, right leg stamps and falls, bend and lift left knee, turn leftward about 45°, left foot strides one step leftward and falls, bend elbow into the left bow stance, at the same time, hands hold broadsword, push it upward, arms straight, broadsword tip upward, broadsword blade forward. Look straight ahead (Figure 5-85 and Figure 5-86).

图 5-85（Figure 5-85）   图 5-86（Figure 5-86）

26.插步反撩（犀牛望月）

（1）接上势，身体重心移至右腿上，上体稍后仰；左脚稍回收，前脚掌着地；同时，两手持刀，右小臂外旋，以刀背领先，翻刀向右前下方挂刀，刀尖向下。目视刀背（图 5-87）。

26. Forward arc kicking (Back leg)

(1) Keep moving, shift gravity center to right leg, slightly lean back, close left foot slightly, front sole touchdown, at the same time, hands hold

296

broadsword, right forearm swings outward, swing broadsword back rightward, forward and downward, broadsword tip downward. Look at broadsword back (Figure 5-87).

图 5-87（Figure 5-87）

（2）上动不停,左脚后撤一步,上体拧腰右转;同时,两手持刀向下、向后挂刀至身体右后侧。目随刀行(图 5-88)。

（2）Keep moving, left foot retreats one step backward, twist waist and turn right, at the same time, hands hold broadsword, swing it downward and backward, and rightward. Look at broadsword (Figure 5-88).

图 5-88（Figure 5-88）

（3）上动不停,上体稍左转,右腿向后撤一步;同时,两手持刀向上、向前、向下绕行。使刀柄挟于右腋下,左手滑把置右腋处。目视刀身(图5-89)。

（3）Keep moving, turn leftward slightly, right leg retreats one step backward, at the same time, hands hold broadsword, swing broadsword blade upward, forward and downward, close broadsword handle in right armpit, left hand slips to right armpit. Look at broadsword (Figure 5-89).

图5-89(Figure 5-89)

(4)上动不停,左腿经右腿后插步,膝关节挺直,前脚掌着地;右腿屈膝半蹲脚尖外展成交叉步,上体拧腰右转;同时,右手持刀直臂向左、向上反撩,刀刃向上;左手脱把变掌,向下绕环后屈肘立于右胸前,掌心向右。目视刀刃(图5-90)。

(4) Keep moving, left leg strides via right leg, knee straight, front sole touchdown, bend right knee on semi-crouch balance, tiptoes outreach into the cross stance, twist waist and turn right, at the same time, right hand holds broadsword and swings it leftward and upward, broadsword blade upward, loosen left hand and change it into palm, swing downward, bend elbow against the right chest, palm center rightward. Look at broadsword blade (Figure 5-90).

图5-90(Figure 5-90)

27.丁步斜架(乌龙戏水)

(1)接上势,身体直起上体左转90°,左腿向前上一步;同时,右手持刀,以刀背领先向前、向上挑起,左手在右腋下接把。目视正前方(图5-91)。

27. T-step obliquely parrying (Switching)

(1) Keep moving, stand, turn leftward 90°, left leg strides one step forward, at the same time, right hand holds broadsword, swing broadsword back

forward and upward, left hand holds broadsword in the right armpit. Look straight ahead (Figure 5-91).

图 5-91(Figure 5-91)

（2）上动不停,右腿向前上一步;同时,两手持刀向后、向下挂刀至身体右后下方时,右手屈肘翻腕并贴于右胯旁,使刀刃斜向上。目视刀尖（图5-92）。

(2) Keep moving, right leg strides one step forward, at the same time, hands hold broadsword and swing it backward, downward and rightward, bend right elbow against right hip, broadsword blade obliquely upward. Look at broadsword tip (Figure 5-92).

图 5-92(Figure 5-92)

（3）上动不停,身体左转90°,右腿屈膝半蹲,左脚并于右脚内侧,脚尖点地成丁步;同时,两手向右前方推架于右上方,刀刃斜向上。目视右前方（图5-93）。

(3) Keep moving, turn leftward 90°, bend right knee on semi-crouch balance, close left foot to the right foot inward, tiptoes touchdown, at the same time, hands push broadsword rightward and forward, broadsword blade obliquely upward. Look rightward and forward (Figure 5-93).

图 5-93（Figure 5-93）

28.舞花下点(凤凰点头)

（1）接上势,身体直起,左脚向左退一步,随即右腿经左腿后侧向左插步;同时,两手持刀向上、向左、向下绕行,刀刃向下。目视左下方(图5-94)。

28. Downward waving (Spotting)

(1) Keep moving, stand, left foot retreats one step leftward, right leg strides leftward via left leg inward, at the same time, hands hold broadsword, swing it upward, leftward and downward, broadsword blade downward. Look leftward and downward (Figure 5-94).

图 5-94（Figure 5-94）

（2）上动不停,左脚尖内扣,以右脚前碾地身体右转约180°;同时,两手持刀随右转身,由左下向右上撩刀,刀刃向上。目视刀身(图5-95)。

(2) Keep moving, left tiptoes buckle inward, front sole grinds, turn rightward about 180°, at the same time, hands hold broadsword, swing it rightward, broadsword blade leftward. Look at broadsword (Figure 5-95).

第五章 少林春秋大刀

图 5-95（Figure 5-95）

（3）上动不停,左脚尖内扣,身体右转 90°；同时,两手持刀以刀背领先向右、向下挂刀。目视前下方（图 5-96）。

(3) Keep moving, left tiptoes buckle inward, turn rightward 90°, at the same time, hands hold broadsword, swing broadsword back rightward and downward. Look forward and downward (Figure 5-96).

图 5-96（Figure 5-96）

（4）上动不停,左脚前上一步,脚尖点地成高虚步；同时,两手指持刀向后经体左侧向上、向前下方呈立圆运行,并用右上臂内侧制动刀柄成切点。目视刀身（图 5-97）。

(4) Keep moving, left foot strides forward, tiptoes touchdown into the high empty stance, at the same time, hands hold broadsword, swing it upward, forward and downward, make left forearm inward broadsword handle the cutting point. Look at broadsword (Figure 5-97).

301

图 5-97（Figure 5-97）

29.绕肩舞花（绕肩花）

（1）接上势，右脚前上一步；两手持刀向上、向后挂刀，右手臂外旋屈肘持刀于腰间，左手持柄直臂上挑（图 5-98）。

29. Shoulder waving (Flowering)

(1) Keep moving, right foot strides one step forward, hands hold broadsword, swing it upward and backward, swing right arm outward, bend elbow and hold broadsword against the waist, left hand holds broadsword handle upward (Figure 5-98).

图 5-98（Figure 5-98）

（2）上动不停，左脚向前上一步；同时，两手持刀向前上撩刀，刀刃向上（图 5-99）。

(2) Keep moving, left foot strides one step forward, at the same time, hands hold broadsword, swing it forward, broadsword blade upward (Figure 5-99).

第五章 少林春秋大刀

图 5-99（Figure 5-99）

（3）上动不停,右腿向前一步;右手持刀臂外旋肘向上后划弧挂刀,并将刀柄扛于肩右上,刀刃向下;左手松开换位前伸接握刀柄中段。目视刀把（图 5-100）。

(3) Keep moving, right leg strides one step forward, right hand holds broadsword, swing elbow outward, make broadsword draw curve backward, swing broadsword handle against right shoulder, broadsword blade downward, loosen left hand, hold broadsword handle center. Look at broadsword (Figure 5-100).

图 5-100（Figure 5-100）

（4）上动不停,右脚尖内扣,身体左转 180°;同时,左把上提,撑肘绕头将刀扛于左肩上,刀尖向后;右手脱把变掌屈肘收于左肩前,以备接把,掌心向上（图 5-101）。

(4) Keep moving, right tiptoes buckle inward, turn leftward 180°, at the same time, lift left elbow and swing broadsword onto the left shoulder, broadsword tip backward, loosen right hand, change right hand into palm, bend elbow against left shoulder, get ready to hold broadsword, supinely (Figure 5-101).

图 5-101(Figure 5-101)

（5）上动不停,左手持刀向上、向前运行;同时,右手接握护手盘处,使刀柄紧贴左腰间,刀身接近水平,刀刃向右。目视刀刃(图 5-102)。

(5) Keep moving, left hand swings broadsword upward and forward, at the same time, right hand holds guard, make broadsword handle against left waist, broadsword nearly horizontal, and broadsword blade rightward. Look at broadsword blade (Figure 5-102).

图 5-102(Figure 5-102)

30.转身云刀(风卷残云)

（1）接上势,左腿向右弧形上步,脚尖内扣,身体右转 180°;同时,两手持刀向后、向上、在头上方沿顺时针方向云刀一周半,两臂交叉于头上方（图 5-103）。

30. Turning and swinging (Sweeping)

(1) Keep moving, left leg strides rightward, tiptoes buckle inward, turn rightward 180°, at the same time, hands hold broadsword, swing it backward and upward, overhead and clockwise one and a half circles, cross arms overhead (Figure 5-103).

第五章 少林春秋大刀

图 5-103（Figure 5-103）

（2）上动不停，以左脚为轴，身体继续右转180°，右腿随之屈膝上提；同时，两手持刀，以刀刃领先向右划弧；右臂屈肘将刀提与胸平，刀刃向外，刀尖斜向前。目视刀刃（图 5-104）。

（2）Keep moving left foot axis, turn rightward 180°, bend and lift elbow, at the same time, hands hold broadsword, make rightward blade draw curve rightward, bend the right arm and lower the elbow, keep broadsword at the chest's level, broadsword blade outward, broadsword tip obliquely forward. Look at broadsword blade (Figure 5-104).

图 5-104（Figure 5-104）

31.弓步提刀（提腰刀）

（1）接上势，右脚向右落步，两腿屈膝半蹲成马步；同时，右手持刀向右下方按压，使刀身与地面平行，刀尖向前，刀刃向下；左手脱把变掌架于头左后上方。目视刀身（图 5-105）。

31. Bow stance lifting (Raising)

（1）Keep moving, right foot falls rightward, bend knees on semi-crouch balance into the horse-riding stance, at the same time, right hand press broadsword rightward and downward, make broadsword parallel to the floor, broadsword tip forward, broadsword blade downward, change left hand into palm overhead. Look at broadsword (Figure 5-105).

图 5-105(Figure 5-105)

(2)上动不停,左腿蹬直成右弓步;同时,右手持刀屈肘上提,手腕内旋使刀刃转向外,刀尖斜向前下方;左掌前臂内旋下按。目视左前方(图5-106)。

(2) Keep moving, left leg kicks straight into the right bow stance, at the same time, right hand holds broadsword, bend and lift elbow, wrist turns inward, swing broadsword blade outward, broadsword tip obliquely forward and downward, left forearm turns inward, press broadsword downward. Look leftward (Figure 5-106).

图 5-106(Figure 5-106)

32.弓步推刀(智斩蔡阳)

(1)接上势,左脚向右脚并拢,前脚掌着地;同时,右手持刀向头上方,刀尖向后,刀把向前,迎头挺胸,左手接握刀柄(图5-107)。

32. Bow stance pushing (Beheading)

(1) Keep moving, close left foot to right foot, front sole touchdown, at the

第五章　少林春秋大刀

same time, right hand swings broadsword overhead, broadsword tip backward, broadsword handle forward, look up and throw out chest, left hand holds broadsword handle (Figure 5-107).

图 5-107 (Figure 5-107)

（2）上动不停,左脚向左前方上步,屈膝半蹲成左弓步;身体左转90°;同时,两手持刀乘云刀之势向左、向下、向前上推刀,左把紧贴左腰前。目视刀尖(图 5-108)。

(2) Keep moving, left foot strides one step leftward and forward, bend knees on semi-crouch balance into the left bow stance, turn leftward 90°, at the same time, hands hold broadsword, swing broadsword leftward, downward and forward, makes broadsword against left waist. Look at broadsword tip (Figure 5-108).

图 5-108 (Figure 5-108)

33.收刀合十(收山势)

（1）接上势,左腿后撤一步,上体稍右转;同时,两手持刀向右后,向下挂刀。目视刀背(图 5-109)。

307

33. Closing and palming (Closing)

(1) Keep moving, left leg retreats one step backward, turn right slightly, at the same time, hands hold broadsword swing it rightward and downward. Look at broadsword back (Figure 5-109).

图 5-109（Figure 5-109）

（2）上动不停,右脚向右后撤步,脚尖内扣,膝关节微屈;同时,两手持刀向后,向上划弧使刀立于身体右侧,刀把戳地,刀刃向外。目视刀身(图5-110)。

(2) Keep moving, right foot retreats rightward and backward, tiptoes buckle inward, bend knee slightly, at the same time, hands hold broadsword, make it draw curve rightward and upward, broadsword handle touchdown, broadsword blade outward. Look at broadsword (Figure 5-110).

图 5-110（Figure 5-110）

（3）上动不停,左脚向右脚并拢直立,上体左转 90°;同时,左手脱把屈肘立掌于胸前。目视前方(图 5-111)。

(3) Keep moving, close left foot to right foot, turn leftward 90°, at the same time, left loosen hand palm, bend elbow and swing palm against the chest.

Look straight ahead (Figure 5-111).

图 5-111(Figure 5-111)

34.收势

左掌自然下垂,贴于身体左侧,还原立正姿势(图 5-112)。

34. Closing

Left palm falls against the left side. Stand at attention (Figure 5-112).

图 5-112(Figure 5-112)

第六章 八段锦

Chapter 6　Baduanjin(Eight-sectioned Exercise)

第一节　【健身气功·八段锦】功法特点

Quarter 1　Features of Fitness Vital Energy—Eight-sectioned Exercise

"健身气功·八段锦"的运动强度和动作的编排次序符合运动学和生理学规律,属于有氧运动,安全可靠。整套功法增加了预备势和收势,使套路更加完整规范。功法动作特点主要体现在以下几个方面。

Fitness Vital Energy—Eight-sectioned Exercise has its exercise intensity and action sequence in line with the kinematics and physiological laws. As an aerobic exercise, it is safe and reliable. The practicing method is added with preparation and closing, making the routine complete and standardized. The practicing and action characteristics are mainly reflected in the following aspects.

一、柔和缓慢,圆活连贯

柔和,是指练习时动作不僵不拘,轻松自如,舒展大方。缓慢,是指练习时身体重心平稳,虚实分明,轻飘徐缓。圆活,是指动作路线带有弧形,不起棱角,不直来直往,符合人体各关节自然弯曲的状态。它是以腰脊为轴带动四肢运动,上下相随,节节贯穿。连贯,是要求动作的虚实变化和姿势的转换衔接无停顿断续之处。动作整体既像行云流水连绵不断,又如春蚕吐丝相连无间,使人神清气爽、体态安详,从而达到疏通经络、畅通气血和强身健体的效果。

1. Slow and soft, harmonious and constant

Soft feature means practicing movements are light and free, generous and poised. Slow feature means practicing movements are smooth and stable, clearly empty and full. Harmonious feature means movements with a curved line, free from edges, consistent with naturally tortuous joints. Arms and legs move with spinal column as the axis, up and down, harmonious and constant. Constant feature means constant movements, empty and full change and posture change convergence, free from pause or intermission, like drifting clouds and flowing water, silkworm threading, achieving blood and vital energy flow and fitness.

二、松紧结合,动静相兼

松,是指习练时肌肉、关节以及中枢神经系统、内脏器官的放松。在意识的主动支配下,逐步达到呼吸柔和、心静体松,同时松而不懈,保持正确的姿态,并将这种放松程度不断加深。紧,是指练习中适当用力,且缓慢进行,主要体现在前一动作的结束与下一动作的开始之前。如"健身气功·八段锦"中的"双手托天理三焦"的上托、"左右弯弓似射雕"的马步拉弓、"调理脾胃须单举"的上举、"五劳七伤往后瞧"的转头旋臂、"攒拳怒目增气力"的冲拳与抓握、"背后七颠百病消"的脚趾抓地与提肛等,都体现了这一点。紧,在动作中只存在一瞬间,而放松须贯穿动作的始终。松紧配合的适度,有助于平衡阴阳、疏通经络、滑利关节、活血化瘀、强筋壮骨、增强体质。

2. Relaxed and tight integration, dynamic and static combination

Relaxed feature means relaxation of muscles, joints, central nervous system, and internal organs in practicing. Dominate consciousness helps achieve soft breathing, calm relaxation, at the same time, correct posture and continuation. Tight feature means appropriate force in practicing, keeping slow, especially before the previous movement ends and the next movement starts. In Fitness

Vital Energy? Eight-sectioned Exercise, Supporting in "Hands Supporting Triple Energizer", Horse-riding Stance Archery in "Leftward and Rightward Arrow-Shooting", Lifting in "Single Lifting for Spleen and Stomach Improvement", Turning and Arm Swinging in "Looking Backward for Diseases Treatment", Punching and Grabbing in "Boxing and Staring", Toe Grinding and Anus Lifting in "Backward Swinging for Diseases Eliminating", are typical manifestations. Tight feature is reflected in an instant movement, while relaxed feature is reflected throughout the movements. Proper tightness and relaxation help to balance Yin-Yang, clear meridians, lubricate joints, improve blood circulation, strengthen tendons and bones, and enhance fitness.

三、神与形合,气寓其中

神,是指人体的精神状态和正常的意识活动,以及在意识支配下的形体表现。"神为形之主,形乃神之宅"。神与形是相互联系、相互促进的整体。本功法每势动作以及动作之间充满了对称与和谐,体现出内实精神、外示安逸,虚实相生、刚柔相济,做到了意动形随、神形兼备。

3. Harmonious mind and form, centering on vital energy

Mind refers to mental state and normal awareness and physical performance under the control of consciousness. "Mind is the base of form, and form is reflection of mind." Mind and form are interrelated and mutually promoted. This art is full of symmetry and harmony, reflecting the mind and connotation, empty and full integration, combination of hardness and softness, mind and form.

气寓其中,是指通过精神的修养和形体的锻炼,促进真气在体内运行,以达到强身健体的效果。习练本功法时,呼吸应顺畅,不可强硬呼吸。

Centering on vital energy refers to that cultural cultivation and physical practice promote vital energy run inside, achieving fitness. In practicing, it is necessary to have smooth breathing, avoiding tough breathing.

第二节 【健身气功·八段锦】习练要领
Quarter 2　Practicing Essentials of Fitness Vital Energy—Baduanjin

一、松静自然

1. Relaxed, calm and natural

松静自然,是练功的基本要领,也是最根本的法则。松,是指精神与形体两方面的放松。精神的放松,主要是解除心理和生理上的紧张状态;形体上的放松,是指关节、肌肉与脏腑的放松。放松是由内到外、由浅到深的锻炼过程,即形体、呼吸、意念轻松舒适、无紧张之感。静,是指思想和情绪要平稳安宁,排除一切杂念。放松与入静是相辅相成的,入静可以促进放松,而放松又有助于入静,二者缺一不可。

Staying relaxed, calm and natural is the practicing essential and rule. Staying relaxed refers to mental and physical relaxation. Mental relaxation relieves psychological and physiological tension while physical relaxation refers to joint, muscle and viscera relaxation. Relaxation means an exercise process from inside to outside and from shallow to deep, making the physique, breaths and mind relaxed and comforted. Free from tension. Staying calm refers to the thoughts and emotions in peace, eliminating all distractions. Staying relaxed and calm is complementary to each other. Staying calm can promote relaxation and staying relaxed can help staying calm. The two are indispensable.

自然,是指形体、呼吸、意念都要顺其自然。具体来说,形体自然,要合于法,一动一势要准确规范;呼吸自然,要莫忘莫助,不能强硬呼吸;意念自然,要"似守非守,绵绵若存",过于用意会造成气滞血瘀,导致精神紧张。需要指出的是,这里的"自然"决不能理解为"听其自然""任其自然",而是指"道法自然",需要习练者在练功过程中仔细体会,逐步把握。

Staying natural refers to that the physique, breath and mind remain natural.

Specifically speaking, physique remaining natural is in line with the law, with each movement exact and standard. Natural breath means free from forced breathing. Mind staying natural refers to "constant and soft", preventing intended thinking from causing vital energy stagnation and blood stasis, as well as mental tension. It is necessary to point out that "staying natural" shall not be understood as "let alone" or "let things take their own course", but as "in line with the natural law", which requires practitioners to appreciate carefully in exercise and gradually grasp.

二、准确灵活

2. Accurate and flexible

准确,主要是指练功时的姿势与方法要正确、合乎规格。在学习初始阶段,基本身形的锻炼最为重要。本功法的基本身形通过功法的预备势进行站桩锻炼即可,站桩的时间和强度可根据不同人群的不同健康状况灵活掌握。在锻炼身形时,要认真体会身体各部位的要求和要领,克服关节肌肉的酸痛等不良反应,为放松入静创造良好条件,为学习掌握动作打好基础。在学习各式动作时,要对动作的路线、方位、角度、虚实、松紧分辨清楚,做到姿势工整、方法准确。

Keeping accurate mainly refers to that the practice position and method should be correct and in line with the regulations. In the initial phase, the basic physical form is the most important. The basic form can be achieved through preparation and piling. Piling time and intensity can be flexible depending on the physical conditions of different people. In form exercising, it is necessary to appreciate carefully requirements and essentials of different parts, overcoming the adverse reaction of joint and muscle, such as aches and pains, and creating conditions for relaxation and meditation, laying down a good foundation for actions. In studying actions, it is necessary to distinguish action route, direction, angle, strength and intensity, achieving neat postures and accurate method.

灵活,是指练习时对动作幅度的大小、姿势的高低、用力的大小、习练的数量、意念的运用、呼吸的调整等都要根据自身情况灵活掌握,特别是老年人群和体弱者,更要注意。

Keeping flexible refers to that action size, position, force, and frequency, mind utilization and breathing adjustment should be flexible according to practical situation of the practitioner, especially the elderly and the infirm.

三、练养相间

3. Practicing and recuperating integration

练,是指形体运动、呼吸调整与心理调节有机结合的锻炼过程。养,是通过上述练习,身体出现的轻松舒适、呼吸柔和、意守绵绵的静养状态。习练本功法,在求动作姿势工整、方法准确的同时,要根据自身的身体情况,调整好姿势的高低和用力的大小,对有难度的动作,一时做不好的,可逐步完成。对于呼吸的调节,可在学习动作期间采取自然呼吸,待动作熟练后再结合动作的升降、开合与自己的呼吸频率有意识地进行锻炼,最后达到"不调而自调"的效果。对于意念的把握,在初学阶段重点应放在注意动作的规格和要点上,动作熟练后要遵循似守非守,绵绵若存的原则进行练习。

Practicing refers to combined physical movements, breathing adjustment and psychological adjustment. Recuperating refers to the physical relaxation, comfort, soft breath and calmness. Practicing needs neat movements and accurate method, and adjustment of the position and force according to physical conditions. Some difficult movements one can not do properly can be gradually completed. For regulation of breathing, it is proper to adopt natural breathing at first, and achieve "automatic regulation" in combination with ups and downs, breathing frequency. Mind grasping at the beginning should focus on action standards and essentials, and constant and harmonious principle through practicing.

练与养,是相互并存的,不可截然分开,应做到"练中有养""养中有练"。特别要合理安排练习的时间、数量,把握好强度,处理好"意""气""形"三者的关系。从广义上讲,练养相兼与日常生活也有着密切的关系。若能做到"饮食有节、起居有常",保持积极向上的乐观情绪,将有助于提高练功效果,增进身心健康。

Practicing and recuperating refers to coexistence instead of separation. It is necessary to achieve practicing in recuperating and recuperating in practicing. In particular, it is necessary to have reasonable arrangements for practicing duration, frequency and intensity, integrating mind, vital energy and form. In a broad sense, practicing and recuperating are closely related to daily life. Regular diet and living, and positive optimism will improve practicing effect and enhance physical and mental health.

四、循序渐进

4. Proceeding in an orderly way

"健身气功·八段锦"对于初学者来说有一定的学习难度和运动强度。因此,在初学阶段,习练者首先要克服练功给身体带来的不适感,如肌肉关节酸痛、动作僵硬、肌肉紧张、手脚配合不协调、顾此失彼等。只有经过一段时间和数量的习练,才会逐渐做到姿势工整、方法逐步准确,动作的连贯性与控制能力得到提高,对动作要领的体会不断加深,对动作细节更加注意,等等。

Fitness Vital Energy? Eight-sectioned Exercise means certain difficulty and intensity for beginners. Therefore, in the beginning stage, practitioners must first overcome physical discomfort caused by practicing, such as muscle and joint pain, stiff movements, strain and in-coordination. Only after a period of time and permanent practicing can the practitioners gradually achieve correct postures and movements, proper continuity and control ability, and right appreciation of movement essentials and details.

在初学阶段,本功法要求习练者采取自然呼吸方法。待动作熟练后,逐步对呼吸提出要求,习练者可采用练功时的常用方法——腹式呼吸。在掌握呼吸方法后,开始注意同动作进行配合。这其中也存在适应和锻炼的过程,不可急于求成。最后,逐渐达到动作、呼吸、意念的有机结合。

In the initial phase, practitioners should take natural breathing. With proficiency, practitioners gradually improve breathing. Practitioners can adopt abdominal breathing, a common practice. The breathing method should cooperate with the actions, which needs adaptation and exercise. It is necessary not to be anxious for success. Finally, combined action, breathing and mind will be achieved.

由于练功者体质状况及对功法的掌握与习练上存在差异,其练功效果不尽相同。良好的练功效果是在科学练功方法的指导下,随着时间和习练数量的积累而逐步达到的。因此,习练者不要"三天打鱼,两天晒网",应持之以恒、循序渐进,合理安排好运动量。

Difference in physical conditions and method mastery causes different practcing effects. Sound practicing effect is achieved under the guidance of scientific method and through gradual practicing. Therefore, practitioners should constantly practice, making progress step by step and reasonably arrange exercising intensity.

第三节 【健身气功·八段锦】动作说明

Quarter 3 Movements Descriptions of Fitness Vital Energy—Baduanjin

一、手型、步型

Section 1 Hand and step

(一)基本手型

Basic hand form

拳

Fist

大拇指抵掐无名指根节内侧,其余四指屈拢收于掌心(即握固,图6-1)。

Thumb pinches ring finger root, close the 4 fingers against the palm center (namely gripping) (Figure 6-1)

图 6-1(Figure 6-1)

掌

Palm

掌一:五指微屈,稍分开,掌心微含(图 6-2)。

(1) Fingers slightly bend and apart, palm center slightly draws (Figure 6-2).

图 6-2(Figure 6-2)

掌二:拇指与食指竖直分开成八字状,其余三指第一、二指节屈收,掌心微含(图 6-3)。

(2) Thumb and index vertically apart into V shape, the first and second knuckles of the remaining three fingers withdraw, and palm center slightly draws (Figure 6-3).

图 6-3(Figure 6-3)

爪

五指并拢,大拇指第一指节,其余四指第一、二指节屈收扣紧,手腕伸直(图 6-4)。

Claw

Fingers together, the first knuckle of the thumb and the first and second knuckles of the four fingers withdraw and fasten, the wrist straightens (Figure 6-4).

图 6-4(Figure 6-4)

(二)基本步型

Basic step form

马步

Horse-riding stance

开步站立,两脚间距约本人脚长的 2~3 倍;屈膝半蹲,大腿略高于水平(图 6-5)。

Stand with feet separated, with the gap between feet 2~3 times the foot length, partly squat, thighs slightly higher (Figure 6-5).

图 6-5(Figure 6-5)

二、动作图解

Section 2　Figures of routine movements

（一）预备势

Preparation

1.动作

1. Movement

动作一：两脚并步站立；两臂自然垂于体侧；身体中正，目视前方（图6-6）。

Movement 1：Stand at attention（Figure 6-6）.

图6-6(Figure 6-6)

动作二：随着松腰沉髋，身体重心移至右腿；左脚向左侧开步，脚尖朝前，约与肩同宽；目视前方（图6-7）。

Movement 2：Relax the waist and lower the hips, shift the physical center of gravity to the right leg, left foot steps leftward with toes forward, the same wide as the shoulders, look straight ahead（Figure 6-7）.

图6-7(Figure 6-7)

动作三:两臂内旋,两掌分别向两侧摆起,约与髋同高,掌心相对;目视前方(图6-8)。

Movement 3: Arms rotate inward, palms swing rightward and leftward respectively, the same high as the hips, palm centers against each other, look straight ahead (Figure 6-8).

图6-8(Figure 6-8)

动作四:上动不停。两腿膝关节稍屈;同时,两臂外旋,向前合抱于腹前呈圆弧形,与脐同高,掌心向内,两掌指间距约10厘米;目视前方(图6-9)。

Movement 4: Keep moving. Slightly bend the knees, at the same time swing arms outward and forward, hold arms in front of the abdomen into a circular arc, the same high as the navel, palm centers inward, the gap between palm fingers about 10cm, look straight ahead (Figure 6-9).

图6-9(Figure 6-9)

2.动作要点

2. Essential of exercise

(1)头向上顶,下颏微收,舌抵上腭,双唇轻闭;沉肩坠肘,腋下虚掩;胸部宽舒,腹部松沉;收髋敛臀,上体中正。

(1) Look up, slightly close the chin, tongue supports palate, shut up, drop shoulders and lower elbows, unlatch armpits, loosen chest and abdomen, close hips and draw buttocks, keep neutral.

(2)呼吸徐缓,气沉丹田,调息6~9次。

(2) Smoothly breathe, vital energy centering on elixir field, regulate breath 6 to 9 times.

3.易犯错误

3. Fallible

(1)抱球势,大拇指上翘,其余四指斜向地面。

(1) In ball holding, thumb upward while the fingers downward.

(2)塌腰,跪腿,八字脚。

(2) Waist drops, kneeling, feet V-shaped.

4.纠正方法

4. Correction method

(1)沉肩,垂肘,指尖相对,大拇指放平。

(1) Drop shoulders and elbows, make finger tips against each other, and level the thumbs.

(2)收髋敛臀,命门穴放松;膝关节不超越脚尖,两脚平行站立。

(2) Drop hips and buttocks, relax the waist, make knees not beyond the toes, and stand with feet parallel.

5.功理与作用

宁静心神,调整呼吸,内安五脏,端正身形,从精神与肢体上做好练功前的准备。

5. Functions and effects

Clarify mind, regulate breath, pacify internal organs, keep figure, get

第六章　八段锦

ready to practice mentally and physically.

（二）第一式　两手托天理三焦

Posture 1　Hands Supporting Triple Energizer

1.动作

1. Movement

动作一：接上式。两臂外旋微下落，两掌五指分开在腹前交叉，掌心向上；目视前方（图6-10）。

Movement 1: Continue the above. Arms swing outward and slightly drop, separate fingers and cross them in front of the abdomen, palm centers upward, look ahead (Figure 6-10).

图 6-10（Figure 6-10）

动作二：上动不停。两腿徐缓挺膝伸直；同时，两掌上托至胸前，随之两臂内旋向上托起，掌心向上；抬头，目视两掌（图6-11）。

Movement 2: Keep moving. Slowly stretch legs and knees, at the same time raise palms to the chest, rotate arms inward and upward, palm centers upward, rise and look at the palms (Figure 6-11).

图 6-11（Figure 6-11）

动作三:上动不停。两臂继续上托,肘关节伸直;同时,下颏内收,动作略停;目视前方(图6-12)。

Movement 3: Keep moving. Continue supporting the arms, stretch the elbows, at the same time withdraw the chin, pause, and look straight ahead (Figure 6-12).

图 6-12(Figure 6-12)

动作四:身体重心缓缓下降;两腿膝关节微屈;同时,十指慢慢分开,两臂分别向身体两侧下落,两掌捧于腹前,掌心向上;目视前方(图6-13)。

Movement 4: Slowly drop the physical center of gravity, slightly bend the knees, at the same time separate fingers, drop arms and hold palms in front of the abdomen, palm centers upward; look ahead (Figure 6-13).

图 6-13(Figure 6-13)

本式托举、下落为一遍,共做六遍。

Repeat the above six times.

2.动作要点

2. Essential of exercise

(1)两掌上托时要舒胸展体,略有停顿,保持抻拉。

（1）Palms support to stretch, slight pause, keeping stretched.

（2）两掌下落时要松腰沉髋，沉肩坠肘，松腕舒指，上体中正。

（2）Palms fall, lower waist and hips, lower shoulders and elbows, relax wrist and fingers, keep neutral.

3.易犯错误

两掌上托时，抬头不够，继续上举时松懈断劲。

3. Fallible

Raise palms but rise improperly, and continue to raise but slack off.

4.纠正方法

两掌上托，舒胸展体缓慢用力，下颏先向上助力，再内收配合两掌上撑，力在掌根。

4. Correction method

Palms support, slowly stretch the chest, raise the chin, and withdraw to support with palms, center on the palm roots.

5.功理与作用

5. Functions and effects

（1）通过两手交叉上托，缓慢用力，保持抻拉，可使"三焦"通畅、气血调和。

（1）Cross hands to support, slowly exert, and keep stretched, making "triple energizer", vital energy and blood circulation smooth.

（2）通过拉长躯干与上肢各关节周围的肌肉、韧带及关节软组织，可有效防治肩部疾患、预防颈椎病等。

（2）Stretch trunk and upper muscles, ligaments and soft tissues, preventing shoulder and cervical vertebrae diseases.

（三）第二式 左右开弓似射雕

Posture 2　Leftward and Rightward Arrow-Shooting

1. 动作

1. Movement

动作一：接上式。身体重心右移；左脚向左侧开站立，两腿膝关节自然伸直；同时，两掌向上交叉于胸前，右掌在外，两掌心向内；目视前方（图6-14）。

Movement 1：Continue the above. Shift rightward the physical center of gravity, shift left foot leftward and stand, straighten knee joints naturally, at the same time, lift palm centers upward and cross them in front of the chest, with the right hand outward and palm centers inward, look ahead (Figure 6-14).

图6-14（Figure 6-14）

动作二：上动不停。两腿徐缓屈膝半蹲成马步；同时，右掌屈指成"爪"，向右拉至肩前；左掌成八字掌，左臂内旋，向左侧推出，与肩同高，坐腕，掌心向左，犹如拉弓射箭之势；动作略停；目视左掌方向（图6-15）。

Movement 2：Keep moving. Slowly bend knees and partly squat into horse-riding stance, at the same time make right palm into "claw", draw it rightward to the front of the shoulder, make the left palm to V shape, rotate the left arm inward, and push it leftward and make it the same high as the shoulder, drop the wrist root, the palm center leftward, like arrow shooting, pause, look at the left palm (Figure 6-15).

第六章 八段锦

图 6-15（Figure 6-15）

动作三:身体重心右移;同时,右手五指伸开成掌,向上、向右划弧,与肩同高,指尖朝上,掌心斜向前;左手指伸开成掌,掌心斜向后;目视右掌(图 6-16)。

Movement 3: Shift the physical center of gravity shifted rightward, at the same time make the right hand into palm and have it draw an arc upward and rightward, have it the same high as the shoulder, fingertips upward, palm center forward, make the left hand into palm, palm center backward, look at the right palm (Figure 6-16).

图 6-16（Figure 6-16）

动作四:上动不停。重心继续右移;左脚回收成并步站立;同时,两掌分别由两侧下落,捧于腹前,指尖相对,掌心向上;目视前方(图 6-17)。

Movement 4: Keep moving. Continue shifting rightward the physical center of gravity, withdraw the left foot and stand, at the same time drop the palms and hold them in front of the abdomen, make fingertips against each other, palm centers upward, look ahead (Figure 6-17).

图 6-17(Figure 6-17)

动作五至动作八：同动作一至动作四，唯左右相反（图6-18~图6-21）。

Movement 5 to movement 8: The same as movement 1 to movement 4, except for changing right into left (Figure 6-18 to Figure 6-21).

图 6-18(Figure 6-18)　　　图 6-19(Figure 6-19)

图 6-20(Figure 6-20)　　　图 6-21(Figure 6-21)

本式一左一右为一遍，共做三遍。

Repeat right-left and left-right three times.

第三遍最后一动时，身体重心继续左移；右脚回收成开步站立，与肩同宽，膝关节微屈；同时，两掌分别由两侧下落，捧于腹前，指尖相对，掌心向上;目视前方(图 6-22)。

In the last movement, Continue shifting leftward the physical center of gravity, withdraw the left foot and stand, make it the same wide as the shoulders, slightly bend knees, at the same time drop the palms respectively and hold them in front of the abdomen, fingertips against each other, palm center upward; look ahead (Figure 6-22).

图 6-22(Figure 6-22)

2.动作要点

2. Essential of exercise

(1)侧拉之手五指要并拢屈紧,肩臂放平。

(1) Close fingers inward, arms and shoulders straight.

(2)八字掌侧撑需沉肩坠肘,屈腕,竖指,掌心涵空。

(2) Splayed palm extend inward, drop shoulders and elbows elbow, bend wrist, fingers upright, palm center empty.

(3)年老或体弱者可自行调整马步的高度。

(3) The elderly or the vulnerable may adjust the height of the horse-riding stance.

3.易犯错误

端肩,弓腰,八字脚。

3. Fallible

Shoulders upward, bend and V-shaped feet

4.纠正方法

沉肩坠肘,上体直立,两脚跟外撑。

4. Correction method

Drop shoulders and elbows, upper part upright, heels stretch outward.

5.功理与作用

(1)展肩扩胸,可刺激督脉和背部俞穴;同时刺激手三阴三阳经等,可调节手太阴肺经等经脉之气。

5. Functions and effects

(1) Shoulders and chest extension and expansion can stimulate governor meridian and back stream point, 3 yin and 3 yang of the hand, adjust lung meridian and other hand meridians.

(2)可有效发展下肢肌肉力量,提高平衡和协调能力;同时,增加前臂和手部肌肉的力量,提高手腕关节及指关节的灵活性。

(2) Effectively develop lower muscle strength, improve balance and coordination, at the same time, increase forearm and hand muscle strength, flexibility of wrist and finger joints.

(3)有利于矫正不良姿势,如驼背及肩内收,很好地预防肩、颈疾病等。

(3) Conducive to correct bad posture, such as humpback and closed shoulders, prevent shoulder or neck disease.

(四)第三式 调理脾胃须单举

Posture 3 Single Lifting for Spleen and Stomach Improvement

1.动作

1. Movement

动作一:接上式。两腿徐缓挺膝伸直;同时,左掌上托,左臂外旋上穿经面前,随之臂内旋上举至头左上方,肘关节微屈,力达掌根,掌心向上,掌指向右;同时,右掌微上托,随之臂内旋下按至右髋旁,肘关节微屈,力达掌根,掌心向下,掌指向前,动作略停;目视前方(图6-23)。

Movement 1: Continue the above. Slowly extend knees, at the same time, left palm supports upward, swing left arm outward through the front and inward and raise it upward and leftward, slightly bend the elbow, center on the palm roots, palm centers upward, fingers rightward, at the same time, slightly raise right palm, swing the arm inward to the right hip, slightly bend the elbow, center on the palm roots, palm center downward, fingers forward, pause, look ahead (Figure 6-23).

图6-23(Figure 6-23)

动作二:松腰沉髋,身体重心缓缓下降;两腿膝关节微屈;同时,左臂屈肘外旋,左掌经面前下落于腹前,掌心向上;右臂外旋,右掌向上捧于腹前,两掌指尖相对,相距约10厘米,掌心向上;目视前方(图6-24)。

Movement 2: Relax the waist and drop the hips, slowly drop the physical center of gravity, slightly bend the knees, at the same time bend the left elbow and swing it outward, drop the left palm to the front of the abdomen, palm centers upward, swing the arm outward, hold the right palm in front of the abdomen, fingertips against each other with a gap of about 10cm, palm centers upward, look ahead (Figure 6-24).

图6-24(Figure 6-24)

动作三、四:同动作一、二,唯左右相反(图6-25和图6-26)。

Movement 3 to movement 4: The same as movement 1 to movement 2, except for changing right into left (Figure 6-25 and Figure 6-26).

图 6-25(Figure 6-25)　　图 6-26(Figure 6-26)

本式一左一右为一遍,共做三遍。

Repeat right-left and left-right three times.

第三遍最后一动时,两腿膝关节微屈;同时,右臂屈肘,右掌下按于右髋旁,掌心向下,掌指向前;目视前方(图6-27)。

In the last movement, slightly bend the knees, at the same time, bend the right elbow, press the right palm on the right hip, palm center downward, fingers forward, look ahead (Figure 6-27).

图 6-27(Figure 6-27)

2.动作要点

力在掌根,上撑下按,舒胸展体,拔长腰脊。

2. Essential of exercise

Exert palm roots, support upward and press downward, chest extending and stretching, spinal column lifting.

3.易犯错误

掌指方向不正,肘关节没有弯曲度,上体不够舒展。

3. Fallible

Palm direction is not positive, not bending the elbow joint, the upper body is not enough to stretch.

4.纠正方法

两掌放平,力在掌根,肘关节稍屈,对拉拔长。

4. Correction method

Make palms flat, center on the palm roots, slightly bend the elbow, draw and lengthen them.

5.功理与作用

5. Functions and effects

(1)通过左右上肢一松一紧的上下对拉(静力牵张),可以牵拉腹腔,对脾胃中焦肝胆起到按摩作用;同时可以刺激位于腹、胸肋部的相关经络以及背部俞穴等,达到调理脾胃(肝胆)和脏腑经络的作用。

(1) Upper limbs stretching (static stretching) can stretch abdomen cavity, massage stomach liver and gall, at the same time, stimulate abdomen, chest and ribs related meridians and back stream points, adjusting spleen and stomach (liver and gall), organs and meridians.

(2)可使脊柱内各椎骨间的小关节及小肌肉得到锻炼,从而增强脊柱的灵活性与稳定性,有利于预防和治疗肩、颈疾病等。

(2) Exercise spine small joints and small muscles, enhancing flexibility and stability of the spine, conducive to the prevention and treatment of shoulder or neck diseases.

（五）第四式 五劳七伤往后瞧

Posture 4　Looking Backward for Diseases Treatment

1.动作

1. Movement

动作一：接上式。

Movement 1: Continue the above.

两腿徐缓挺膝伸直；同时，两臂伸直，掌心向后，指尖向下，目视前方（图6-28）。

Slowly stretch legs and knees, at the same time stretch arms, palm centers backward, fingers downward, look ahead (Figure 6-28).

图6-28(Figure 6-28)

然后上动不停。两臂充分外旋，掌心向外；头向左后转，动作略停；目视左斜后方(图6-29)。

Pause, swing arms outward, palm centers outward, turn left, pause, look leftward and backward (Figure 6-29).

图6-29(Figure 6-29)

第六章 八段锦

动作二:松腰沉髋,身体重心缓缓下降;两腿膝关节微屈;同时,两臂内旋按于髋旁,掌心向下,指尖向前;目视前方(图 6-30)。

Movement 2: Relax the waist and drop the hips slowly drop the physical center of gravity, slightly bend the knees, at the same time swing the arms inward to the hips, palm centers downward, fingers forward; look ahead (Figure 6-30).

图 6-30(Figure 6-30)

动作三:同动作一,唯左右相反(图 6-31 和图 6-32)。

Movement 3: The same as movement 1, except for changing right into left (Figure 6-31 and Figure 6-32).

图 6-31(Figure 6-31)   图 6-32(Figure 6-32)

动作四:同动作二(图 6-33)。

Movement 4: The same as movement 2 (Figure 6-33).

图 6-33(Figure 6-33)

本式一左一右为一遍，共做三遍。

Repeat right-left and left-right three times.

第三遍最后一动时，两腿膝关节微屈；同时，两掌捧于腹前，指尖相对，掌心向上；目视前方（图6-34）。

In the last movement, slightly bend the knees, at the same time, hold palms in front of the abdomen, fingertips against each other, palm centers upward, look ahead (Figure 6-34).

图 6-34（Figure 6-34）

2.动作要点

2. Essential of exercise

（1）头向上顶，肩向下沉。

(1) Look up, shoulders sink.

（2）转头不转体，旋臂，两肩后张。

(2) Look over shoulder, stand upright, turn arms, shoulders extend backward.

3.易犯错误

上体后仰，转头与旋臂不充分或转头速度过快。

3. Fallible

The upper part backward, turn and swing arms insufficiently or turn too fast.

4.纠正方法

下颏内收,转头与旋臂幅度宜大,速度均匀。

4. Correction method

Withdraw the chin inward, turn and swing sufficiently at a uniform speed.

5.功理与作用

5. Functions and effects

(1)"五劳"指心、肝、脾、肺、肾五脏劳损,"七伤"指喜、怒、悲、忧、恐、惊、思七情伤害。本式动作通过上肢伸直外旋扭转的静力牵张作用,可以扩张牵拉胸腔、腹腔内的脏腑。

(1) "Exhaustion or lesion of the five internal organs" refer to the heart, liver, spleen, lung and kidney, and "seven injuries" refer to injuries caused by emotions of joy, anger, sadness, worry, fear, panic and thinking. Upper limbs stretching and swinging can expand organs affecting chest cavity and abdomen cavity.

(2)本式动作中往后瞧的转头动作,可刺激颈部大椎穴,达到防治"五劳七伤"的目的。

(2) Looking Backward can stimulate cervical spine, preventing diseases.

(3)可增加颈部及肩关节周围参与运动肌群的收缩力,增加颈部运动幅度,活动眼肌,预防眼肌疲劳以及肩、颈与背部等疾患。同时,改善颈部及脑部血液循环,有助于解除中枢神经系统疲劳。

(3) Increase contractility of neck and shoulder joint and muscles, range of neck motions, eye muscles, prevent muscle fatigue, diseases of shoulders, neck and back, at the same time, and improve neck and brain blood circulation, relieving central nervous system fatigue.

(六) 第五式 摇头摆尾去心火

Posture 5 Shaking and turning for eliminating internal heat

1.动作

1. Movement

动作一:接上式。身体重心左移;右脚向右开步站立,两腿膝关节自然伸直;同时,两掌上托与胸同高时,两臂内旋,两掌继续上托至头上方,肘关节微屈,掌心向上,指尖相对;目视前方(图6-35)。

Movement 1: Continue the above. Shift leftward physical center of gravity, right foot rightward and stand, straight knees naturally, at the same time support palms up to the chest, swing arms inward, continue supporting palms overhead, slightly bend the elbow, palm centers upward, fingers against each other, look ahead (Figure 6-35).

图 6-35(Figure 6-35)

动作二:上动不停。两腿徐缓屈膝半蹲成马步;同时,两臂向两侧下落,两掌扶于膝关节上方,肘关节微屈,小指侧向前;目视前方(图6-36)。

Movement 2: Keep moving. Slowly withdraw knees and partly squat into a horse-riding stance, at the same time drop arms, put palms the upper parts of the knees, slightly bend the elbow, little finger forward, look ahead (Figure 6-36).

第六章 八段锦

图 6-36（Figure 6-36）

动作三：身体重心向上稍升起，而后右移；上体先向右倾，随之俯身；目视右脚（图 6-37）。

Movement 3: Slightly shift the physical center of gravity upward, then rightward, rise and lean rightward, and bend, look at the right foot (Figure 6-37).

图 6-37（Figure 6-37）

动作四：上动不停。身体重心左移；同时，上体由右向前、向左旋转；目视右脚（图 6-38）。

Movement 4: Keep moving. Shift the physical center of gravity leftward, at the same time, the upper part forward and then leftward, look at the right foot (Figure 6-38).

图 6-38（Figure 6-38）

动作五：身体重心右移,成马步;同时,头向后摇,上体立起,随之下颏微收;目视前方(图6-39)。

Movement 5: Slightly shift the physical center of gravity rightward into a horse-riding stance, at the same time, turn back, upper part upright, slightly withdraw the chin, and look ahead (Figure 6-39).

图6-39(Figure 6-39)

动作六至动作八：同动作三至动作五,唯左右相反(图6-40~图6-42)。

Movement 6 to movement 8: The same as movement 3 to movement 5, except for changing right into left (Figure 6-40 to Figure 6-42).

图6-40(Figure 6-40)　　　　图6-41(Figure 6-41)

图6-42(Figure 6-42)

本式一左一右为一遍,共做三遍。

Repeat right-left and left-right three times.

做完三遍后,身体重心左移,右脚回收成开步站立,与肩同宽;同时,两掌向外经两侧上举,掌心相对;目视前方(图6-43)。

In the last movement, shift leftward the physical center of gravity, withdraw the right foot and stand, the same wide as the shoulders, at the same time, palms outward and upward, palm centers against each other, look ahead (Figure 6-43).

图6-43(Figure 6-43)

随后松腰沉髋,身体重心缓缓下降。两腿膝关节微屈;同时屈肘,两掌经面前下按至腹前,掌心向下,指尖相对;目视前方(图6-44)。

Then relax the waist and drop the hips, and slowly drop the physical center of gravity. Slightly bend the knees and elbows, press palms to the abdomen, palm centers downward, fingers against each other, and look ahead (Figure 6-44).

图6-44(Figure 6-44)

2.动作要点

2. Essential of exercise

(1)马步下蹲要收髋敛臀,上体中正。

(1)Horse-riding downward, close hips and buttocks, keep neutral.

(2)摇转时,颈部与尾闾对拉伸长,好似两个轴在相对运转,速度应柔和缓慢,动作圆活连贯。

(2) In shaking and turning, neck and coccyx stretch, like two axes running against each other, softly and slowly, harmonious and constant.

(3)年老或体弱者要注意动作幅度,不可强求。

(3) The elderly or the vulnerable should properly adjust the movement range.

3.易犯错误

3. Fallible

(1)摇转时颈部僵直,尾闾摇动不圆活,幅度太小。

(1) In turning, stiff neck, coccyx shaking not flexible, margin too small.

(2)前倾过大,使整个上身随之摆动。

(2) Lean forward too much, making the upper part swing accordingly.

4.纠正方法

4. Correction method

(1)上体侧倾与向下俯身时,下颏不要有意内收或上仰,颈椎部肌肉尽量放松伸长。

(1) When the upper part leans and bends, don't intentionally withdraw or raise the chin, relax and extend the cervical muscles as much as possible.

(2)加大尾闾摆动幅度,应上体左倾尾闾右摆,上体前俯尾闾向后划圆,头不低于水平,使尾闾与颈部对拉拔长,加大旋转幅度。

(2) Swing the coccyx greatly, making upper part lean leftward and the coccyx swing rightward, upper part bend and the coccyx draw circles backward, look up, extend the coccyx and the neck, swing them greatly.

5.功理与作用

5. Functions and effects

(1)心火,即心热火旺的病症,属阳热内盛的病机。通过两腿下蹲,摆动尾闾,可刺激脊柱、督脉等;通过摇头,可刺激大椎穴,从而达到疏经泄热的作用,有助于祛除心火。

(1) Internal heat refers to syndrome of true heat disease with false cold manifestation. Squatting and swinging coccyx can stimulate the spine and governor meridian, and cervical spine, dredging and removing internal heat.

(2)在摇头摆尾过程中,脊柱腰段、颈段大幅度侧屈、环转及回旋,可使整个脊柱的头颈段、腰腹及臀、股部肌群参与收缩,既增加了颈、腰、髋的关节灵活性,也增强了这些部位的肌力。

(2) In shaking and turning, spine, waist and neck significantly bend inward, ring and turn backward, making head and neck, spine, waist, abdomen, buttocks, thigh muscles involved in contraction, increasing neck, waist, hip joint flexibility muscle strength.

(七)第六式 两手攀足固肾腰

Posture 6　Holding feet to reinforce the kidney

1.动作

1. Movement

动作一:接上式。两腿挺膝伸直站立;同时,两掌指尖向前,两臂向前、向上举起,肘关节伸直,掌心向前;目视前方(图6-45)。

Movement 1: Continue the above. Stretch knees and stand, at the same time fingers forward, arms forward and upward, stretch elbows, palm centers forward, look ahead (Figure 6-45).

图 6-45(Figure 6-45)

动作二：两臂外旋至掌心相对，屈肘，两掌下按于胸前，掌心向下，指尖相对；目视前方（图 6-46）。

Movement 2: Swing arms outward and make palm centers against each other, bend elbows, press palms on the chest, palm centers downward, fingertips against each other, look ahead (Figure 6-46).

图 6-46(Figure 6-46)

动作三：上动不停。两臂外旋，两掌心向上，随之两掌掌指顺腋下向后插；目视前方（图 6-47）。

Movement 3: Keep moving. Swing arms outward, palm centers upward, bend the upper part, insert fingers backward, and look ahead (Figure 6-47).

图 6-47(Figure 6-47)

第六章　八段锦

动作四:两掌心向内沿脊柱两侧向下摩运至臀部;随之上体前俯,两掌继续沿腿后向下摩运,经脚两侧置于脚面;抬头,动作略停;目视前下方(图 6-48)。

Movement 4: Shift palm centers inward along both sides of the spine and to the hips, bend the upper part, continue shifting palms downward and to the ground, look up, pause, look forward and downward (Figure 6-48).

图 6-48(Figure 6-48)

动作五:两掌沿地面前伸,随之用手臂举动上体起立,两臂伸直上举,掌心向前;目视前方(图 6-49)。

Movement 5: Stretch palms along the ground, raise arms, palm centers forward, look ahead (Figure 6-49).

图 6-49(Figure 6-49)

本式一上一下为一遍,共做六遍。

Repeat right-left and left-right six times.

做完六遍后,松腰沉髋,重心缓缓下降;两腿膝关节微屈;同时,两掌向前下按至腹前,掌心向下,指尖向前;目视前方(图 6-50)。

In the last movement, relax the waist and drop the hips, slowly drop the physical center of gravity, slightly bend the knees, press palms to the abdomen, palm centers downward, fingertips forward, look ahead (Figure 6-50).

图 6-50（Figure 6-50）

2.动作要点

2. Essential of exercise

（1）反穿摩运要适当用力,至足背时松腰沉肩、两膝挺直,向上起身时手臂主动上举,带动上体立起。

(1) Exerting hard, before reaching the instep, loosen waist and lower shoulders, knees straight, rise and arms lift.

（2）年老或体弱者可根据身体状况自行调整动作幅度,不可强求。

(2) The elderly or the vulnerable should properly adjust the movement range.

3.易犯错误

3. Fallible

（1）两手向下摩运时低头,膝关节弯曲。

(1) Hands drop and the head lowers, and knees bend.

（2）向上起身时,起身在前,举臂在后。

(2) Rise followed by arm lift.

4.纠正方法

4. Correction method

（1）两手向下摩运要抬头,膝关节伸直。

(1) Hands drop and look up, stretch the knees.

(2)向上起身时要以臂带身。

(2) Rise driven by with arms.

5.功理与作用

5. Functions and effects

(1)通过前屈后伸可刺激脊柱、督脉以及命门、阳关、委中等穴,有助于防治生殖泌尿系统方面的慢性病,达到固肾壮腰的作用。

(1) Bending forward and stretching backward stimulate the spine, governor meridian and acupoints of gate of vitality, yang pass and bilateral meridian, controlling genitourinary system chronic disease, reinforcing the kidney.

(2)通过脊柱大幅度前屈后伸,可有效发展躯干前、后伸屈脊柱肌群的力量与伸展性,同时对腰部的肾、肾上腺、输尿管等器官有良好的牵拉、按摩作用,可以改善其功能,刺激其活动。

(2) Spine bending forward and stretching backward can effectively develop trunk spinal muscle strength and extension, at the same time, pull and massage waist, kidney, adrenal glands, ureters and other organs, improving their functions and stimulating their activities.

(八)第七式 攒拳怒目增气力

Posture 7　Boxing and Staring

接上式。身体重心右移,左脚向左开步;两腿徐缓屈膝半蹲成马步;同时,两掌握固,抱于腰侧,拳眼朝上;目视前方(图 6-51)。

Keep moving. Shift rightward the physical center of gravity, left foot leftward, slowly bend the knees and partly squat into a horse-riding stance, at the same time, grip palms, hold them on the waist, fist eyes upward, look ahead (Figure 6-51).

图 6-51（Figure 6-51）

动作一：左拳缓慢用力向前冲出，与肩同高，拳眼朝上；瞪目，视左拳冲出方向（图 6-52）。

Movement 1: Lowly punch the left fist forward, the same high as the shoulder, fist eye upward, stare, look at the left fist (Figure 6-52).

图 6-52（Figure 6-52）

动作二：左臂内旋，左拳变掌，虎口朝下；目视左掌（图 6-53）。

Movement 2: Swing the left arm inward, change the left fist into palm, the point between thumb and forefinger downward, look at the left palm (Figure 6-53).

图 6-53（Figure 6-53）

左臂外旋，肘关节微屈；同时，左掌向左缠绕，变掌心向上后握固；目视左拳(图 6-54)。

Swing the left arm outward, slightly bend the elbow, at the same time swing the left palm leftward, palm center upward and grips, look at the left fist (Figure 6-54).

图 6-54(Figure 6-54)

动作三：屈肘，回收左拳至腰侧，拳眼朝上；目视前方(图 6-55)。

Movement 3: Bend the elbow, withdraw the left fist to the waist, fist eye upward, look ahead (Figure 6-55).

图 6-55(Figure 6-55)

动作四至动作六：同动作一至动作三，唯左右相反(图 6-56~图 6-59)。

Movement 4 to movement 6: The same as movement 1 to movement 3, except for changing right into left (Figure 6-56 to Figure 6-59).

图 6-56(Figure 6-56)　　图 6-57(Figure 6-57)

图 6-58(Figure 6-58)

图 6-59(Figure 6-59)

本式一左一右为一遍,共做三遍。

Repeat right-left and left-right three times.

做完三遍后,身体重心右移,左脚回收成并步站立;同时,两拳变掌,自然垂于体侧;目视前方(图 6-60)。

In the last movement, shift rightward the physical center of gravity, withdraw the left foot and stand, at the same time, change fists into palms and have them hang naturally, look ahead (Figure 6-60).

图 6-60(Figure 6-60)

2.动作要点

2. Essential of exercise

(1)马步的高低可根据自己的腿部力量灵活掌握。

(1) Horse-riding stance level may be flexible according to one's leg strength.

(2)冲拳时要怒目瞪眼,注视冲出之拳,同时脚趾抓地,拧腰顺肩,力达拳面;拳回收时要旋腕,五指用力抓握。

(2) In punching, it is necessary to stare, and gaze the fists, at the same

time, make toes grind, twist waist and shoulders, deliver force to fist face, recover fist and swing wrist, fingers grasp.

3.易犯错误

3. Fallible

(1)冲拳时上体前俯,端肩,掀肘。

(1) Punch and the upper part bends and shoulders upward and elbow upward.

(2)拳回收时旋腕不明显,抓握无力。

(2) Withdraw the fist without obvious swinging, grasping weakly.

4.纠正方法

4. Correction method

(1)冲拳时头向上顶,上体立直,肩部松沉,肘关节微屈,前臂贴肋前送,力达拳面。

(1) Punch and look up, the upper part straight, relax shoulders, slightly bend the elbow, and swing the forearm forward against the ribs, center on the fist.

(2)拳回收时,先五指伸直充分旋腕,再屈指用力抓握。

(2) To withdraw the fist, spread the fingers and rotate the wrist, and grasp.

5.功理与作用

5. Functions and effects

(1)中医认为,"肝主筋,开窍于目"。本式中的"怒目瞪眼"可刺激肝经,使肝血充盈,肝气疏泄,有强健筋骨的作用。

(1) TCM believes that "liver determines tendon, and sight determines resuscitation." Staring stimulates the liver, improving its blood circulation, dredging diarrhea, and enhancing bones.

(2)两腿下蹲十趾抓地、双手攒拳、旋腕、手指逐节强力抓握等动作,可刺激手、足三阴三阳十二经脉的俞穴和督脉等;同时,使全身肌肉、筋脉受到静力牵张刺激,长期锻炼可使全身筋肉结实,气力增加。

(2) Legs squat and toes grind, change hands into fists, turn wrist, exert fingers, stimulating hand and foot 12 meridians and governor meridian, muscles, tendons. Long-term practicing can enhance muscles strong and strength.

(九)第八式 背后七颠百病消

Posture 8　Backward Swinging for Diseases Eliminating

1.动作

1. Movement

动作一:接上式。两脚跟提起;头上顶,动作略停;目视前方(图6-61)。

Movement 1: Continue the above. Raise the heels, look up, pause, look ahead (Figure 6-61).

图6-61(Figure 6-61)

动作二:两脚跟下落,轻震地面;目视前方(图6-62)。

Movement 2: Drop the heels and lightly shake the ground, look ahead (Figure 6-62).

图 6-62（Figure 6-62）

本式一起一落为一遍，共做七遍。

Repeat up and down seven times.

2.动作要点

2. Essential of exercise

（1）上提时脚趾要抓地，脚跟尽力抬起，两腿并拢，百会穴上顶，略有停顿，要掌握好平衡。

（1）Lift and toes touchdown, left heels vigorously, close legs, head center buts, slight pause, keep balance.

（2）脚跟下落时，咬牙，轻震地面，动作不要过急。

（2）Tap feet, clench teeth, stamp slightly, and keep slow

（3）沉肩舒臂，周身放松。

（3）Drop shoulders and stretch arms, relax.

3.易犯错误

提时，端肩，身体重心不稳。

3. Fallible

Rise and shoulders upward, he physical center of gravity instable.

4.纠正方法

五趾抓住地面，两腿并拢，提肛收腹，肩向下沉，百会穴上顶。

4. Correction method

Toes grip the ground, legs together, raise the archos and withdraw the abdomen, drop the shoulders, raise the middle top.

5.功理与作用

5. Functions and effects

(1)脚趾为足三阴、三阳经交会之处,脚十趾抓地,可刺激足部有关经脉,调节相应脏腑的功能;同时,颠足可刺激脊柱与督脉,使全身脏腑经络气血通畅,阴阳平衡。

(1) Toes at the junction of 3 yin and 3 yang. Toes grinding can stimulate foot meridians, regulate the function of the corresponding organs, at the same time, stimulate the spine and governor meridian, making organs and meridians smooth and keep balance.

(2)颠足而立可发展小腿后部肌群力量,拉长足底肌肉、韧带,提高人体的平衡能力。

(2) Tapping feet and standing may develop forelegs muscle strength, stretch plantar muscles, ligaments, improving balance.

(3)落地震动可轻度刺激下肢及脊柱各关节内外结构,并使全身肌肉得到放松复位,有助于解除肌肉紧张。

(3) Falling and stamping can slightly stimulate legs and spinal joints internal and external structures, relax and reset muscles, relieving muscle tension.

(十)收势

Closing

1.动作

1. Movement

动作一:接上式。两臂内旋,向两侧摆起,与髋同高,掌心向后;目视前方(图6-63)。

第六章 八段锦

Movement 1: Continue the above. Swing arms inward and to both sides, the same high as the hips, palm center backward, look ahead (Figure 6-63).

图 6-63(Figure 6-63)

动作二:两臂屈肘,两掌相叠置于丹田处(男性左手在内,女性右手在内);目视前方(图 6-64)。

Movement 2: Bend elbows, overlap palms against the pubic region (man left hand inward, woman right hand inward), and look ahead (Figure 6-64).

图 6-64(Figure 6-64)

动作三:两臂自然下落,两掌轻贴于腿外侧;目视前方(图 6-65)。

Movement 3: Arms hang naturally, palms against the legs, look ahead (Figure 6-65).

图 6-65(Figure 6-65)

2.动作要点

体态安详,周身放松,呼吸自然,气沉丹田。

2. Essential of exercise

Calm and quiet, relax, breathe naturally, vital energy centering on elixir field.

3.易犯错误

收功随意,动作结束后或心浮气躁,或急于走动。

3. Fallible

Closing at will, flighty and impetuous, or eager to walk

4.纠正方法

收功时要心平气和,举止稳重。收功后可适当做一些整理活动,如搓手浴面和肢体放松等。

4. Correction method

To close, be calm and prudent, appropriately practice, such as rubbing, washing or relaxing.

5.功理与作用

气息归元,放松肢体肌肉,愉悦心情,进一步巩固练功效果,逐渐恢复到练功前安静时的状态。

5. Functions and effects

Keep vital energy, relax limb muscles, keep pleasant mood, consolidate practice effect, gradually restore to the state before practice.

第七章 易筋经
Chapter 7　Yijinjing

第一节 【健身气功·易筋经】功法特点
Quarter 1　Features of Fitness Vital Energy—Yijinjing

一、动作舒展，伸筋拔骨

1. Stretching smoothly

本功法中的每一势动作，不论是上肢、下肢还是躯干，都要求有较充分的屈伸、外展内收、扭转身体等运动，从而使人体的骨骼及大小关节在传统定势动作的基础上，尽可能的呈现多方位和广角度的活动。其目的就是要通过"拔骨"的运动达到"伸筋"，牵拉人体各部位的大小肌群和筋膜，以及大小关节处的肌腱、韧带、关节囊等结缔组织，促进活动部位软组织的血液循环，改善软组织的营养代谢过程，提高肌肉、肌腱、韧带等软组织的柔韧性、灵活性和骨骼、关节、肌肉等组织的活动功能，达到强身健体的目的。

All movements, including movements of upper limbs, legs and trunk, must have bending and stretching, outreaching and closing, twisting and turning, so as to make bones and joints follow traditional movements and multiple and wide-range activities. Its purpose is to "pull bones" and "stretch tendons", involving various muscles and fascia, tendons, ligaments, joint capsules, promote moving parts blood circulation, improve soft tissue nutrition metabolism, improve flexibility and agility of muscles, tendons, ligaments and other soft tissues, functions of bones, joints, muscles and other tissues, achieving fitness.

二、柔和匀称,协调美观

2. Soft and well-proportioned, coordinated and elegant

本功法是在传统"易筋经十二定势"动作的基础上进行了改编,增加了动作之间的连接,每势动作变化过程清晰、柔和。整套功法的运动方向,为前后、左右、上下;肢体运动的路线,为简单的直线和弧线;肢体运动的幅度,是以关节为轴的自然活动角度所呈现的身体活动范围;整套功法的动作速度,是匀速缓慢的移动身体或身体局部。动作力量上,要求肌肉相对放松,不僵硬,用力圆柔而轻盈,不使蛮力,刚柔相济。每势之间无繁杂和重复动作,便于中老年人学练。同时,对部分动作难度作了不同程度的要求,也适合青壮年学练。

Based on traditional "Channel-changing Scriptures 12-Set" movements, this art has made certain improvement and increased linking between movements, making every movement clear and soft, focusing on forward and backward, leftward and rightward, upward and downward simple straight lines and arcs, limb movement natural range with joints as the axis, low and uniform speed, muscle relaxation, soft and light movements, free from stiffness and hardness, complicated or repetitive movements, suitable to the elderly. It has some difficult requirements, suitable to young people.

本功法动作要求上下肢与躯干之间、肢体与肢体之间的左右上下、以及肢体左右的对称与非对称,都应有机的整体协调运动,彼此相随,密切配合。因此,"健身气功·易筋经"呈现出动作舒展、连贯、柔畅、协调、动静相兼。同时在精神内涵的神韵下,给人以美的享受。

It requires symmetric and asymmetric upward and downward, leftward and rightward movements between upper and lower limbs and the trunk should be comprehensively coordinated and organic. "Fitness Vital Energy—Channel-changing Scriptures" is characterized by smooth, constant, soft, coordinated and elegant movements.

三、注重脊柱的旋转屈伸

3. Turn, bend and stretch the spine

脊柱是人体的支柱,又称"脊梁"。由椎骨、韧带、脊髓等组成,具有支持体重、运动、保护脊髓及其神经根的作用。神经系统是由位于颅腔和椎管里的脑和脊髓以及周围神经组成。神经系统控制和协调各个器官系统的活动,使人体成为一个有机整体以适应内外环境的变化。因此,脊柱旋转屈伸的运动有利于对脊髓和神经根的刺激,以增强其控制和调节功能。本功法的主要运动形式是以腰为轴的脊柱旋转屈伸运动,如"九鬼拔马刀式"中的脊柱左右旋转屈伸动作,"掉尾势"中脊柱前屈并在反伸的状态下做侧屈、侧伸动作。因此,本功法是通过脊柱的旋转屈伸运动以带动四肢、内脏的运动,在松静自然、形神合一中完成动作,达到健身、防病、延年、益智的目的。

The spine is the backbone, also known as the "back", consisting of vertebrae, ligaments and spinal cord, supporting weight, motion, protecting spinal cord and nerve roots. Nervous system consists of brain, spinal cord and peripheral nerves in the cranial cavity and the spinal cord. Nervous system controls and coordinates activities of the various organ systems, making the body an organic whole to adapt to changes in internal and external environments. Turning, bending and stretching of the spine benefit spinal cord and nerve root stimulation, enhance control and regulation functions. The main movements refer to turning, bending and stretching of the spine with the waist as the axis, such as spine leftward and rightward turning, bending and stretching movements, such as spine leftward and rightward turning, bending and stretching movements in "Sabre swinging" and spine forward bending, lateral bending and stretching in "Whipping with tail". Spine turning, bending and stretching promote limbs and visceral movements, achieving fitness, disease prevention, longevity and intelligence reinforcements.

第二节 【健身气功·易筋经】习练要领
Quarter 2 Practicing Essentials of Fitness Vital Energy—Yijinjing

一、精神放松,形意合一

1. Relax, form and mind integration

习练本功法要求精神放松,意识平静,不做任何附加的意念引导。通常不意守身体某个点或部位,而是要求意随形体动作的运动而变化。即在习练中,以调身为主,通过动作变化导引气的运行,做到意随形走、意气相随,起到健体养生的作用。同时,在某些动作中,需要适当的配合意识活动。如"韦驮献杵第三势"中双手上托时,要求用意念观注两掌;"摘星换斗势"中要求目视上掌,意存腰间命门处;"青龙探爪"时,要求意存掌心。而另一些动作虽然不要求配合意存,但却要求配合形象的意识思维活动。如"三盘落地势"中下按、上托时,两掌犹如拿重物;"出爪亮翅势"中伸肩、撑掌时,两掌有排山之感;"倒拽九牛尾势"中拽拉时,两膀如拽牛尾;"打躬势"中脊椎屈伸时,应体会上体如"勾"一样的卷曲伸展运动。这些都要求意随形走,用意要轻,似有似无,切忌刻意、执著于意识。

It is necessary to make mind relax and awareness calm, free from idea guidance, concentration on a certain point or part. It is proper to change the mind to follow the movements. Practicing focuses on adjustment, achieving mind and movement integration and fitness. Certain movements need appropriate awareness activities. For example, in "Wei Tuo Presenting the Pestle 3", hands support posture requires concentration on palms. In "Plucking a Star and Exchanging a Star Cluster", it is required to look at the palms and concentration on waist life-gate. In "Black Dragon Displaying Its Claws", it is necessary to concentrate on the palm centers. Other movements do not require concentration, but require thinking against images. For example, in "Three Plates Falling on the Floor", pressing and supporting should make palms seem to support heavy objects. In "Displaying Paw-Style Palms like a White Crane Spreading Its Wings" shoulders stretching and palms supporting should make palms have a sense of mountain pushing. In "Pulling Nine Cows by Their Tails", pulling should make shoulder seem to pull an ox by the tail. In "Bowing Down in Salutation", spine bending and stretching should make bending and stretching similar to "hooking". The requirements should integrate mind and form, easy minded, avoiding deliberation and clinging to consciousness.

二、呼吸自然,贯穿始终

2. Breathe naturally, throughout

习练本功法时,要求呼吸自然、柔和、流畅,不喘不滞,以利于身心放松、心平气和及身体的协调运动。相反,若不采用自然呼吸,而执著于呼吸的深长绵绵、细柔缓缓,则会在于导引动作的匹配过程中产生"风""喘""气"三相,即呼吸中有声(风相),无声而鼻中涩滞(喘相),不声不滞而鼻翼扇动(气相)。这样,习练者不但不受益,反而会导致心烦意乱,动作难以松缓协调,影响健身效果。因此,习练本功法时,要以自然呼吸为主,动作与呼吸始终保持柔和协调的关系。

In practicing, it is necessary to breathe naturally, keep soft and smooth, avoid delay, so as to facilitate physical and mental relax, keep coordinated. Centering on breathing deeply and persistently will witness breath sound (wind phase), silent and nasal astringent stagnation (asthma phase), silent and nose flap (nasal flaring phase) will make the upset, movements coordination difficult, affecting the effect. Therefore, in practicing, it is necessary to breathe naturally, keep movements and breathing soft and coordinated.

此外,在功法的某些环节中也要主动配合动作进行自然呼或自然吸。如"韦驮献杵第三势"中双掌上托时自然吸气;"倒拽九牛尾势"中收臂拽拉时自然呼气;"九鬼拔马刀式"中展臂扩胸时自然吸气,松肩收臂时自然呼气,含胸合臂时自然呼气,起身开臂时自然吸气;"出爪亮翅势"中两掌前推时自然呼气,等等。因为人体胸廓会随着这些动作的变化而扩张或缩小,吸气时胸廓会扩张,呼气时胸廓会缩小。因此,习练本功法时,应配合动作,随胸廓的扩张或缩小而自然吸气或呼气。

In addition, it is necessary to take the initiative to keep in line with movements and have natural exhale and inhale, such as natural inhale for palms supporting in "Wei Tuo Presenting the Pestle 3", natural exhale for arms closing and pulling in "Pulling Nine Cows by Their Tails", natural inhale for arm and chest extending in "Nine Ghosts Drawing Saber", natural exhale for arm closing and shoulders relaxing, and chest drawing and arms closing, natural inhale for rising and arms opening, and arms pushing in "Displaying Paw-Style Palms like a White Crane Spreading Its Wings". The thorax expands with inhale and shrinks with exhale. Therefore, in practicing, it is necessary to keep in line with movements, conduct natural inhale or exhale when thorax expands or shrinks.

三、刚柔相济、虚实相兼

3. Hard and soft, empty and full

本功法动作有刚有柔,且刚与柔是在不断相互转化的;有张有弛,有沉有轻,是阴阳对立统一的辩证关系。如"倒拽九牛尾势"中,双臂内收旋转逐渐拽拉至止点是刚,为实;随后身体以腰转动带动两臂伸展至下次手臂拽拉前是柔,为虚。又如"出爪亮翅势"中,双掌立于胸前呈扩胸展肩时,肌肉收缩的张力增大为刚,是实;当松肩伸臂时,两臂肌肉等张收缩,上肢是放松的,为柔;两臂伸至顶端,外撑有重如排山之感时,肌肉张力再次增大为刚,是实。这些动作均要求习练者在用力之后适当放松,松柔之后尚需适当有刚。这样,动作就不会出现机械、僵硬或疲软无力的松弛状况。

The movements are rigid and soft, tense and relaxed, heavy and light and constantly variable, witnessing dialectical relations. For example, in "Pulling Nine Cows by Their Tails", arms closing and turning gradually to the end means hard and full, turning with the waist as the axis and arms stretching and extending means soft and empty. In "Displaying Paw-Style Palms like a White Crane Spreading Its Wings", palms in front of the chest and chest and shoulders extending and expanding, and muscle tension increasing, means hard and full. Shoulders relaxing and arms closing, muscles and upper limbs relaxing mean soft. Arms stretching to the end, outward extending witnesses a sense of mountain pushing, and muscle tension increasing again, mean hard and full. In practicing, it is necessary to appropriately relax after exerting, and exert after relaxing so as to avoid inability, stiffness or weakness.

四、循序渐进，个别动作配合发音习练

4. Progressive, movements with articulation

练本功法时,不同年龄、不同体质、不同健康状况、不同身体条件的练习者,可以根据自己的实际情况灵活的选择各式动作的活动幅度或姿势,如"三盘落地势"中屈膝下蹲的幅度、"卧虎扑食势"中十指是否着地姿势的选择,等等。习练时还应遵循由易到难、由浅到深、循序渐进的原则。

In practicing, practitioners of different ages and physiques can make proper selection. For example, squatting in "Three Plates Falling on the Floor" and fingers touchdown in "Lying Tiger Pouncing for Food" are optional in degrees and extents. In practicing, it is necessary to follow the progressive principle.

另外,本功法在练习某些特定动作的过程中要求呼气时发音(但不需出声)。如"三盘落地势"中的身体下蹲、两掌下按时,要求配合动作口吐"嗨"音,目的是为了下蹲时气能下沉至丹田,而不因下蹲造成下肢紧张,引起气上逆至头部;同时口吐"嗨"音,气沉丹田,可以起到强肾、壮丹田的作用。因此,在该势动作中要求配合吐音、呼气,并注意口型,吐"嗨"音口微张,音从喉发出,上唇着力压于龈交穴,下唇松,不着力于承浆穴。这是本法中"调息"的特别之处。

In addition, it is necessary to make articulation for exhale in certain movements. For example, in "Three Plates Falling on the Floor", squatting and palms pressing require to cry "Hey" so as to center on elixir field, avoid leg and head tension, at the same time, enhance the kidney and elixir field. It is necessary to make mouth properly shaped, cry from the throat, press upper lip, and relax lower lip. It is special breath adjustment.

第三节 【健身气功·易筋经】动作说明

Quarter 3 Movements Descriptions of Fitness Vital Energy—Yijinjing

一、手型、步型

Section 1 Hand and step

(一)基本手型

Basic hand form

握固

Grip

大拇指抵掐无名指根节,其余四指屈拢收于掌心(图7-1)。

Thumb pinches ring finger root, closed the 4 fingers against the palm (Figure 7-1).

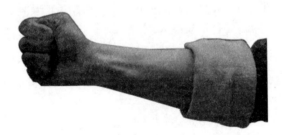

图7-1(Figure 7-1)

荷叶掌

Lotus palm

五指伸直,张开(图7-2)。

Fingers straight, open (Figure 7-2).

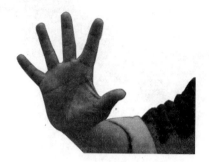

图 7-2(Figure 7-2)

柳叶掌

Willow leaf palm

五指伸直,并拢(图 7-3)。

Fingers straight, closed (Figure 7-3).

图 7-3(Figure 7-3)

龙爪

Dragon claw

五指伸直、分开,拇指、食指、无名指、小指内收(图 7-4)。

Fingers straight and separated, thumb, index finger, ring finger and little finger closed inward (Figure 7-4).

图 7-4(Figure 7-4)

虎爪

Tiger claw

五指分开,虎口撑圆,第一、二指关节弯曲内扣(图 7-5)。

Fingers apart, the part between the thumb and the forefinger stays round, the first and second finger joints buckle inward (Figure 7-5).

图 7-5(Figure 7-5)

(二)基本步型

Basic steps

弓步

Bow-step

两腿前后分开一大步,横向之间保持一定宽度,前腿屈膝前弓,大腿斜向地面,膝与脚尖上下相对,脚尖微内扣;后腿自然伸直,脚跟蹬地,脚尖微内扣,全脚掌着地(图 7-6)。

Legs one step apart forward and backward, feet apart, bend forelegs, thighs obliquely downward, knees and tiptoes against each other, tiptoes slightly buckle inward, hind leg naturally straight, heel stamps, tiptoes slightly buckle inward, soles touchdown (Figure 7-6).

图 7-6(Figure 7-6)

丁步

T-step

两脚左右分开,间距约 10~20 厘米。两腿屈膝下蹲,前腿脚跟提起,脚尖着地,虚点地面,置于后脚足弓处;后腿全脚掌着地踏实(图 7-7)。

Feet apart leftward and rightward, spacing of about 10cm~20cm. Bend knees and squat, foreleg heel rises, tiptoes touchdown, imaginary pointing the floor and against heel, sole touchdown (Figure 7-7).

图 7-7(Figure 7-7)

马步

Horse-riding stance

开步站立,两脚间距约为本人脚长的 2~3 倍,屈膝半蹲,大腿略高于水平(图 7-8)。

Stand into the horse-riding stance, feet spacing about 2~3 times the foot, bend knees on semi-crouch balance, thighs slightly upward (Figure 7-8).

367

图 7-8(Figure 7-8)

二、动作图解
Section 2　Figures of movements

(一)预备势

Preparation

1.动作

两脚并拢站立,两手自然垂于体侧;下颏微收,百会虚领,唇齿合拢,舌自然平贴于上腭;目视前方(图 7-9)。

1. Movement

Stand at attention, hands fall naturally, slightly close the chin, head middle raises naturally, close lips and teeth, and tongue naturally against palate. Look straight ahead (Figure 7-9).

图 7-9(Figure 7-9)

第七章　易筋经

2.动作要点

全身放松,身体中正,呼吸自然,目光内含,心平气和。

2. Essential of exercise

Relax, keep neutral, breathe naturally, keep calm.

3.易犯错误

手脚摆站不自然,杂念较多。

3. Fallible

Stand unnaturally, with distracting thoughts.

4. 纠正方法

调息数次,逐渐进入练功状态。

4. Remedy

Adjust breathing, gradually enter practice state.

5.功理与作用

宁静心神,调整呼吸,内安五脏,端正身形。

5. Functions and effects

Keep calm and upright, adjust breathing.

(二)第一势　韦驮献杵第一势

Form 1　Wei Tuo Presenting the Pestle 1

1.动作

1. Movement

动作一:左脚向左侧开半步,约与肩同宽,两膝微屈,成开立姿势;两手自然垂于体侧(图7-10)。

Movement 1: Left foot strides half a step leftward, about the same wide as the shoulders, bend knees slightly, stand with feet slightly apart, hands fall naturally to the sides (Figure 7-10).

图 7-10(Figure 7-10)

动作二：两臂自体侧向前抬至前平举，掌心相对，指尖向前（图 7-11）。

Movement 2: Lift arms forward, palm centers against each other, fingertips forward (Figure 7-11).

正(Front)   侧(Side)
图 7-11(Figure 7-11)

动作三、四：两臂屈肘，自然回收，指尖向斜前上方约 30°，两掌合于胸前，掌根于膻中穴同高，虚腋；目视前下方（图 7-12）。动作稍停。

Movements 3 and 4: Bend elbows, close naturally, fingertips obliquely above about 30°, palms in front of the chest, palm root at the chest center level, empty armpit, look forward and downward (Figure 7-12). Pause.

图 7-12(Figure 7-12)

2.动作要点

2. Essential of exercise

(1)松肩虚腋。

(1) Relax shoulders and keep armpit empty.

(2)两掌合于胸前,应稍停片刻,以达气定神敛之功效。

(2) Palms together in front of the chest, and pause, keep calm and quite.

3.易犯错误

两掌内收胸前时,或松肩抬肘或松肩坠肘。

3. Fallible

Close palms in front of the chest, relax shoulders and lift elbows, or relax shoulders lower elbow.

4.纠正方法

动作自然放松,注意调整幅度,应虚腋如挟鸡蛋。

4. Remedy

Naturally relax, keep adjustment proper, make empty armpit similar to egg holding.

5.功理与作用

5. Functions and effects

(1)古人云:"神住气自回。"通过神敛和两掌相合的动作,可起到气定神敛、均衡身体左右气机的作用。

(1) As an old saying goes, "Keep calm and balanced." Keeping calm and shifting palms can stabilize vital energy and balance leftward and rightward vital energy mechanism.

(2)可改善神经、体液调节功能,有助于血液循环,消除疲劳。

(2) It can improve nerve and body fluid regulation, blood circulation, eliminating fatigue.

(三)第二势 韦驮献杵第二势

Form 2 Wei Tuo Presenting the Pestle 2

动作一:接上势。两肘抬起,两掌平伸,手指相对,掌心向下,掌臂约与肩呈水平(图7-13)。

Movement 1: Keep moving, lift elbows, palms straight, fingers against each other, palm centers downward, arms and shoulders at the same level (Figure 7-13).

正(Front)　　　　侧(Side)

图 7-13(Figure 7-13)

动作二:两掌向前伸展,掌心向下,指尖向前(图7-14)。

Movement 2: Palms stretch forward, palm center downward, fingertips forward (Figure 7-14).

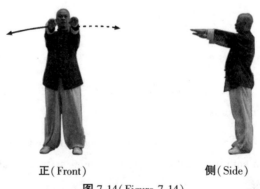

正(Front)　　　　侧(Side)

图 7-14(Figure 7-14)

动作三:两臂向左右分开至侧平举,掌心向下,指尖向外(图7-15)。

Movements 3: Arms apart leftward and rightward, palm centers downward, fingertips outward (Figure 7-15).

图 7-15(Figure 7-15)

动作四:五指自然并拢,坐腕立掌;目视前下方(图 7-16)。

Movement 4: Close fingers naturally, raise palms, look forward and downward (Figure 7-16).

图 7-16(Figure 7-16)

2.动作要点

2. Essential of exercise

(1)两掌外撑,力在掌根。

(1) Palms outward, power palm roots.

(2)坐腕立掌时,脚趾抓地。

(2) Raise palms, foot toes touchdown.

(2)自然呼吸,气定神敛。

(3) Breathe naturally, keep calm and quite.

3.易犯错误

两臂侧举时不呈水平状。

3. Fallible

Lift arms inward, not horizontal.

4.纠正方法

两臂侧平举时自然伸直,与肩同高。

4. Remedy

Lift arms and make them straight, keep at the shoulder's level.

5.功理与作用

5. Functions and effects

(1)通过伸展上肢和立掌外撑的动作导引,起到疏理上肢等经络的作用,并具有调练心、肺之气,改善呼吸功能及气血运行的作用。

(1) Upper limbs and palms stretching and extending can adjust upper limb meridians, improving mind, lungs, and respiratory functions, and blood circulation.

(2)可提高肩、臂的肌肉力量,有助于改善肩关节的活动功能。

(2) Improve shoulder and arm muscles, and shoulder joint functions.

(四)第三势 韦驮献杵第三势

Form 3　Wei Tuo Presenting the Pestle 3

1.动作

1. Movement

动作一:接上式。松腕,同时两臂向前平举内收至胸前平屈,掌心向下,掌与胸相距约一拳;目视前下方(图7-17)。

Movement 1: Keep moving, relax wrists, at the same time arms forward and bend against the chest, palm centers downward, palm and chest one fist apart, look forward and downward (Figure 7-17).

图 7-17(Figure 7-17)

动作二:两掌同时内旋,翻掌至耳垂下,掌心向上,虎口相对,两肘外展,约与肩平(图 7-18)。

Movement 2: Palms swing inward, turn palms to the earlobes, supinely, the parts between the thumb and the forefinger against each other, elbows outreach, at about the shoulders' level (Figure 7-18).

图 7-18(Figure 7-18)

动作三:身体重心前移至前脚掌支撑,提踵;同时,两掌上托至头顶,掌心向上,展肩伸肘;微收下颏,舌抵上腭,咬紧牙关(图 7-19)。

Movements 3: Shift gravity center to front sole, lift toes, at the same time, palms support overhead, supinely, extend shoulders and stretch elbows, slightly close lower chin, tongue supports palate, clench teeth (Figure 7-19).

正(Front)   侧(Side)

图 7-19(Figure 7-19)

动作四:静立片刻。

Movement 4: Pause.

2.动作要点

2. Essential of exercise

(1)两掌上托时,前脚掌支撑,力达四肢,下沉上托,脊柱竖直,同时身体重心稍前移。

(1) Palms butt, front sole support, exert force to the limbs, spine upright, at the same time, shift gravity center slightly forward.

(2)年老或体弱者可自行调整两脚提踵的高度。

(2) The elderly or the vulnerable can adjust foot height.

(3)上托时,意想通过"天门"观注两掌,目视前下方,自然呼吸。

(3) Butt, make "Heavenly Gate" center on palms, and look forward and downward, breathe naturally.

3.易犯错误

3. Fallible

(1)两掌上托时,屈肘。

(1) Palms support, bend elbow.

(2)抬头,目视上方。

(2) Look up, look at the top.

4.纠正方法

4. Remedy

(1)两掌上托时,伸肘,两臂夹耳。

(1) Palms support, stretch elbow, arms clip ears.

(2)上托时强调的是意注两掌,而不是目视两掌。

(2) Support, center on palms, rather than look at palms.

5.功理与作用

5. Functions and effects

(1)通过上肢撑举和下肢提踵的动作导引,可调理上、中、下三焦之气,并且将三焦及手足三阴五脏之气全部发动。

(1) Upper limbs and palms stretching and extending can regulate triple energizer, mobilize triple energizer, hands and feet and five internal organs.

(2)可改善肩关节活动功能及提高上下肢的肌肉力量,促进全身血液循环。

(2) Improve muscles of shoulder joints and legs, promote blood circulation.

(五)第四势 摘星换斗势

Form 4 Plucking a Star and Exchanging a Star Cluster

1.动作

左摘星换斗势

1. Movement

Left Plucking a Star and Exchanging a Star Cluster

动作一:接上式。两脚跟缓缓落地;同时,两手握拳,拳心向外,两臂下落至侧上举(图7-20)。

Movement 1: Keep moving, feet slowly fall, at the same time, clench fists, fist centers outward, arms fall inward and upward (Figure 7-20).

图7-20(Figure 7-20)

随后两拳缓缓伸开变掌,掌心斜向下,全身放松;目视前下方(图7-21)。

Fists slowly stretch and become palms, palm center obliquely downward, relax, look forward and downward (Figure 7-21).

图 7-21(Figure 7-21)

身体左转;屈膝;同时,右臂上举经体前下摆至左髋关节外侧"摘星",右掌自然张开;左臂经体侧下摆至体后,左手背轻贴命门;目视右掌(图7-22~图7-24)。

Turn left, bend knees, at the same time, right arm swings upward, forward and downward to "pick a star", right palm naturally opens, left arm swings inward, downward and backward, look at right palm (Figure 7-22 to Figure 7-24).

图 7-22(Figure 7-22)   图 7-23(Figure 7-23)

正(Front)   侧(Side)

图 7-24(Figure 7-24)

第七章　易筋经

动作二：直膝，身体转正；同时，右手经体前向额上摆至头顶右上方，松腕，肘微屈，掌心向下，手指向左，中指尖垂直于肩髃穴；左手背轻贴命门，意注命门；右臂上摆时眼随手走，定势后目视掌心(图 7-25)。

Movement 2: Knees straight, turn upright, at the same time, swing right hand overhead, forehead, rightward and upward, relax wrists, bend elbows slightly, palm centers downward, fingers leftward, middle fingertip perpendicular to the shoulder end, left hand back slightly against life-gate, center on life-gate, look at right arm, set and look at palm center (Figure 7-25).

图 7-25(Figure 7-25)

静立片刻，然后两臂向体侧自然伸展(图 7-26)。

Pause, arms naturally stretch to the sides (Figure 7-26).

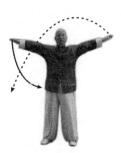

图 7-26(Figure 7-26)

右摘星换斗势

Right Plucking a Star and Exchanging a Star Cluster.

右摘星换斗势与左摘星换斗势动作相同，唯方向相反(图 7-27 和图 7-28)。

Right Plucking a Star and Exchanging a Star Cluster is the same as Left Plucking a Star and Exchanging a Star Cluster, except the direction (Figure 7-27 and Figure 7-28).

379

图 7-27（Figure 7-27）　　　图 7-28（Figure 7-28）

2.动作要点

2. Essential of exercise

（1）转身以腰带肩，以肩带臂。

(1) Turn and make waist drive shoulders, shoulders drive arms.

（2）目视掌心，意注命门，自然呼吸。

(2) Look at palm center, center on life-gate, breathe naturally.

（3）颈、肩病患者，动作幅度的大小可灵活掌握。

(3) Practitioners suffer neck or shoulder disease can flexibly adjust movement amplitude.

3.易犯错误

3. Fallible

（1）目上视时挺腹。

(1) Look up, throw out abdomen

（2）左右臂动作不协调，不到位。

(2) Leftward and rightward arm movements uncoordinated, not in place.

4.纠正方法

4. Remedy

（1）目上视时，注意松腰、收腹。

(1) Look up, and relax the waist, close abdomen.

(2)自然放松,以腰带动。

(2) Naturally relax, driven with the waist.

5.功理与作用

5. Functions and effects

(1)通过本势阳掌转阴掌(掌心向下)的动作导引,目视掌心,意存腰间命门,将发动的真气收敛,下沉入腰间两肾及命门,可达到壮腰健肾、延缓衰老的功效。

(1) Change yin palm into yang palm (palm center downward). Look at palm center, center on waist life gate, close vital energy downward to kidneys and life gate, improving waist and kidney and delaying aging.

(2)可增加颈、肩、腰等部位的活动功能。

(2) Improve neck, shoulder and waist functions.

(六)第五势 倒拽九牛尾势

Form 5 Pulling Nine Cows by Their Tails

1.动作

右倒拽九牛尾势

1. Movement

Right Pulling Nine Cows by Their Tails

动作一:接上式。双膝微屈,身体重心右移,左脚向左侧后方约45°撤步;右脚跟内转,右腿屈膝成右弓步;同时,左手内旋,向前、向下划弧后伸,小指到拇指逐个相握成拳,拳心向上;右手向前上方划弧,伸直与肩平时,小指到拇指逐个相握成拳,拳心向上,稍高于肩;目视右拳(图7-29)。

Movement 1: Keep moving, slightly bend knees, shift gravity center rightward, left foot retreats leftward and backward about 45°, right heel turns inward, bend right knee into the bow stance, at the same time, left hand turns inward, draws curve forward and downward, and stretches, hold fingers and thumb into fists, fist centers upward, slightly higher than shoulders, look at right fist (Figure 7-29).

图 7-29(Figure 7-29)

动作二:身体重心后移,左膝微屈;腰稍右转,以腰带肩,以肩带臂;右臂外旋,左臂内旋,屈肘内收;目视右拳(图 7-30)。

Movement 2: Shift gravity center backward, slightly bend left knee, waist turns slightly rightward, make waist drive shoulders, shoulders drive arms, right arm swings outward, left arm turns inward, bend and close elbows, look at right fist (Figure 7-30).

图 7-30(Figure 7-30)

动作三:身体重心前移,屈膝成弓步;腰稍左转,以腰带肩,以肩带臂,两臂放松前后伸展;目视右拳(图 7-31)。

Movements 3: Shift gravity center forward, bend elbow into the bow stance, make waist drive shoulders, shoulders drive arms, arms relax and stretch, look at right fist (Figure 7-31).

第七章 易筋经

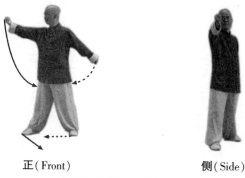

正(Front)　　　　　侧(Side)

图 7-31(Figure 7-31)

重复二至三动作三遍。

Repeat Movement 2 to 3 for 3 times.

动作四：身体重心前移至右脚，左脚收回，右脚尖转正，成开立姿势；同时，两臂自然垂于体侧；目视前下方（图7-32）。

Movement 4: Shift gravity center to right foot, close left foot, right tiptoes upright into standing with feet slightly apart, at the same time, arms fall naturally to the sides, look forward and downward (Figure 7-32).

图 7-32(Figure 7-32)

左倒拽九牛尾势

Left Pulling Nine Cows by Their Tails

左倒拽九牛尾势与右倒拽九牛尾势动作、次数相同，唯方向相反（图7-33~图7-35）。

Left Pulling Nine Cows by Their Tails is the same as Right Pulling Nine Cows by Their Tails in movements and umber of times, but the directions are

383

different. (Figure 7-33 to Figure 7-35).

图 7-33(Figure 7-33)　　　图 7-34(Figure 7-34)

正(Front)　　　　　　　侧(Side)

图 7-35(Figure 7-35)

2.动作要点

2. Essential of exercise

(1)以腰带肩,以肩带臂,力贯双膀。

(1) Make waist drive shoulders, shoulders drive arms, exert shoulders

(2)腹部放松,目视拳心。

(2) Relax abdomen, look at fist centers.

(3)前后拉伸,松紧适宜,并于腰的旋转紧密配合。

(3) Stretch front and back, keep proper, keep waist turning coordinated.

(4)后退步时,注意掌握重心,身体平稳。

(4) Retreat and coordinate gravity center, keep stable.

3.易犯错误

3. Fallible

(1)两臂屈拽用力僵硬。

(1) Bend and pull arms stiff

(2)两臂旋拧不够。

(2) Turn arms insufficient.

4.纠正方法

4. Remedy

(1)两臂放松,动作自然。

(1) Relax arms, move naturally

(2)旋拧两臂时,注意拳心向外。

(2) Twist arms, fist centers outward.

5.功理与作用

5. Functions and effects

(1)通过腰的扭动,带动肩胛活动,可刺激背部夹脊、肺腧、心腧等穴,达到疏通夹脊和调练心肺之作用。

(1) Waist twisting and driving shoulders can stimulate back point, lung point, and heart point, smoothing and improving back, lung and heart functions.

(2)通过四肢上下协调活动,可改善软组织血液循环,提高四肢肌肉力量及活动功能。

(2) Coordination between upper and lower limbs can improve soft tissue blood circulation, limb muscle functions.

（七）第六势　出爪亮翅势

Form 6　Displaying Paw-Style Palms like a White Crane Spreading Its Wings

1.动作

1. Movement

动作一：接上式。身体重心移至左脚,右脚收回,成开立姿势；同时,右臂外旋,左臂内旋,摆至侧平举,两掌心向前,环抱至体前,随之两臂内收,两手变柳叶掌立于云门穴前,掌心相对,指尖向上；目视前下方（图7-36~图7-38）。

Movement 1: Keep moving, shift gravity center to left foot, close right foot into standing with feet slightly apart, at the same time, swing right arm outward, twist left arm inward, lateral raising, palm centers forward and to the front, close arms, change hands into willow leaf palm against cloud gate point, palm centers against each other, fingertips upward, look forward and downward (Figure 7-36 to Figure 7-38).

图7-36(Figure 7-36)

正(Front)　　　　　　　　侧(Side)

图7-37(Figure 7-37)

第七章 易筋经

图 7-38（Figure 7-38）

动作二：展肩扩胸，然后松肩，两臂缓缓前伸，并逐渐转掌心向前，成荷叶掌，指尖向上；瞪目（图 7-39）。

Movement 2: Extend shoulders and expand chest, relax shoulders, slowly stretch arms forward, palm centers forward into the lotus leaf palm, fingertips upward, and stare (Figure 7-39).

正（Front）　　　侧（Side）
图 7-39（Figure 7-39）

动作三：松腕，屈肘，收臂，立柳叶掌于云门穴；目视前下方（图 7-40 和图 7-41）。重复二至三动作七遍。

Movements 3: Relax wrists, bend elbows, close arms, make willow palm to the Cloud Gate point, look forward and downward (Figure 7-40 and Figure 7-41). Repeat the movement twice to 7 times.

正（Front）　　　侧（Side）
图 7-40（Figure 7-40）

图 7-41（Figure 7-41）

2.动作要点

2. Essential of exercise

（1）出掌时身体正直,瞪眼怒目,同时两掌运用内劲前伸,先轻如推窗,后重如排山；收掌时如海水还潮。

（1）Keep upright, stare, at the same time, exert and stretch palms, slightly as if pushing a window and vigorously as if pushing a mountain, close palms as if tide returns.

（2）注意出掌时为荷叶掌,收掌于云门穴时为柳叶掌。

（2）Palm pushing for lotus palm, closing palm to cloud gate point for willow leaf palm.

（3）收掌时自然吸气,推掌时自然呼气。

（3）Palm closing for inhale and palm pushing for exhale.

3.易犯错误

3. Fallible

（1）扩胸展肩不充分。

（1）Extend shoulders and expand chest insufficiently.

（2）两掌前推时,不用内劲,而是用力。

（2）Push palms forward with force instead of interior strength.

（3）呼吸不自然,强呼强吸。

(3) Breathe forcibly instead of naturally.

4.纠正方法

4. Remedy

（1）出掌前,肩胛内收。

(1) Before palm pushing, close shoulders.

（2）两掌向前如推窗、排山。

(2) Palms pushing forward such as pushing a window and a mountain.

（3）按照"推呼收吸"的规律练习。

(3) Pushing for inhale and closing for exhale.

5.功理与作用

5. Functions and effects

（1）中医认为"肺主气,司呼吸"。通过伸臂推掌、曲臂收掌、展肩扩胸的动作导引,可反复启闭云门、中府等穴,促进自然之清气与人体之真气在胸中交汇融合,达到改善呼吸功能及全身气血运行的作用。

(1) TCM believes that "the lungs focus on breathing". Arms stretching and palms pushing, shoulders extending and chest expanding can repeatedly close and open Cloud Gate and outward and upward chest, promoting integration of natural clear air and human vital energy, improving respiratory function and blood circulation.

（2）可提高胸背部及上肢肌肉力量。

(2) Improve chest back and upper back muscles.

（八）第七势 九鬼拔马刀势

Form 7　Nine Ghosts Drawing Swords

1.动作

右九鬼拔马刀势

1. Movement

Right Nine Ghosts Drawing Swords

动作一:接上式

Movement 1: Keep moving,

躯干右转。同时,右手外旋,掌心向上;左手内旋,掌心向下(图 7-42)。

Turn right, at the same time, swing right hand outward, supinely, swing left hand inward, palm centers downward (Figure 7-42).

正(Front)　　　　　　　侧(Side)

图 7-42(Figure 7-42)

随后右手由胸前内收经右腋下后伸,掌心向外;同时,左手由胸前伸至前上方,掌心向外(图 7-43)。

Close right hand downward via right armpit, palm center outward, at the same time, stretch left hand to the front of the chest and forward, palm center outward (Figure 7-43).

正(Front)　　　　　　　侧(Side)

图 7-43(Figure 7-43)

第七章 易筋经

躯干稍左转；同时，右手经体侧向前上摆至头前上方后屈肘，由后向左绕头半周，掌心掩耳；左手经体左侧下摆至左后，屈肘，手背贴于脊柱，掌心向后，指尖向上；头右转，右手中指按压耳廓，手掌扶按玉枕；目随右手动，定势后视左后方（图7-44和图7-45）。

Turn left slightly, at the same time, make right hand upwardly and overhead, and bend elbow forward and upward, swing the head half a circle from rightward to leftward, palm center cover ears, swing left hand leftward and downward, bend elbow, hand back against the spine, palm center backward, fingertips upward, turn right, right middle finger presses the ear, palm presses Jade Pillow, look at the right hand, set, look leftward and backward (Figure 7-44 and Figure 7-45).

图 7-44（Figure 7-44）

正（Front）　　　　　背（Back）
图 7-45（Figure 7-45）

动作二：身体右转，展臂扩胸；目视右上方，动作稍停（图7-46）。

Movement 2: Turn right, extend arms and expand chest, look upward and rightward, pause (Figure 7-46).

图 7-46(Figure 7-46)

动作三：屈膝；同时，上体左转，右臂内收，含胸；左手沿脊柱尽量上推；目视右脚跟，动作稍停(图 7-47)。

Movements 3: Bend elbow, at the same time, turn left, close right arm inward, draw the chest, push left hand upward along the spine as far as possible, look at right heel, pause (Figure 7-47).

正(Front)　　　　背(Back)

图 7-47(Figure 7-47)

重复二至三动作三遍。

Repeat Movement 2 to 3 for 3 times.

动作四：直膝，身体转正；右手向上经头顶上方向下至侧平举，同时，左手经体侧向上至侧平举，两掌心向下；目视前下方(图 7-48)。

Movement 4: Knees straight, upright, make right hand upward, overhead and downward to lateral raising, at the same time, left hand upward and downward to lateral raising, palm centers downward, look forward and downward (Figure 7-48).

图 7-48（Figure 7-48）

左九鬼拔马刀势

Left Nine Ghosts Drawing Swords

左九鬼拔马刀势与右九鬼拔马刀势动作、次数相同，唯方向相反（图 7-49～图 7-51）。

Left Nine Ghosts Drawing Swords is the same as Right Nine Ghosts Drawing Swords in movements and number of times, but the directions are different. (Figure 7-49 to Figure 7-51).

图 7-49（Figure 7-49）　　图 7-50（Figure 7-50）

图 7-51（Figure 7-51）

2.动作要点

2. Essential of exercise

(1)动作对拔拉伸,尽量用力;身体自然弯曲转动,协调一致。

(1) Try hard to stretch and pull, bend and turn naturally, coordinated and consistent.

(2)扩胸展臂时自然吸气,松肩合臂时自然呼气。

(2) Expand chest and extend arms for inhale, relax shoulders and close arms for exhale.

(3)两臂内合、上抬时自然呼气,起身展臂时自然吸气。

(3) Close arms inward and upward for exhale, rise for inhale.

(4)高血压、颈椎病患者和年老体弱者,头部转动的角度应小,且轻缓。

(4) Suffers of hypertension, cervical vertebrae and the elderly and vulnerable should turn slightly and slowly.

3.易犯错误

3. Fallible

(1)屈膝合臂时,身后之臂放松。

(1) Bend elbows and close arms, arms relaxed behind.

(2)屈膝下蹲时,重心移至一侧。

(2) Bend knees and squat, shift gravity center inward.

(3)头部左右转动幅度过大。

(3) Turn leftward and rightward too much.

4.纠正方法

4. Remedy

(1)合臂时,身后之臂主动上推。

(1) Close arms, arms push behind initiatively.

(2)重心稳定,上下起伏。

(2) Stabilize gravity center, up and down.

(3)动作放松,切忌着意转动头部。

(3) Movements relaxed, avoid deliberate turning.

5.功理与作用

5. Functions and effects

(1)通过身体的扭曲、伸展等运动,使全身真气开、合、启、闭,脾胃得到摩动,肾得以强健;并具有疏通玉枕关、夹脊关等要穴的作用。

(1) Twisting, stretching and extending achieve vital energy opening and closing, improving spleen, stomach and kidney, Jade Pillow and back point.

(2)可提高颈肩部,腰背部肌肉力量,有助于改善人体各关节的活动功能。

(2) Improve neck, shoulder, waist back muscles, and functions of joints.

(九)第八势 三盘落地势

Form 8　Three Plates Falling on the Floor

1.动作

1. Movement

左脚向左侧开步,两脚距离约宽于肩,脚尖向前;目视前下方(图7-52)。

Left foot strides leftward with feet apart, feet gap similar to width of shoulders, tiptoes forward, look forward and downward (Figure 7-52).

图 7-52(Figure 7-52)

动作一:屈膝下蹲;同时,沉肩、坠肘,两掌逐渐用力下按至约与环跳穴同高,两肘微屈,掌心向下,指尖向外;目视前下方(图 7-53)。同时,口吐"嗨"音,音吐尽时,舌尖向前轻抵上下牙之间,终止吐音。

Movement 1: Bend knees and squat, at the same time, lower shoulders and elbows, press palms gradually to the level of loop jump point, slightly bend elbows, palm centers downward, fingertips outward, look forward and downward (Figure 7-53), at the same time, cry "Hey", then tongue tip against the gap between the upper and lower teeth, terminate tonguing.

图 7-53(Figure 7-53)

动作二:翻掌心向上,肘微屈,上托至侧平举;同时,缓缓起身直立;目视前方(图 7-54 和图 7-55)。

Movement 2: Turn, supinely, bend elbows slightly, support to lateral raising, at the same time, slowly rise, look straight ahead (Figure 7-54 and Figure 7-55).

第七章 易筋经

图 7-54（Figure 7-54）

图 7-55（Figure 7-55）

重复一至二动作三遍。第一遍微蹲（图 7-56）；

Repeat Movement 1 and 2 for 3 times. The first time, slightly squat (Figure 7-56),

图 7-56（Figure 7-56）

第二遍半蹲（图 7-57）；

The second time, partly squat (Figure 7-57),

图 7-57（Figure 7-57）

第三遍全蹲（图 7-58）。

The third time spring sitting (Figure 7-58).

图 7-58（Figure 7-58）

2.动作要点

2. Essential of exercise

（1）下蹲时,松腰、裹臀,两掌如负重物;起身时,两掌如托千斤重物。

(1) Squat, relax waist, bind buttocks, palms seem heavy object bearing, rise, palms seem to support extremely heavy object.

（2）下蹲依次加大幅度。年老和体弱者下蹲深度可灵活掌握,年轻体健者可半蹲或全蹲。

(2) Squat dramatically. The elderly and vulnerable can make squat depth flexible while young people can partly squat or have spring sitting.

（3）下蹲与起身时,上体始终保持正直,不应前俯或后仰。

(3) Squat and rise, keep upright, avoid bending forward or leaning backward.

（4）吐"嗨"音时,口微张,上唇着力压龈交穴,下唇松,不着力于承浆穴,音从喉部发出。

(4) Cry "Hey", slightly open the mouth, press upper lip to upper labial frenum, lower lip relaxes, avoid shifting gravity center to mandibular fossa, tonguing from the throat.

（5）瞪眼闭口时,舌抵上腭,身体中正安舒。

(5) Stare and close the mouth, tongue supports palate, keep neutral and relaxed.

3.易犯错误

3. Fallible

（1）下蹲时,直臂下按。

(1) Squat, arms straight and downward.

(2)忽略口吐"嗨"音。

(2) Ignore crying "Hey".

4.纠正方法

4. Remedy

(1)下蹲按掌,要求屈肘,两掌水平下按。

(1) Squat and press palms, bend elbows, palms downward.

(2)下蹲时注意口吐"嗨"音。

(2) Squat and cry "Hey".

5.功理与作用

5. Functions and effects

(1)通过下肢的屈伸活动,配合口吐"嗨"音,使体内真气在胸腹间相应的降、升,达到心肾相交、水火既济。

(1) Bend and stretch lower limbs, cry "Hey", make vital energy drop and rise between the chest and abdomen, reaching the kidneys intersection and integration.

(2)可增强腰腹及下肢力量,起到壮丹田之气、强腰固肾的作用。

(2) Enhance waist, abdomen and leg strength, improving elixir field and kidney.

(十)第九势 青龙探爪势

Form 9 Black Dragon Displaying Its Claws

1.动作

1. Movement

左青龙探爪势

Left Black Dragon Displaying Its Claws

动作一:接上式。左脚收回半步,约与肩同宽(图 7-59);

Movement 1: Keep moving, left foot strides half a step backward, about the same wide as the shoulders (Figure 7-59),

图 7-59(Figure 7-59)

两手握固,两臂屈肘内收至腰间,拳轮贴于章门穴,拳心向上;目视前下方(图 7-60)。

Hands grip, bend elbows against the waist, fist centers against rib edge, palm centers upward, look forward and downward (Figure 7-60).

图 7-60(Figure 7-60)

然后右拳变掌,右臂伸直,经下向右侧外展,略低于肩,掌心向上;目随手动(图 7-61 和图 7-62)。

Change right fist into palm, right arm straight, make it outreach downward and rightward, slightly lower than the shoulder, supinely, look at the hands (Figure 7-61 and Figure 7-62).

图 7-61（Figure 7-61）　　　图 7-62（Figure 7-62）

动作二：右臂屈肘、屈腕，右掌变"龙爪"，指尖向左，经下颏向身体左侧水平伸出，目随手动；躯干随之向左转约 90°；目视右掌指所指方向（图 7-63 和图 7-64）。

Movement 2: Bend the right arm and lower the elbow, bend the wrist, change right palm into "dragon claw", fingertips leftward, make it leftward via the chin, look at the hands, turn leftward about 90°, look at right fingers (Figure 7-63 and Figure 7-64).

图 7-63（Figure 7-63）

正（Front）　　　侧（Side）

图 7-64（Figure 7-64）

动作三："右爪"变掌，随之身体左前屈，掌心向下按至左脚外侧；目视下方（图 7-65 和图 7-66）。

Movements 3: Change "right claw" into palm, turn left and bend forward, palm centers downward and press to left foot outward, look downward (Figure 7-65 and Figure 7-66).

图 7-65(Figure 7-65)   图 7-66(Figure 7-66)

躯干由左前屈转至右前屈,并带动右手经左膝或左脚前划弧至右膝或右脚外侧,手臂外旋,掌心向前,握固;目随手动视下方(图 7-67 和图 7-68)。

Turn leftward and bend rightward, make right hand draw curve to outside of left right knee or right foot in front of left knee or left foot, swing arm outward, palm center forward, grip, look at the hand and downward (Figure 7-67 and Figure 7-68).

图 7-67(Figure 7-67)   图 7-68(Figure 7-68)

动作四:上体抬起,直立;右拳随上体抬起收于章门穴,拳心向上;目视前下方(图 7-69)。

Movement 4: Rise and stand, and close right fist against rib edge, fist center upward, look forward and downward (Figure 7-69).

图 7-69(Figure 7-69)

右青龙探爪势

Right Black Dragon Displaying Its Claws

右青龙探爪势与左青龙探爪势动作相同,唯方向相反(图 7-70~图 7-74)。

Right Black Dragon Displaying Its Claws is the same as Left Black Dragon Displaying Its Claws in movements, but directions are different (Figure 7-70 to Figure 7-74).

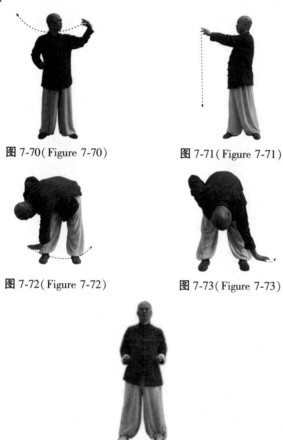

图 7-70(Figure 7-70)　　图 7-71(Figure 7-71)

图 7-72(Figure 7-72)　　图 7-73(Figure 7-73)

图 7-74(Figure 7-74)

2.动作要点

2. Essential of exercise

(1)伸臂探"爪",下按划弧,力注肩背,动作自然、协调,一气呵成。

(1) Stretch arm into "claw", draw curve downward, exert force to shoulder back, make movements natural, coordinated and constant.

(2) 目随"爪"走,意存"爪"心。

(2) Look at the "claw", centering on "claw".

(3)年老和体弱者前俯下按或划弧时,可根据自身状况调整幅度。

(3) The elderly and vulnerable bend forward, press downward or draw curve according to their practical situation.

3.易犯错误

3. Fallible

(1)身体前俯时,动作过大,重心不稳,双膝弯曲。

(1) Bend forward too much, gravity center in stable, knees bent.

(2)做"龙爪"时,五指弯曲。

(2) "Dragon claw" with fingers bent.

4.纠正方法

4. Remedy

(1)前俯动作幅度适宜、直膝。

(1) Bend properly, keep knees straight

(2)五指伸直分开,拇指、食指、无名指、小指内收,力在"爪"心。

(2) Fingers straight and separated, close thumb, index finger, ring finger and little finger, exert "claw" center.

5.功理与作用

5. Functions and effects

(1)中医认为"两肋属肝""肝藏血,肾藏精",二者同源。通过转身、左右探爪及身体前屈,可使两肋交替松紧开合,达到疏肝理气、调畅情志的功效。

(1) TCM believes that "both sides of the chest focus on the liver," "liver stores blood, kidney stores essence", homologous. Turning leftward and rightward, forming claw and bend forward can alternately relax and tighten opening and closing of both sides of the chest, improving the liver and regulating emotions.

(2)可改善腰部及下肢肌肉的活动功能。

(2) Improve waist and leg muscle functions.

(十一)第十势 卧虎扑食势

Form 10   Tiger Springing on Its Prey

1.动作

1.Movement

左卧虎扑食势

Left Tiger Springing on Its Prey

动作一:接上式。右脚尖内扣约45°,左脚收至右脚内侧成丁步;同时,身体左转约90°;两手握固于腰间章门穴不变;目随转体视左前方(图7-75)。

Movement 1: Keep moving, buckle right tiptoes inward approximately 45°, close left foot to right foot inward into the T-step, at the same time, turn leftward about 90°, grip hands against the rib edge, look leftward and forward (Figure 7-75).

正(Front)

侧(Side)

图 7-75(Figure 7-75)

动作二:左脚向前迈一大步,成左弓步;同时,两拳提至肩部云门穴,并内旋变"虎爪",向前扑按,如虎扑食,肘稍屈;目视前方(图7-76)。

Movement 2: Left foot strides a big step forward into the left bow stance, at the same time, lift fists to shoulder Cloud Gate Point, swing them into "tiger claw", make them forward, like Tiger Springing on Its Prey, bend elbows slightly, look straight ahead (Figure 7-76).

正(Front)　　　　　侧(Side)

图7-76(Figure 7-76)

动作三:躯干由腰到胸逐节屈伸,重心随之前后适度移动;同时,两手随躯干屈伸向下、向后、向上、向前绕环一周(图7-77~图7-79)。

Movements 3: Bend and stretch from the waist to the chest, shift gravity center back and forth properly, at the same time, swing hands downward, backward, upward and forward a circle (Figure 7-77 to Figure 7-79).

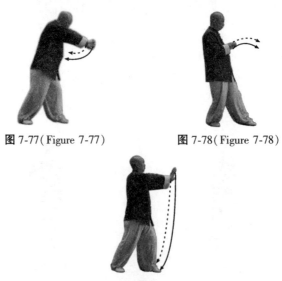

图7-77(Figure 7-77)　　图7-78(Figure 7-78)

图7-79(Figure 7-79)

第七章 易筋经

随后上体下俯,两"爪"下按,十指着地;后腿屈膝,脚趾着地;前脚跟稍抬起;随后塌腰、挺胸、抬头、瞪目;动作稍停,目视前上方(图7-80)。

Bend, press "claws" downward, 10 fingers touchdown, bend hind legs, toes touchdown, lift front heel, lower waist, throw out chest, look up, stare, pause, look forward and upward (Figure 7-80).

正(Front)　　　　　　侧(Side)

图7-80(Figure 7-80)

年老体弱者可俯身,两"爪"向前下按至左膝前两侧,顺势逐步塌腰、挺胸、抬头、瞪目。动作稍停。

The elderly and vulnerable may bend and stretch "claws" forward and downward to knees forward and inward, turn waist downward, throw out chest, look up, stare and pause.

动作四:起身,双手握固收于腰间章门穴;身体重心后移,左脚尖内扣越135°;身体重心左移;同时,身体右转180°,右脚收至左脚内侧成丁步(图7-81)。

Movement 4: Rise, close fists against waist rib edge, shift gravity center backward, buckle left tiptoes inward 135°, shift gravity center leftward, at the same time, turn rightward 180°, close right foot to left foot inward into the T-step (Figure 7-81).

图7-81(Figure 7-81)

407

右卧虎扑食势

Right Tiger Springing on Its Prey

右卧虎扑食势与左卧虎扑食势动作相同,唯方向相反(图7-82和图7-83)。

Right Tiger Springing on Its Prey is the same as Left Tiger Springing on Its Prey, but the directions are different (Figure 7-82 and Figure 7-83).

图7-82(Figure 7-82)

图7-83(Figure 7-83)

2.动作要点

2. Essential of exercise

(1)用躯干的蛹动带动双手前扑绕环。

(1) Trunk worm to drive hands pounce and swing.

(2)抬头、瞪目时,力达指尖,腰背部呈反弓形。

(2) Look up and stare, deliver the force to fingertips, make waist back arched.

(3)年老和体弱者可根据自身状况调整动作幅度。

(3) The elderly and vulnerable can adjust movement amplitude according to their practical situation.

3.易犯错误

3. Fallible

(1)俯身时耸肩,含胸,头晃动。

(1) Bend and shrug, draw the chest and shake head.

(2)做"虎爪"时,五指微屈或过屈。

(2) "Tiger claw" with too much or too little fingers bending.

4.纠正方法

4. Remedy

(1)躯干直立,目视前上方。

(1) Trunk upright, look forward and upward.

(2)五指末端弯曲,力在指尖。

(2) Bend fingertips, and exert them.

5.功理与作用

5. Functions and effects

(1)中医认为"任脉为阴脉之海",统领全身阴经之气。通过虎扑之势,身体的后仰,胸腹的伸展,可使任脉得以疏伸及调养,同时可以调和手足三阴之气。

(1) TCM believes that "conception vessel is the source of yin", commanding yin vital energy. Tiger Springing on Its Prey, backward leaning, chest and abdomen stretching and extending can smoothen and improve conception vessel, at the same time, and 3 yin meridians of the hands and feet.

(2)改善腰腿肌肉活动功能,起到强健腰腿的作用。

(2) Improve waist and leg muscle functions, enhancing waist and legs.

(十二)第十一势　打躬势

Form 11　Bowing Down in Salutation

1.动作

1. Movement

动作一:接上式。起身,身体重心后移,随之身体转正;右脚尖内扣,脚尖向前,左脚收回,成开立姿势;同时,两手随身体左转放松,外旋,掌心向前,外展至侧平举后,两臂屈肘,两掌掩耳,十指扶按枕部,指尖相对,以两手食指弹拨中指击打枕部7次(即"鸣天鼓");目视前下方(图7-84和图7-85)。

Movement 1: Keep moving, rise, shift gravity center backward, and stand at attention, buckle right tiptoes inward, tiptoes forward, close left foot, stand with feet slightly apart, at the same time, turn left and relax hands, swing them outward, palm centers forward, stretch to lateral raising, bend elbows, palms cover ears, make 10 fingers press occiput, fingertips against each other, knock occiput with index fingers and middle fingers 7 times (occipital knocking), look forward and downward (Figure 7-84 and Figure 7-85).

图 7-84(Figure 7-84)   图 7-85(Figure 7-85)

动作二:身体前俯由头经颈椎、胸椎、腰椎、骶椎,由上向下逐节缓缓牵引前屈,两腿伸直;目视脚尖,停留片刻(图7-86)。

Movement 2: Bend forward the head, cervical vertebrae, thoracic vertebrae, lumbar vertebrae and sacral vertebrae, legs straight, look at tiptoes, and pause (Figure 7-86).

正(Front)   侧(Side)
图 7-86(Figure 7-86)

动作三:由骶椎至腰椎、胸椎、颈椎、头,由下向上依次缓缓逐节伸直后成直立;同时两掌掩耳,十指扶按枕部,指尖相对;目视前下方(图7-87)。

Movements 3: Turn upright the sacral vertebrae, lumbar vertebrae, thoracic vertebrae, cervical vertebrae and head, at the same time palms cover ears, 10 fingers hold and press occiput, fingertips against each other, look forward and downward (Figure 7-87).

图 7-87(Figure 7-87)

重复二至三动作三遍,逐渐加大身体前屈幅度,并稍停。第一遍前屈小于 90°,第二遍前屈约 90°,第三遍前屈大于 90°(图 7-88~图 7-90)。年老体弱者可分别前屈约 30°,约 45°,约 90°。

Repeat movement twice to three times, increasingly bend forward, and pause. The first time bend less than 90°, the second time bend about 90°, the third time bend greater than 90° (Figure 7-88 to Figure 7-90). The elderly and vulnerable can bend respectively about 30°, about 45° and about 90°.

正(Front)　　　　侧(Side)

图 7-88(Figure 7-88)

正(Front)　　　　侧(Side)

图 7-89(Figure 7-89)

正(Front)　　　　侧(Side)

图 7-90(Figure 7-90)

2.动作要点

2. Essential of exercise

(1)体前屈时,直膝,两肘外展。

(1) Bend, knee straight, and outreach elbows.

(2)体前屈时,脊柱自颈向前拔伸卷曲如勾;后展时,从尾椎向上逐节伸展。

(2) Bend, stretch the spine forward like hooking, and retreat it the caudal vertebra.

(3)年老和体弱者可根据自身状况调整前屈的幅度。

(3) The elderly and the vulnerable can adjust bending amplitude according to their practical situation.

3.易犯错误

体前屈和起身时,两腿弯曲,动作过快。

3. Fallible

Bend and rise, legs bent, and movements too fast.

4.纠正方法

体松心静,身体缓缓前屈和起身,两腿伸直。

4. Remedy

Relax and keep calm, slowly bend and rise, legs straight.

第七章 易筋经

5.功理与作用

5. Functions and effects

(1)中医认为"督脉为阳脉之海",总督一身阳经之气。通过头、颈、胸、腰、骶椎逐节牵引屈、伸,背部的督脉得到充分锻炼,可使全身经气发动,阳气充足,身体强健。

(1) TCM believes that "governor meridian is the source of yang", governing yang vital energy. The head, neck, chest, waist and sacral vertebrae drag, bend and stretch, exercising back governor meridians, mobilizing vital energy, improving yang and health.

(2)可改善腰背及下肢的活动功能,强健腰腿。

(2) Improve waist back and legs functions, improving waist and legs.

(3)"鸣天鼓"有醒脑、聪耳、消除大脑疲劳功效。

(3) "Occipital knocking" refreshes, improving hearing, and eliminating mental fatigue.

(十三)第十二势　掉尾势

Form 12 Swinging the Tail

1.动作

1. Movement

动作一:接上式。起身直立后,两手猛然拨离开双耳(即"拔耳")(图7-91)。

Movement 1:Keep moving, rise, hands suddenly leave ears (ear drawing) (Figure 7-91).

图 7-91(Figure 7-91)

手臂自然前伸,十指交叉相握,掌心向内(图 7-92 和图 7-93)。

Arms naturally stretch forward, 10 fingers cross, palm center inward (Figure 7-92 and Figure 7-93).

图 7-92(Figure 7-92)　　图 7-93(Figure 7-93)

屈肘,翻掌前伸,掌心向外(图 7-94)。

Bend elbows, turn and stretch palms, palm centers outward (Figure 7-94).

正(Front)　　　　侧(Side)

图 7-94(Figure 7-94)

然后屈肘,转掌心向下内收于胸前;身体前屈塌腰、抬头,两手交叉缓缓下按;目视前方(图 7-95 和图 7-96)。

第七章 易筋经

Bend elbow, turn palm centers downward and against the front chest, bend and turn waist downward, look up, hands cross and slowly press down, look straight ahead (Figure 7-95 and Figure 7-96).

图 7-95(Figure 7-95)

正(Front)　　　　　　侧(Side)

图 7-96(Figure 7-96)

年老和体弱者身体前屈,抬头,两掌缓缓下按可至膝前。

The elderly and vulnerable bend, look up, and press downward palms to the knees.

动作二:头向左后转,同时,臀向左前扭动;目视尾闾(图 7-97)。

Movement 2: Turn leftward, at the same time, swing buttocks forward and leftward, look at coccyx (Figure 7-97).

正(Front)　　　　　　侧(Side)

图 7-97(Figure 7-97)

动作三:两手交叉不动,放松还原至体前屈(图7-98)。

Movement 3: Cross hands and keep still, relax and bend them (Figure 7-98).

图 7-98(Figure 7-98)

动作四:头向右后转,同时,臀向右前扭动;目视尾闾(图7-99)。

Movements 4: Turn rightward and backward, at the same time, swing buttocks forward and rightward, look at coccyx (Figure 7-99).

图 7-99(Figure 7-99)

动作五:两手交叉不动,放松还原至体前屈(图7-100)。

Movement 5: Cross hands and keep still, relax and bend them (Figure 7-100).

图 7-100(Figure 7-100)

重复一至四动作三遍。

Repeat Movement 1 to 4 for 3 times.

2.动作要点

2. Essential of exercise

(1)转头扭臀时,头与臀部作相向运动。

(1) Turn and twist buttocks, head and buttocks move in opposite directions.

(2)高血压、颈椎病患者和年老体弱者,头部动作应小而轻缓。另外,应根据自身情况调整身体前屈和臀部扭动的幅度和次数。

(2) Suffers of hypertension and cervical vertebrae disease, the elderly and vulnerable, should have minor and slight movements. In addition, it is necessary for them to adjust bending and buttocks twisting magnitude and frequency according to their practical situation.

(3)配合动作,自然呼吸,意识专一。

(3) Keep coordinated and consistent, breathe naturally

3.易犯错误

摇头摆臀,交叉手及重心左右移动。

3. Fallible

Shake head and swing buttocks, cross hands and shift gravity center leftward and rightward.

4.纠正方法

交叉手下按固定不动,同时注意体会同侧肩与髋相合。

4. Remedy

Cross hand and press down in a fixed manner, at the same time, make shoulders and hips consistent.

5.功理与作用

5. Functions and effects

(1)通过体前屈及抬头、掉尾的左右屈伸运动,可使任、督二脉及全身气脉在此前各势动作锻炼的基础上得以调和,练功后全身舒适、轻松。

(1) Bending and look up, swing the back leftward and rightward can improve conception vessel and governor vessel and overall vital energy, achieving comfort and relaxation.

(2)可强化腰背肌肉力量的锻炼,有助于改善脊柱各关节和肌肉的活动功能。

(2) Improve waist back muscles, spinal joints and muscle functions.

(十四)收势

Closing

1.动作

1. Movement

动作一:接上式。两手松开,两臂外旋;上体缓缓直立;同时,两臂伸直外展呈侧平举,掌心向上,随后两臂上举,肘微屈,掌心向下;目视前下方(图7-101~图7-103)。

Movement 1: Keep moving, relax hands, swing arms outward, slowly rise, at the same time, outreach arms straight to lateral raising, supinely, arms upward, bend elbows slightly, palm centers downward, look forward and downward (Figure 7-101 to Figure 7-103).

第七章 易筋经

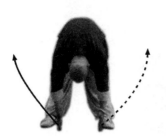

图 7-101（Figure 7-101）

图 7-102（Figure 7-102）

图 7-103（Figure 7-103）

动作二：松肩，屈肘，两臂内收，两掌经头、面、胸前下引致腹部，掌心向下；目视前下方（图 7-104）。

Movement 2: Relax shoulders, bend elbows, close arms, swing palms downward to abdomen via the head, face and chest, palm centers downward, look forward and downward (Figure 7-104).

图 7-104（Figure 7-104）

重复一至二动作三遍两臂放松还原，自然垂于体侧；左脚收回，并拢站立；舌抵上腭；目视前方（图 7-105）。

Repeat movements 1 and 2 three times, relax and restore arms, fall naturally to the sides, close left foot, stand, tongue supports palate, look

419

straight ahead (Figure 7-105).

图 7-105(Figure 7-105)

2.动作要点

2. Essential of exercise

(1)第一、二次双手下引至腹部以后,意念继续下引,经涌泉穴入地。最后一次则意念随双手下引至腹部稍停。

(1) After the fist and second hands guiding downward to abdomen, keep guiding idea downward, pass through sole to the floor. The last time, guide idea to follow hands downward and to abdomen, pause.

(2)下引时,两臂匀速缓缓下行。

(2) Guide the idea downward, lower arms slowly.

3.易犯错误

两臂上举是仰头上视。纠正方法头正,目视前下方。

3. Fallible

Arms upward and look up.

4.纠正方法

头正,目视前下方。

4. Remedy

Keep upright, look forward and downward.

5.功理和作用

5. Functions and effect

(1)通过上肢的上抱下引动作,可引气回归于丹田。

(1) Upper limbs holding upward and guiding downward can return vital energy to elixir field.

(2)起到调节全身肌肉、关节的放松。

(2) Adjust and relax muscles and joints.